T0306771

The First English Hero

THE FIRST ENGLISH HERO

THE LIFE OF RANULF DE BLONDEVILLE

IAIN SODEN

AMBERLEY

In the Name of Jesus Christ, Lord and Saviour

First published 2009
This edition published 2021

Amberley Publishing
The Hill, Stroud
Gloucestershire, GL5 4EP

www.amberley-books.com

Copyright © Iain Soden 2009, 2021

The right of Iain Soden to be identified as the Author of this work has been asserted in accordance with the Copyright, Designs and Patents Act 1988.

ISBN 978 1 3981 0674 1 (print)
ISBN 978 1 4456 1998 9 (ebook)

All rights reserved. No part of this book may be reprinted or reproduced or utilised in any form or by any electronic, mechanical or other means, now known or hereafter invented, including photocopying and recording, or in any information storage or retrieval system, without the permission in writing from the Publishers.

British Library Cataloguing in Publication Data.
A catalogue record for this book is available from the British Library.

Printed in the UK.

CONTENTS

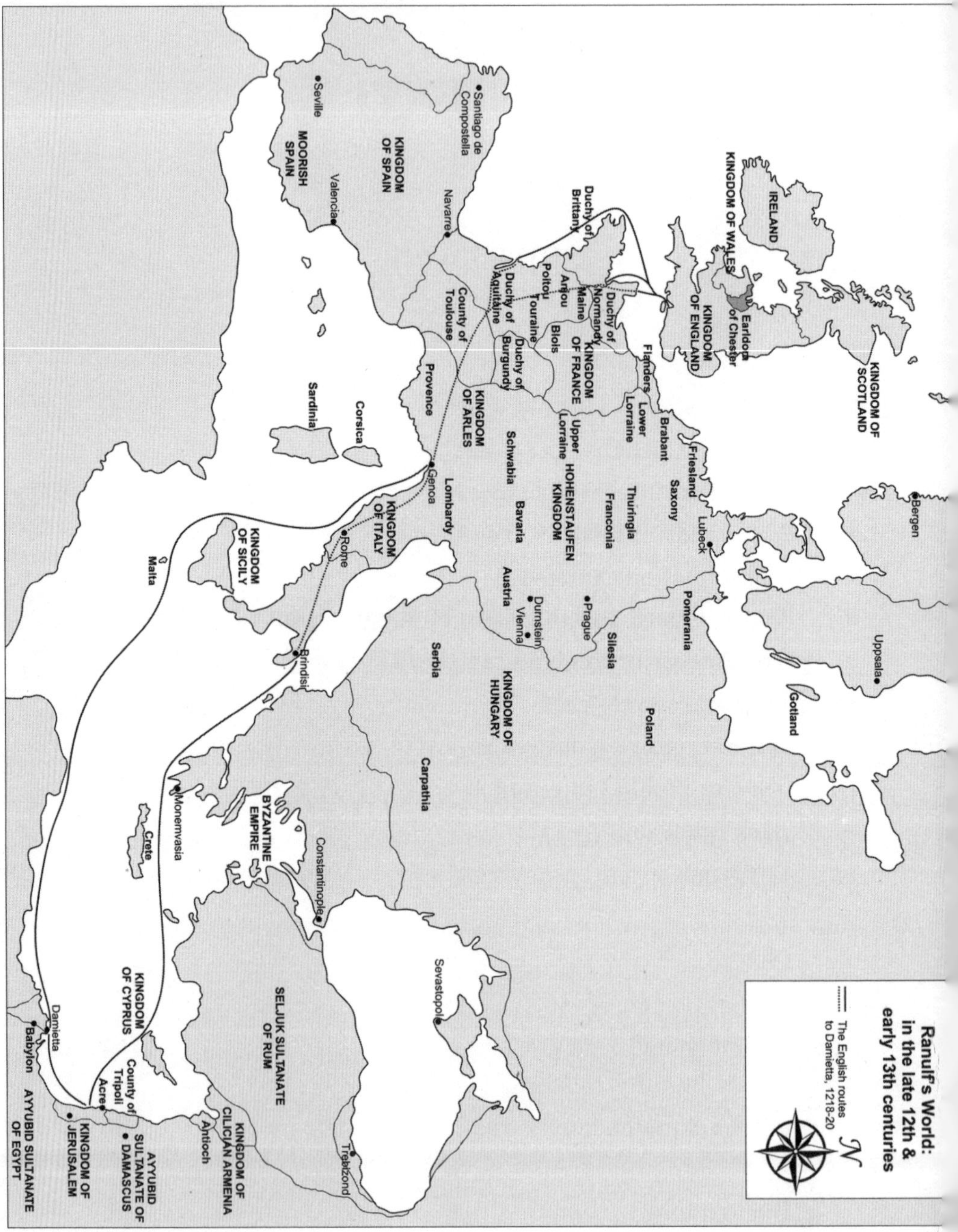

Ranulf's world in the late twelfth and early thirteenth centuries. *Drawn by Jacqueline Harding.*

PREFACE

I first became interested by Ranulf de Blondeville as an archaeologist in Coventry, my home city, a quarter of a century ago. Ranulf owned half the city. However, neither historian nor archaeologist I spoke to ever seemed to know much about him, nor could they point me to relevant books from which I might learn more. Therein lay a challenge it took me many years to find time to take up. Not before time, either, since my work has been all over the former Honour of Chester and his name just keeps cropping up.

Ranulf de Blondeville, sixth Earl of Chester lived at a challenging time for many historians and archaeologists working today, since the sources are relatively obscure and elusive. They are almost all in Latin or French, sometimes Norman French, most never translated, with the result that they are given a wide berth by all but a few university departments. Internet coverage is, as yet, negligible. I am fortunate to have a relevant academic and professional background and, with accessibility in mind, I have been able to return to the original documents to proffer translation and point out some subtle nuances, sometimes with additional archaeological evidence. I have sought to avoid the rather sparing language of the original documents, along with the largely obscure, restrictive and generally unhelpful legal terminologies often used in weighty academic tomes. I have standardised spellings, adopting the simplest modern English and French versions of Anglo-Norman or Latin names (thus William Marshall, not Guillaume le Maréchal, Geoffrey Goldsmith, not Galfridus Aurifaber or Geoffrey Orfever). However, in cases where common Latin usage prevails in English, I have not tried to change it (such as Philip Augustus, not Philippe Auguste).

For over a century historians have concentrated on the two gigantic figures of the fraternal Angevin kings, Richard the Lionheart and John and to an extent, their opponent, the acquisitive but hugely able King Philip Augustus of France.[1] The Angevin kings were certainly impressive rulers, distinctive in their utterly opposed styles of kingship, the first portrayed as a charismatic and tough soldier (hero), his younger brother a weak schemer (villain). Since Victorian times their *Boys' Own* stories of derring-do and villainy, told by the dying embers of imperial British campfires, have largely been simplistically re-hashed and only in the last two decades has some circumspection, if not revisionism, appeared in print.[2]

For Richard the Lionheart, historians have laboured excessively over his prominent part in the Third Crusade (although he really did make it his own) and the results in England of his distant captivity in Austria and Germany. Latterly they have dwelt on his possible homosexuality. To some extent these are all distractions and certainly are to the detriment of study of his last five years spent vigorously defending Normandy and Poitou.[3] To harp on, as many do, that he visited England only twice in ten years as king is to miss a point entirely. Once he returned from crusade and helped end English unrest inspired by John, he was far more sorely needed in Normandy than in England.

Conversely John did abandon Normandy and, through poor judgement, undid all the meticulous administrative and military work Henry II and Richard had done there. However, his lot was to have his incompetence always misinterpreted as villainy. John was neither decisive nor intuitive as a leader and tended to surround himself with rogues and sycophants, making poor decisions worse. He was only truly a villain when he had to deal with people on a personal level, whether male or female.

Contemporary twelfth- and thirteenth-century historians were relatively numerous, although many took a similar view of the same events. This was partly because most were monks and wrote from similarly cloistered surroundings, relying upon the same news reaching them from the same sources. Thus some of the stories told by Ralph of Diss, Roger of Hoveden, Ranulf Higden, Matthew Paris and Benedict of Peterborough bear very close similarities, together with a host of anonymous monastic annalists: Tewkesbury, Burton, Chester, Dieulacres, Dunstable, Worcester. In one case, Roger of Hoveden and Benedict of Peterborough are likely to be the same person, the author adopting a self-effacing pen-name. One work of history is sadly absent, the purported '*Geste*' of Earl Randal, a fabled thirteenth-century eulogy, perhaps written soon after Ranulf's death and probably unashamedly panegyric in tone, if it was real. Perhaps written in the style of the surviving *History of William Marshall* and in Norman French, it was probably lost long ago.

Amongst the nineteenth-century editors of the predominantly Latin manuscripts stand some giants of scholarship, such as Hardy, Stapleton and Stubbs, editors of the Rolls Series. I marvel at their output and weighty textual criticism. In the twentieth century the works of Maurice Powicke and Geoffrey Barraclough are standing the test of time and must be visited. Professors Painter and Alexander in the USA a generation ago, promoted a wider understanding of the Earl of Chester's part in Angevin England but their studies were narrower and concentrated largely on politics under John and Henry III. I owe them all my gratitude. Other historians have done Ranulf a great dis-service by not looking closely enough. One Breton scholar perhaps mixed him up with his long-dead grandfather, Ranulf de Gernons, when he described him at the time of his marriage, aged about 19, to Constance of Brittany as '*vieux, grossier et brutal*' (old, coarse and brutal).[4] Otherwise perhaps his chagrin is understandable Breton indignation at the treatment of his homeland by its neighbours, both English and French. To this day Brittany retains a proud, independent air. It can be a wild place and is steeped in legends of its struggles for freedom and independence.

Any study of Ranulf and his contemporaries must look to both sides of the Channel and beyond. The Angevin Empire stretched from Berwick to Bordeaux, from Ireland to Angers, its influence reaching far beyond through marriage and alliance. Until 1204, for English kings and nobility, Normandy was home; England was the office where money was to be made. Interaction between the two was constant from 1066 and for the decade 1194 to 1204 Normandy drained the manpower and finances of England to the dregs. Long after 1204, when John lost Normandy to the King of France, the lure of a Norman homeland remained. For many English men and women it remains today. If I have learnt anything from laying bare the life of Ranulf, sixth Earl of Chester, it is that when he was forced to leave his home behind, the homeland echoes can still be found in old loyalties, in piety and, most of all, in obligations and duties to family and to friends to the very end. In the early thirteenth century, any idea of the distinct national and cultural identities we see today was still some way off. Ranulf spoke French as his mother-tongue, but saw himself as distinctly Norman. Ironically he died very much an Englishman, in a realm struggling to become independent of Normandy for the first time in seven generations. Professor Powicke once astutely observed that for this reason, 1204 is a date which defines England every bit as much as 1066.

In the centuries since Ranulf's day, many differences of perception have emerged but can so easily be overlooked. Firstly there is our perception of the passage of time and the sequence of events. Instantaneous communication in the twenty-first century is taken for granted. In the medieval world (and up until the invention of the telegraph) long-distance communication was entirely by letter or word-of-mouth and took as long as the length of journey on foot, on horseback or under sail. The lands of Western Europe contained huge forested and arable tracts between towns and villages, castles and abbeys. For this reason, spies, agents and messengers were everywhere. Nothing happened quickly, and nothing happened which did not pass before the eyes of an intelligence-gathering class of spy-clerks, monk-agents, knightly messengers and minor royal informers. Intelligence and rumour were paramount. While sieges were relatively common, pitched battles in the field were only fought because two converging armies deliberately manoeuvred for days or weeks with the aid of spies and contrived to meet each other at almost pre-arranged places, vying for the better approach, the favourable ground, sometimes almost missing each other in a forest or during darkness. Surprise was rare – except perhaps for the astounding forced marches of Richard and John who, at their best, shared an uncanny ability to turn up when and where least expected, although either could themselves be surprised in this way. Armies normally took weeks to notify, months to muster. A fleet of ships might need a year to assemble and could wait tied up in port for months on end (as at Brindisi in 1217–18, or Portsmouth in 1229–30) for its troop complement to arrive and then be delayed by bad weather or its commander's whim. For a historian the joy of all this is that our forebears made the time to sit and record it.

Sadly war has always been painful for all, both combatants and civilians. Armies, once under way, generally travelled amidst a ten mile-wide landscape stripped bare of food for the troops and forage for the horses, the column stained and polluted by a trail of its own ordure, leaving behind blood and heartbreak and casualties whose demise resulted simply in their silence and no return home. As in all ages, to be maimed in war was to be stripped of livelihood and injuries could be unspeakable.

We forget that many ordinary people experienced the poorest quality of life, such as is only seen today in what is usually referred to as 'the developing world'. Slavery was widespread and accepted across all of Northern Europe; whole families of serfs of every nationality were bought and sold as part of the land they occupied. Famine, the lingering results of natural disaster, high infant mortality and the like were not unusual – although sometimes notable – occurrences in both England and Normandy. Thus, when fire broke out in Chester in 1180, half the town was lost in a day and when a series of great storms descended on Normandy in 1197 the harvest was ruined and a winter of famine ensued. Life for many ordinary people was precarious most of the time. Healthcare was minimal and frighteningly rudimentary, not to say improper, even for the wealthiest individuals. In short, even though aspects of the rural landscapes of medieval England and Normandy might be familiar to us today, the most able among us would struggle to survive in the feudal world of the twelfth and thirteenth centuries.

For the privileged few who had the benefit of high birth, honouring one's knightly service was a constant bone of contention. In theory a knight ought to stay at his lord's side to finish a job once started. In reality he could consider his obligations fully met if he spent as little as 40 days in the field. Even in the midst of a crusade, knights came and went once they themselves considered their work done. Few stayed on in the term such as Ranulf undertook on crusade – two years – amidst appalling privation and constant danger (in addition to the two consecutive years he had already spent under arms in England). Such personal limitations on service robbed the defence of Normandy in 1200–1204 of experienced, battle-hardened knights time and again. No amount of fresh taxation could raise enough cash to pay enough mercenaries to take their place. The concept of a permanent, professional army was a long way off, although perhaps Ranulf of Chester was as near as anyone in that generation of nobles might come to a professional soldier.

Finally something must be said regarding loyalty. The modern western concept of loyalty carries with it no idea of being slightly loyal or incompletely loyal, or of switching allegiance with the reasonable hope of a later pardon. Yet loyalty in a medieval sense was a saleable commodity as part of the feudal contract between lord and vassal, King and Earl. Castles, honours and lands were bargaining chips in the hands of the King or one of his nobles, who could confer them or remove them in order to reward, punish or simply remind his vassal of his previous or new-found obligations or fidelity. No conferral or distraint need be final or binding to the last. For this reason some changed allegiances frequently. It was unusual to find individuals whose words and actions were in accord and constistent throughout their lives, their allegiances unwavering. It is this aspect which makes Ranulf of Chester unusual in his own generation, and his peers themselves recognised that. They all came to know that if he disagreed with someone, it was firmly stated, but it did not mean he would desert them. Henry II, Richard I, John and Henry III all had good reason to be grateful for Ranulf's support at key moments, as had John de Brienne, King of Jerusalem, and King Andrew of Hungary in the Fifth Crusade. Without Ranulf, England, and perhaps even Western Europe, would have been very different today.

I

EARL IN WAITING (1170–89)

Western Europe in the late twelfth century would look most peculiar to the modern observer. England, Scotland, Wales and Ireland were all, to some extent, self-governing countries, although they meddled constantly with each other and borders which today are fixed lines on maps could be very fluid indeed. The Kingdom of Wales amounted to little more than the wilder central portion of that country we know today; its northern and southern shores owed allegiance to England. France, already fabulously wealthy, was a fifth of its modern size, nestling around the modern Ile de France and its capital, Paris. It was dominated on the one side by England's Angevin Empire, which stretched from the English Channel to the Pyrenees and from the Atlantic Coast to Burgundy. On its other side lay Germany and its Holy Roman Empire, from the Baltic to the Mediterranean, via Burgundy, western Switzerland, northern Italy and Provence.

Between the kingdoms lay the dukes, counts and viscounts whose complex allegiances changed like the wind and whose backing could make or break the aspirations of a king. Thus a balance of power might be held by the choice of allegiance of a

Count of Toulouse or a Duke of Brabant. Most often in this story, it was the Duke of Brittany. In order for either England or France to advance growing territorial ambitions, they played politics on a grand diplomatic scale, courting one, then another, marrying a countess here or a duke there, until marital aspiration and intrigue at court could mean the rise and fall of a nation, almost (but not quite) irrespective of military might.

In all this the sanctity of the Holy Mother Church was supposedly immutable and universal. Sin brought the Church's retribution, even in this life. A great man could not do great wrongs without it becoming the stuff of widespread condemnation and the threat of everlasting damnation. Similarly fame which was backed by the Church spread far and wide. It was in this multi-layered world that the first five earls of Chester ruled their lands, owing allegiance to the King of England for the English portion and to the Duke of Normandy for the Norman. It was a lesson of history for them that in 1170, when the 6th earl-in-waiting, Ranulf of Chester was born, king and duke amounted, inseparably, to the same person – Henry II.

The energetic and immensely able Henry II was tempestuously married to Eleanor, Duchess of Aquitaine, the most formidable woman in Western Europe and a politician of huge note. Previously briefly married to the King of France, she had played court politics on a grand scale and as Henry's wife produced a veritable brood of in-fighting sons whose ambitions outstripped and bewildered their father. The eldest – briefly made Duke of Normandy, was Henry 'The Young King,' who forced his father to have him crowned while he himself was still king. He died young. Then the impetuous but pious Richard, made Duke of Aquitaine. His star would burn very brightly as King Richard the Lionheart and burn out just as quickly. There was Geoffrey, who was briefly Duke of Brittany. He too died young but not before he sired children whose place in English history would be pivotal. Then stood John, infamous for being given no significant lands of his own, yet always his father's favourite. When lands he had eventually, he could not keep them and infamously lost the crown jewels too. His (partly) unjust fate has been to remain one of England's most reviled Kings. The modern western world, obsessed with its own view of exemplary governance, merely paints him, through Magna Carta, as democracy's first stumbling block with 800 years of hindsight. Would that it was so simple – Magna Carta spawned immediate disaster for England. The trio of Richard, Geoffrey and John are central to this story, together with their heirs; so too the power-struggle between England's Angevin Empire and its small but fabulously wealthy and acquisitive neighbour, the Kingdom of France.

For Ranulf de Blondeville, the singular title of Earl of Chester is somewhat misleading since his power and estates in England stretched far and wide beyond Chester, or even the English Midlands. Progressively historians such as Barraclough and Husain have dealt in detail with his lands in Cheshire; [1] they have always made sufficient mention of that, but usually to the exclusion of all the other far flung lands and property attached to the *honour* of the earldom across half a dozen Midland counties of England and into North Wales. However, all the earls of Chester up to and including Ranulf were not even from England. They were Normans. It is equally to Normandy where the trail first of all leads anyone who would follow any of their startling lives and careers.

Ranulf was the sixth Norman Earl of Chester and the first to have any real deep-seated links with England, although they were forced upon him by the events in which he was caught up as a young man. He became the most celebrated soldier of his age, an astute politician at the centre of government. His support was courted by Popes and his firm stance in support of Papal authority won a civil war when England was invaded by France. Although Earl of Chester always remained his foremost title, to his contemporaries and to the commentators of his generation, he was at one time or another also Duke of Brittany, Earl of Lincoln, of Richmond and of Leicester. He was hereditary Viscount of the Bessin in central and western Normandy, encompassing the Viscounties of Bayeux and of Avranches; he was also Viscount of St Sauveur-le-Vicomte, Viscount of the Val de Vire and Baron of St Sever.[2] He was a strong family-man, who married twice, once politically, a second time (probably) for love, but who was never blessed with the gift of children, for reasons unknown. He was a loyal supporter in peace and war to five kings, alongside four of whom he fought in battle. He was the most faithful of friends to a group of less constant nobles whose machinations would have tried the patience of a saint, but who he seems to have tried to understand. He made a few bitter enemies, who all eventually showed him the utmost respect. With his death one historian (Stubbs) notes that almost the last link to England's feudal Norman heritage had passed.

Ranulf (the third earl to bear the name) was probably born in 1170, either in England's Shropshire or western Normandy.[3] Later medieval historians named him 'de Blondeville', 'de Blundeville', 'Blonville' or 'Blunville'. Their spellings vary somewhat. The name was not his surname; indeed many Norman nobles bore no such thing. It was simply to distinguish him from his grandfather Ranulf de Gernons (fourth Earl 1128–53) and his great-grandfather Ranulf de Meschines (third Earl 1121–28), both prominent men in their own time. Ranulf de Meschines had married the daughter of Henry I, so the line was closely linked to the Anglo-Norman royal house.

Some historians associate Blonde-Ville with his purported birth at Oswestry in Shropshire, although in another spelling it is uncannily similar to the village of Blanville near Avranches in Normandy.[4] In fact in the area of his family's authority in the Cotentin peninsula, it seems that almost every third village ends in *-ville*, even today. Without stronger evidence, the Norman seaside location seems as probable a place as a damp frontier town in the Welsh Marches for the confinement of a very young Norman lady giving birth to her first child.

Ranulf's parents were Hugh Kevelioc and Bertrada d'Evreux. Hugh was twenty-three and his new wife only fourteen when their son was born. Noble, political marriages in the twelfth century often involved wives so young. They had married the previous year, when Bertrada was just thirteen and she was quickly pregnant with Ranulf. Hugh already had a daughter, Amicia, born out of wedlock to an unknown mistress. Bertrada was cousin to the King, Henry II, who had knighted Hugh as his wedding gift. More particularly, Hugh was Earl of Chester and hereditary Viscount of the Bessin; Bertrada was the daughter of Simon, Count of Evreux in eastern Normandy, and brought with her valuable lands in dowry. The union of two powerful families bound together the Viscounties of the Bessin and the Vexin in Normandy and made for strong, peaceful internal relations.

In due course Ranulf would be joined by four sisters: Matilda, Mabel, Hawise and Alice (also known as Agnes). Perhaps Hugh and Bertrada's marriage was not all-consuming, since the Earl also openly found time to father a second son, Roger of Chester, perhaps by the same mistress as Amicia.[6] One day Ranulf would become responsible for his younger sisters and their welfare although his half-siblings would never be his legal responsibility – however he took a keen interest in Amicia's family and their wellbeing. He would make strong political marriages for all of his sisters and help ensure the good fortune of their children. His half-brother also served alongside him on campaign for some years.

It was Ranulf's lot to have a warlike but ultimately rebellious ancestry from which to take a lead. His grandfather, Ranulf de Gernons, a celebrated soldier, had rebelled against King Stephen during the anarchy of the 1140s and had lost his lands when defeated.[7] Although he regained them just before his death in 1153, his own young sons, Hugh and Richard, were viewed with suspicion. Hugh lived at court until he came of age and could be trusted with the earldom. Richard, as younger son, would never inherit. He lived and died in relative obscurity, possibly some of it in Coventry, where he was buried in the Benedictine Cathedral Priory of St Mary before 1173.[8]

In due course the young Hugh gained a fearsome reputation for waging brutal war. While the Countess Bertrada still carried the unborn Ranulf he defeated the Welsh at Baldert near Chester; then made a mound of their severed heads at a hospital outside the town.[9] However, in 1173 he followed his own father's unpredictable lead, becoming instrumental in a rebellion against Henry II in what became known as the War of Earl Hugh.[10] Fighting alongside an old family friend, Ralph, Baron de Fougères, together they ravaged the King's interests in Normandy and Brittany until both were captured and imprisoned at the castle of Dol-de-Bretagne.

Henry II now had two important hostages whom he could execute (although such important prisoners rarely were), imprison indefinitely, or whose future allegiance he could purchase. He chose the last course although Hugh was carted as prisoner from Dol to the castle at Falaise, to the Tower of London, to Caen and back again to Falaise, for two full years as a political hostage until he was felt trustworthy enough to receive back his lands in return for his allegiance. Meanwhile Henry sent his son, Prince Geoffrey, to Brittany before Easter 1175 to take possession of the castles Hugh and Ralph had held against him, principally Dol and Fougères.[11]

In 1177 Hugh received back his lands but retained only one castle at Chester. His others were held of the King's hands, including all those in Normandy. Some of his English castles, like Coventry, were slighted.[12] He campaigned along the Welsh border, winning a famous battle at Bromfield on 13 June 1177 but was then sent to Ireland with Hugh de Lacy, Constable of Chester, as part of the advance guard to prepare the ground for Henry's fourth son, Prince John, who was to become Earl of Ulster.[13] They were natural choices since Cheshire controlled lucrative trade routes to Ireland out of the River Dee, trading mainly for corn – witness *garbs* or wheat-sheaves which are part of the arms of the earls of Chester. Though this was ultimately a futile expedition (the young John made a mess of it), it did show a degree of trust in Hugh, albeit very much at arms' length and, however much he was trusted, he was watched over by his own junior constable. His earldom was his, but he remained in a political straightjacket.

He was possibly brought back from Ireland by dire news from Chester. On a Sunday afternoon in April 1180, fire had broken out and before the conflagration burnt itself out more than half of the town was reduced to ashes.[14] This was the hub of Hugh's remaining power in England, held by his ancestors by right of conquest. It was a desperate blow and the town would not recover overnight. Whatever remedial measures he may have been able to put in place, Hugh was unable to reap many rewards. Within the year he was dead, probably poisoned, like his father before him. He died at Leek in Staffordshire and, like his father, was buried in the chapter-house of St Werburgh's Benedictine Abbey, Chester (now Chester Cathedral).[15]

Hugh's death left Bertrada a widow of twenty-five, with six children. Ranulf, his heir, was only eleven years old, too young to receive his rightful lands yet and held at the King's court in Domfront, Normandy, with his mother and sisters. He was not quite a hostage but a ward of King Henry, sharing his days with others who found themselves landless sureties for the good behaviour of their dominions until the King should see fit to grant them full possession. His early companions at court probably included the young Constance, daughter of Duke Conan IV of Brittany and his wife Margaret, sister of William the Lion, King of Scotland. Constance had been betrothed to King Henry's son, Prince Geoffrey, since 1166, when he was eight and she perhaps six. Conan was forced to abdicate his Dukedom in 1181, apparently bypassing his own son Richard, in favour of Prince Geoffrey (under extreme pressure from King Henry).[16] That same year Geoffrey and Constance were married, binding an unhappy Brittany to England.[17] From this simple union began forty years of regional strife which would suck in Ranulf again and again. Constance and Ranulf developed what was probably a lifelong mutual loathing, further stirred up by events in their individual, rapidly-converging lives.

Ranulf received a simple education in war and chivalry as befitted a young Norman noble. He was literate and wrote (or dictated) in competent Latin, as the style of his few surviving letters shows, and he grew up at a royal court well-known for its espousal of the arts. That said, he probably had little spare time on his hands, while being prepared for the rigours as well as the chivalry of Norman knighthood. We know his tutor as one Alexander, son of Ralph.[18] He was almost certainly a minor Norman steward who married Annabella de Savage, daughter of a Norman lord from Caen.[19] He would have taught Ranulf Latin and English (somewhere between late Anglo-Saxon and a pre-Chaucerian middle English); his mother-tongue, of course, was Norman French. Some mathematics (in terms of accounting) and some geometry would also have been on the curriculum. He would certainly have been able to ride almost as soon as he could walk, since like all noble Normans he would live a mounted life, in peace and war.

Ranulf would probably have received his spiritual guidance from a succession of family priests who were retained by the Earl throughout his life and who would travel with him, becoming his confidantes. Such a priest or clerk was usually a Benedictine monk. However, Ranulf seemingly was slightly different, since in his teens he was probably attended by his half-sister's husband, Sir Ralph Mainwaring, a man who seems to have enjoyed a varied career. Sir Ralph, who had already served Ranulf's father, Earl Hugh, became embroiled in a controversy over whether his young wife, Ranulf's half-sister Amicia, was legitimate. She was not.[20] Amicia probably died not long after, since she disappears totally from records; the debate over her legitimacy would have clouded her rights to any inheritance, in any case. She and Ralph did, however, have a son, Thomas (later Sir Thomas) Mainwaring and a daughter, deferently named Bertrada. The family, from 'St Jean de Mesnil-Guerin' (ie the root of *Mainwaring*) near Vire in Normandy, owed knightly service to the earls of Chester as Viscounts of the Val de Vire and Ralph was involved in the issue of Earl Hugh's charters in Coventry before 1181. He seems to have taken holy orders, possibly being described as Ranulf's chaplain in the 1190s.[21] He was made Justice of Chester in 1196, a post he held until 1202. By 1208 he was in receipt of the lucrative benefice of St Michael's Church, Coventry. Ralph was replaced as Ranulf's personal chaplain around 1196 by John, Augustinian Prior of Trentham Priory who was himself succeeded about 1204 by another cleric named Thomas. Another is known, by the name of Roger. This seems to have been a regular, contract-based appointment and the dates of each known contract equate well with 'chapters' in Ranulf's life.

In 1187 Ranulf lost his maternal grandfather, Simon (he never knew Ranulf de Gernons, his eponymous paternal grandfather). Simon, Count of Evreux (Count is the nearest French equivalent of Earl) was killed at the battle of Hattin in the Holy Land, as Jerusalem was lost to Saladin and the armies of Islam.[22] It is not known whether Simon had ever had any real influence on the young Ranulf, by now aged seventeen, but this was the first time that his young life would be touched by events in the Holy Land. It would not be the last.

In 1188 Ranulf's mother, the dowager Countess, still aged only thirty-two, made a rare appearance in records in her own right. Gerald of Wales tells a curious story of her keeping tame does for milking purposes.[23] On a particular occasion Gerald was present when she presented three cheeses made with this deer-milk to the Archbishop of Canterbury. Far from being one of his fanciful stories, for which he is known, he added the detail that they were made in small wicker or wooden containers, very much like small Norman cheeses such as Pavé d'Auge and Camembert still are today. On this evidence alone she seems to have been a woman in touch with her surroundings. Little else is heard of her, except in relation to the dower-lands and manors which she retained after Earl Hugh's death or when she attended Ranulf as Earl.[24] She made one or two grants to monasteries in common with her husband and her widowhood was spent mainly at her chief manor of Brècy, Normandy, until her death in 1227.[25]

We know little about the teenage Ranulf, since he lived out of the limelight at court amongst his peers. His martial training would have been constant. Any remaining parental guidance was abrogated to his tutor and older nobles. We do not even know what he looked like, there being no paintings or certain sculpture of him. He would have worn his hair short and probably worn a beard as soon as he could grow one. From a later description we know that adulthood brought him no great physical stature although this is not apparent on the surviving figurative seals which show him mounted and resplendent in full armour, a formulaic view. He took his military bearing seriously and while he rightly used the Arms of Chester as his own, he also employed a personal seal showing a lion-rampant, a common symbol of strength and ferocity[26]. Linked to that is the fact that in adult life he was taunted by an enemy as being noticeably shorter than many of his contemporaries, a taunt he bitterly resented and quickly saw avenged in battle. Amongst the tall Viking-descended Norman nobles, where good nourishment, careful marriage-choices and constant physical training lent themselves towards a prominent stature, he was perhaps a good few inches shorter than his immediate peers. We also know he developed a fearsome temper, not a bad thing in a battle, but something which might just as easily get him into trouble as out of it. Combined with impetuosity and occasional tactlessness, it would flare up at inopportune moments in his life and had the potential to cause him difficulties. Later references also suggest that in adulthood he grew fond of wine, while his later dealings with King John indicate he also acquired a liking for gambling. Neither made for easy bed-fellows. In common with his kings, however, it would be hunting which was to be his life-long passion and he would come to maintain numerous hunting parks.

At sixteen, Ranulf was nearing his 'majority', an ill-defined term in late twelfth-century Normandy. He was still at court where an ailing Henry II was less and less in control of his Empire, which stretched from Berwick-upon-Tweed in the north, beyond Bordeaux in the south, from Ireland in the west to the upper reaches of the Loire in the east. Henry II was estranged from his wife Eleanor, who held Aquitaine, but hardly in his name. His rebellious eldest son, Henry, who had actually been sensationally crowned 'the young king' while his father was alive, had died. On 19 August 1186, another son, Prince Geoffrey, now Duke of Brittany, fell from his horse in a tournament and was crushed when the horse fell on him. His funeral briefly brought the rival kingdoms of England and France together, since the young French King Philip Augustus the year before had successfully courted Geoffrey's allegiance. He apparently had to be restrained from throwing himself into the grave in a great show of grief. He had just lost a golden opportunity to use Geoffrey and Brittany against the aged King Henry.

Philip might almost have been weeping for the chaos to come for, with his power waning and the charismatic but rebellious soldier-prince, Richard, Duke of Aquitaine, next in line to the throne (as Richard the Lionheart), a rudderless Brittany threatened the delicate balance between England and France. It was on a collision course with Normandy.

As his own opposition to his aged father grew into open revolt, and with John, his able but fractious and impetuous younger brother in-tow, Richard sought new allies in his bid for the throne. Poitou and Anjou came to him. Following on, the great lords of Normandy flocked to him, although many held back while others tested the waters. Ralph de Fougères, perhaps mindful of the onerous personal terms he had endured after the disastrous revolt of 1173, was one of the first to turn to Richard, bringing with him the brittle border-lands of eastern Brittany.

The old King was not done for just yet, however. Although the empire threatened to split apart, Henry now betrothed his trump card, Ranulf of Chester, to his widowed daughter-in-law Constance of Brittany. During their short, five-year marriage she and Prince Geoffrey had had a daughter, Eleanor and at the time of Geoffrey's death, she had been carrying his second child. In March 1187 she gave birth to a son; generating grave concerns at court, and deliberately egging on Breton aspirations to independence, she named him Arthur, evoking the myths of a rose-tinted Arthurian past which Celtic parts of Britain and Brittany have always shared.[27] She and both her children, however, were Henry's prisoners at court, hostages for Brittany's continued peaceful acquiescence. Her support for Breton aspirations to independence were ironic since her grandfather, Duke Alan, had been an English-born lord (described as such in 1137–46) and her mother, Margaret, was a Scot. Constance had little Breton blood in her.[28] It may have been a not-unnatural opposition to her early status of pawn at court which drove her gradually into the arms of the nationalist movements for Breton independence.

The French historian M. Menard described Constance as enraged by her lot, since she felt that her new husband, a mere earl and as yet landless, was a snub to the Breton ducal house. Her first husband had been a Prince and Duke of Brittany; the natural choice for his replacement, which would have suited the Church, would have been Prince Richard, but he was already spoken for – not that a betrothal could not have been undone if the will was there. However, Richard was now at odds with Henry and the succession of the English crown was far from assured. The price Constance paid was that her son had been relegated (in her eyes) from possible heir to the Kingdom of England back to heir to the Duchy of Brittany and, until majority, the ward of an unknown English earl, not even yet a knight, who might use and abuse her son's hereditary titles at will. Ranulf, as his new step-father and guardian, became a political pawn in a power-struggle bigger than any teenager could ever fear. At first, he may not have fully realised what was happening to him, but his advisors were aware. If he wanted his earldom, he had to fall in line. On 1 January 1189 he was knighted by the King at Caen; he was officially of-age and took formal possession of his lands which had been in the King's 'safe-keeping' since Earl Hugh's death in 1181. His wedding to Constance followed soon after on 3 February,[29] a date deliberately chosen as the feast of St Werburgh the Virgin, which mirrored the dedication of St Werburgh's Abbey at Chester (now Chester Cathedral). Ranulf was now officially Earl of Chester and Viscount of his Norman lands, and by right of his wife's inheritance he was now Duke of Brittany and Earl of Richmond. Before long he would be sorely tested. He was not yet nineteen years old.

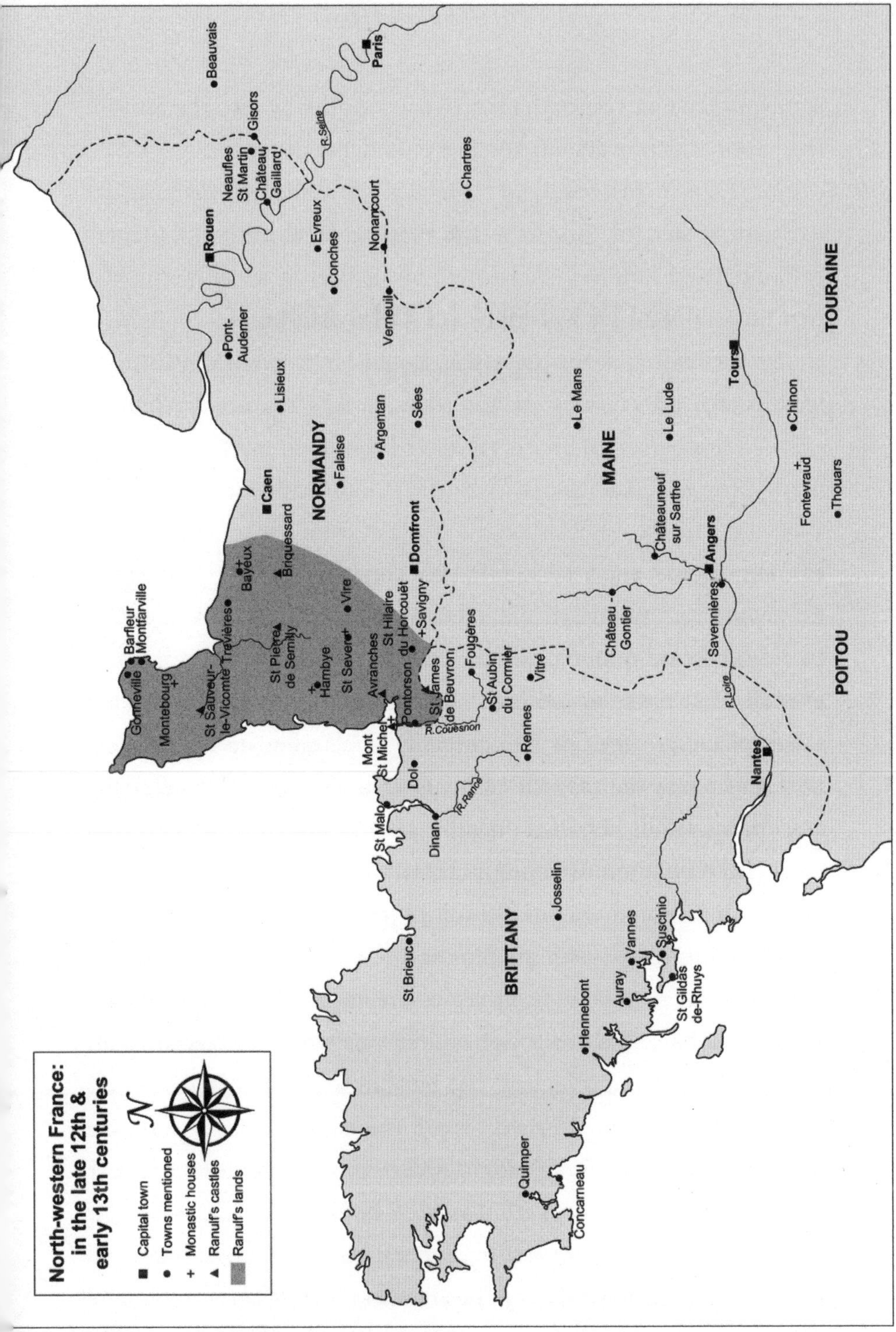

North-western France in the late twelfth and early thirteenth centuries. *Drawn by Jacqueline Harding.*

2

INTO THE LIMELIGHT (1189–94)

Having come of age and been freshly knighted, Ranulf set to work. Following his marriage, the young Earl was naturally required to attend to his dominions and some immediate travel was to be expected, on both sides of the Channel. This does appear to have taken place, presumably beginning in England since his earldom of Chester was the taproot of his wealth. Geoffrey Barraclough's work on Ranulf's personal documents shows that in that first year or so he was certainly issuing charters at Coventry and Chester before all England was overtaken by the death of the old King, Henry II, on 6 July 1189 at Chinon.[1]

By now the succession had been assured and Richard was quickly proclaimed king. What was not assured was whether everyone else's face would fit the new regime. The factions which had existed in the late 1180s had totally divided Henry and Richard. Prince John did not even wait for Henry's death to declare for the ambitious Richard, breaking his ailing father's heart even as he lay on his death-bed. As one of the last of Henry's newly-knighted nobles, Ranulf now found himself in a potentially difficult position, as did all who had followed Henry. How much he had been in Henry's thrall is difficult to gauge;

some have suggested that Henry had him make a vow of crusade on his behalf in 1188.[2] Certainly he might have felt he had cause, his grandfather having died at Hattin the year before. He was very young yet, however, and such a promise may have been felt to be premature. The Dieulacres Chronicle actually says that he did go on crusade with Richard in 1190 and that he shared similar adventures.[3] This, however, is a single source and is uncorroborated by any other although some have believed it. Certainly the normally reliable Ralph of Coggeshall lists the nobles who did accompany Richard and Ranulf was not amongst them.[4] Roger of Hoveden too omits him – and he himself went on the crusade with Richard, so ought to have known who was there and who was not.

In order to prevent a power-vacuum yawning, Richard's coronation took place relatively quickly, on 3 September, at Westminster Abbey.[5] He moved to reassure by rewarding the existing nobility and drawing new nobles to himself, many of whom paid huge sums for numerous high offices, their outlay designed to fill the coffers ready for the coming crusade. There was little of material significance the King could lavish upon the young Ranulf which might mean something – he was already becoming aware of his new wealth; he controlled lands and property without compare on both sides of the Channel. He and Richard were related distantly, sharing Henry I as an ancestor. Ranulf's reward, therefore, was the prestige of being given pride of place in the coronation procession. Matthew Paris states of the procession to the coronation chair:

> Then there followed them six earls and counts, carrying a single coffer, on which were laid out the royal insignia and garments; following them was the Earl of Chester, holding up high the crown,

which was of gold and wonderfully set with jewels.[6]

There followed a huge all-male banquet (at which, amongst other things a phenomenal 5000 chickens were consumed), a celebration of chivalry and knight-service designed to cement allegiance across an empire. Nevertheless, for Ranulf certainties were few. Richard kept one of his younger sisters at court as a family ward, if not perhaps as an outright hostage. Here she lived with Ranulf's wife, his step-daughter Eleanor and his step-son, the toddler Arthur, who were definitely there for Britanny's acquiescence.[7]

In early March 1190 Richard held a great council at Nonancourt, Normandy. Most of the leading men in England attended. Here Richard intended to set his affairs in order on both sides of the Channel before embarking on what would become known to history as the Third Crusade.[8] He appointed his officers to look after England, auctioning off most of the county sheriffdoms to raise money for the crusade. His judge of character in this was seriously flawed and his officials quarreled almost immediately he left. He also made Prince John swear not to enter England for three years, an oath he broke as soon as Richard was out of sight. At Dreux on 16 March Richard met the French King, Philip Augustus, to discuss the coming crusade before moving off to tour his continental dominions and at the same time saw to treaty arrangements for his forthcoming marriage to Berengaria of Navarre. On 2 July he linked up with Philip again at Vezelay (Burgundy) before their two armies set out for the Holy Land.[9]

For Ranulf the situation he inherited, just as Richard left, was precarious, despite his wealth. His new family was the nub of the problem. Richard, prior to his departure, announced his heir – a necessary step since he was about to go on crusade and might not return; his recklessness in battle was already well known.

However, he stirred up trouble by stating formally that his brother Prince John, Count of Mortain would be overlooked in favour of the three-year-old Arthur of Brittany, Ranulf's step-son. Richard even began to make plans for Arthur's betrothal to the daughter of Tancred, King of Sicily. Large sums of gold changed hands to secure it – more funds for the crusade.[10] In the late twelfth century the rules of succession were far from clear and while *primogeniture* (first-born male inherits all) was becoming normal, both John and Arthur had good claims to the English throne by blood. In addition it may be that Richard harboured some resentment that Ranulf had been married to Constance, when he should have been the more likely choice, a view put forward by one French historian.[11] Henry, of course, had been implacably opposed to his son's growing power which was a real threat. Conferring Brittany upon him would have played into his hands. The simmering Constance may have been mollified by Richard's statement of support, since it seemed to elevate Arthur to a better place and Brittany to the centre of affairs. It might, however, have the effect of rendering Ranulf's wardship an irrelevance. Constance, never one to shy away from court intrigue, possibly along her twin brother Richard, became the young Arthur's advisors and as stepfather, Ranulf was bypassed.[12] Constance chose to remain largely in Brittany while Ranulf had to tend to his lands in England and Normandy. It was fast becoming a marriage in name only. Indeed Constance justified her distance from Ranulf on grounds of an illegal union.[13] She sought the support of the Breton Bishops and the Pope in stating that she and Ranulf were too closely related for the marriage to be valid (they were indeed cousins through their great-grandparents). She conveniently ignored the fact that she and her first husband Geoffrey had also shared a similar consanguinity. Rome kept silent and no annulment ever came.

Ranulf soon had much to attend to; King Richard's departure had been swiftly followed by major unrest on both sides of the Channel, stirred up principally by Prince John and his adherents. John was Ranulf's neighbour in England (John's Derbyshire lands were contiguous with Ranulf's in Cheshire and Staffordshire), while in Normandy, John was not only his neighbour but Ranulf also held some of his lands of him as Count of Mortain (principally the 'Terre Venions' around Vire).

In England Ranulf was surrounded by John's followers. This even extended to the Church, where John's man, the Bishop of Coventry, Hugh Nonant, had fomented serious trouble at his Benedictine Cathedral, ejecting the monks and taking over their possessions (he is reputed to have said 'To hell with monks!'). In their place he instituted his own community of canons (probably Augustinians). He also began to amass great personal wealth from secular sources, legitimately buying the sheriffdoms of Warwickshire, Staffordshire and Leicestershire for 300 marks.[14] Although he was made to promise not to exercise this authority by Baldwin, Archbishop of Canterbury, he broke his promise as soon as Baldwin died on crusade in 1190 and began to render fraudulent accounts to the exchequer, lining his own pockets. Letters written by his uncle, Arnulf of Lisieux, show that he had always been a rash character, attracting condemnation; clearly age had not mellowed him. Nonant's lead was, however, the start of a pattern John's allies repeated across the country. As sheriff, Nonant then began to send in accounts for the Earl of Chester's properties including his castles at Chartley and Newcastle under Lyme. The young Ranulf in Normandy did not yet have the personal support to stand in the Bishop's way. Like the timing of his own accession to the earldom, Nonant's appointment to the See of Coventry was a late move by Henry II, after he had been something of a diplomatic star in the dying days of the former regime. Since he now had the ear of Prince John, and Richard was 2000 miles away, Ranulf sensibly kept a low profile. He was forced on 30 July 1192 to appear to offer support to Nonant. He issued a charter to the Cathedral Priory of Coventry, formally giving control of the nearby (and rich) St Michael's parish church in Coventry to Nonant's reordered Priory community.[15] He attached his ring as a mark of his good faith. Why he chose not to formally seal it is unclear. Perhaps by doing so he held back from condoning Nonant's actions at a time when ambiguity might be the key to his safety.

By 1192 the Third Crusade had ended on a sour note with the leaders having fallen out. The King of France had returned home early and began plotting with Prince John to oust Richard who was amongst the last to leave Palestine. He immediately took up arms against Richard's vassals and all along the frontiers of Normandy, Anjou, the Touraine, Poitou and Gascony, constables began to fortify their castles against the coming onslaught.[16] John sought to secure the succession, freeze out the young Arthur, and trust that the reckless Richard would die of wounds or disease. He was part way to his goal.

Richard, his interests supposedly still protected by Papal decree while away on crusade, had concluded a three-year truce with Saladin and set out for home, alarmed by the months-old rumours which had reached him.[17] Had he stayed, he might well have died of disease or wounds and John would have succeeded. The reality was that Richard's army was worn out and he himself was very ill; he had lost many men, either to sickness or wounds, including a number of major allies, not least Ranulf's neighbours and family friends Ralph de Fougères from the Breton border and William Ferrers the elder, Earl of Derby.[18] Richard's return was suddenly halted by shipwreck in the northern Adriatic, forcing him overland into hostile country. Shortly before Christmas 1192, travelling in disguise, he was riding hard for Vienna, rumours of his identity and wherabouts preceding him. Eventually his party was recognised and captured by men of Duke Leopold of Austria, vassal of the German Emperor Henry VI, to whom Richard was then sold. He was first of all imprisoned for a short while in Dürnstein Castle, one of a chain of castle-eyries high above the River Danube.[19] Thereafter he was too valuable to leave alone in one place for long so was moved about constantly with the emperor's court, sitting mostly at Worms (Germany). Ransom and freedom would eventually follow in February 1194, draining England and Normandy of finances; more damaging though was the intrigue of Philip Augustus and Prince John, who offered counter-ransom for the Duke to hang on to Richard, while both still thought they could come out on top in their scheming. In reality, the inept John was outmatched in Normandy again and again by an able and acquisitive Philip Augustus, who flattered and mollified John on the one hand and then promptly outmanoeuvred him in battle.

During his captivity, Richard was able to exercise some power, living in quarters befitting his station. He received guests and messengers from England, although few were official – except those whose message was either sent by or sanctioned by John or his party. Some emissaries were even those clearly in John's camp, such as Bishop Nonant.[20]

In 1193 Ranulf received his first official post, almost certainly from Richard's Justiciar, Walter of Coutances, when he was appointed a judge in the King's court.[21] For the first time he now served alongside trusted and time-served royal supporters trying to maintain order in the face of John's tiresome scheming. Some provided lifelong constancy and friendship, such as the superbly able William Marshall, the most celebrated knight of his generation. They were all his elders; he could learn much from them of the workings of both the dispensation of royal authority and the royal court.

As the King's party sought to maintain (or re-establish) control, Ranulf joined his fellow justices under the Archbishop of Rouen in successfully besieging John's party at Windsor Castle until, in April 1193, a negotiated truce ensured a peaceful outcome. No one was over-eager to get too far on the wrong side of John since Richard's release was still uncertain; John might yet be king. However, the spiralling military situation along Normandy's south-eastern border was dire and the south coast of England was put on high alert, fearing a French invasion.

Attempts to oust Richard continued on both sides of the Channel, unrest fomented by John, aided by his closest followers and abetted by the King of France, whose potential support John could neither count on nor dispense with. Whole tracts of the Norman frontier were ceded to Philip Augustus in return for his support for John's claim to the throne.[22] Gaining Philip's support was costing both crown and duchy dear, however. Even as he negotiated, Philip continued to exert pressure all along the eastern and south-eastern Norman frontier, in 1193–4 taking state-of-the-art castles such as Conches, one after another.[23] Countess Bertrada's own family home, Evreux, encircled once Conches fell, held out for the moment and re-supplied, nervously awaiting relief; eastern Normandy seemed beyond help.

Many thought Richard dead and John was not about to tell them otherwise. However, with the ransom of 100,000 marks eventually paid, hostages exchanged and the humiliating grant of all England to the Emperor of Germany, Richard was finally released on about 4 February 1194.[24] Standing hostage for a king was an honour; a number were asked but only one man refused – Robert Nonant, Bishop Hugh's brother. The whole family was firmly against Richard, even as the King's captivity was clearly nearing its end. Hugh and Robert's treachery forced them to flee, Hugh's departure in particular taking pressure off Ranulf's Midland dominions and allowing the Cathedral Priory in Coventry to begin to restore the *status quo*.[25]

Richard's release was certainly not without pain. He was almost re-arrested in Germany on trumped-up murder charges but narrowly escaped this reversal due to help from allies made during his captivity. However, his parole came at a heavy price. As Duke of Normandy he owed allegiance to the King of France; for his Kingdom of England he now swore allegiance to the Emperor of Germany. His return to England thereafter was swift but known only to a few – and he remained under guard by the emperors' soldiers. Nevertheless, it was cause for his party to rally. He bypassed Normandy, side-stepping Philip's armies for now and headed straight for England. He landed at Sandwich in Kent and stopped only at Canterbury to give thanks for his safe return. At London his German guards finally departed, astonished by what they saw and declaring that they would have asked for a higher ransom had they had the slightest idea of how rich England's capital looked. As Richard headed north, one by one the rebel strongholds gave up their opposition, abandoning John without a fight, until only two remained, Tickhill (Derbyshire) and Nottingham.

Ranulf was among those few who knew Richard's return was imminent. Even as Richard headed across Europe he himself led an army into the East Midlands, aided by his brother-in-law of four years, David, Earl of Huntingdon (whom he had married to his oldest sister, Matilda). David was the brother of the King of Scotland, William the Lion, and had considerable lands in the Midlands. Marriage had also made him Constance's uncle. He was also a valuable ally for Ranulf to bring to Richard's aid since he gave his help of his own free will; no demands for troops or war taxes were ever levied on the earldom of Huntingdon.[26] His was not an altruistic appearance, however, since he also represented the King of Scotland, who was pressing for possession of Northumberland and Cumberland. His Breton links cannot have gone unnoticed. Even without further allies the Earls' entourages were likely to exceed 200 knights with ten times that number of men at arms. It was a formidable array. Tickhill quickly capitulated without a fight but Nottingham was proving tougher, partly because the rumours of Richard's return could not yet be substantiated. Roger of Hoveden recounts that a great army under the Earls of Chester and Huntingdon, aided by William Ferrers the Younger, Earl of Derby (but still probably uninvested with the earldom, since his father's death on the recent crusade) marched on Nottingham.[27] Presumably all winter in the mustering, they laid siege to the castle in February 1194, as soon as the early spring weather allowed the campaigning season to begin and the roads were sufficiently passable for a full siege train. It was also timed to perfection, with Richard himself thought to be only weeks away.

The town of Nottingham, perched on its high sandstone cliff, was quickly occupied by Ranulf and its great urban castle full of John's rebels was surrounded. Ranulf and the Earl of Huntingdon brought up siege equipment, alleged to include, for the first time in England, machines designed to throw 'Greek Fire', a flamethrower-cum-fireball catapult, a terror-weapon adapted from the Saracens during the crusade. The knightly scribe Jean de Joinville, a generation later (1249), described the desperate efforts of one French knight to throw off his outer clothes in the midst of a siege in Egypt when he could not put out the napalm-like substance.[28] It must have terrified the inhabitants of Nottingham shut up inside the castle with the rebels.

The screw tightened gradually within the town, but the castle was stoutly defended. Siegeworks were dug and attempts repeatedly made to gain a toehold on the castle defences, which had themselves been given extra defensive works, including an added barbican. Both sides were taking casualties but the defenders could not be persuaded that their cause was lost. News that Richard had landed in Kent was met with incredulity; still they expected John to be declared king. Finally on 25 March Richard himself arrived with reinforcements, to the sound of trumpets, and ordered the all-out frontal attack which Ranulf and his brother-in-law had been preparing. The sight of the royal standard and the sound of the fanfare should have been enough to make the defenders give up but they probably thought it merely propaganda.

An all-out attack began and Roger of Hoveden speaks of terrible casualties, both dead and injured on both sides.[29] Richard, ever the action-man, himself took part in the melée and his own bodyguard was hit by a volley of arrows, but by evening they had taken the barbican and the outer bailey. Overnight the siege engines were moved forward, although the defenders sallied out to burn the defences which had fallen to the royal army, denying them cover. By the light of the following day an enraged Richard had some of the previous day's prisoners hanged in full view of the castle. The defenders knew what to expect if they continued to hold out. The following day, 27 March, he gave safe conduct to envoys from the castle, simply to prove to them that it was indeed the King who had arrived. On their return to their own lines the castle capitulated after a six week siege. A relieved Richard celebrated by going hunting in Sherwood Forest for the day.[30]

Within a month Ranulf found himself at court in Winchester as Richard on 17 April underwent a public 'crown-wearing', not strictly a second coronation but a second chance to demonstrate his God-given authority and for miscreant nobles to return to his peace. The procession had all the pomp of a coronation, however, and just as in 1189 a train of nobles followed him up the cathedral nave. Having previously carried the crown at the coronation, Ranulf now carried one of the three swords of state, named *Curtana*, the other two were borne by William, King of Scotland and Hamelin, Earl of Warrenne.[31] Within days Ranulf and the royal justices met once more, chiefly to levy fines on those who had abandoned the King since 1190.[32] He was constantly at court for those few days, witnessing charters and seeing the King's justice in operation.[33] Richard's mind, however, was elsewhere. With government in England returned to the hands of trustworthy men, he set out once more for Normandy where his decisive leadership in war was desperately needed. With him he took an army headed by some of his most trusted young nobles, among them Ranulf, whose stature at Windsor and then Nottingham had come so obviously to the King's attention. Richard also had affairs of state to settle, which involved Ranulf.

3

WAR UNDER RICHARD (1194–99)

The army of the Lionheart swept through Normandy and headed for a showdown meeting with Prince John. They met at Lisieux, the first time in over three years. It was understandably fraught but Richard, who had a reputation for intemperate rage, was uncharacteristically gentle with his brother, whom he forgave, describing him as merely a child. This was indeed a cruel jibe as in 1194 John was 28 and Richard 37. He was less inclined to forgive John's self-seeking counsellors who had incurred his wrath. The vile Nonant had already been forced to flee from Coventry in February, taking refuge in the abbey of Bec-Helhouin in Normandy. Although he eventually received a royal pardon of sorts, and the Coventry Bishopric remained his (the lucrative sheriffdoms did not), his last years were spent in disgrace, under threat of a huge fine if he ever stepped out of line. It was said that when he lay on his deathbed in 1198, the list of his sins was so long and heinous, no one could be found who was willing to absolve him.[1] Richard's policy to keep John quiet was to give him back his few lands, (Mortain, Eye, Gloucester) but to withhold all the castles which normally came with them; it was political emasculation.

With John in his place Richard moved on to his father's great castle of Verneuil, invested by Philip Augustus since 10 May. On 29 May Philip panicked at news of Richard's approach and, raising the siege, withdrew in some disarray, suggesting to some that this was the moment of Normandy's liberation.[2] Normans of all ranks were now tired by three years of war along the frontiers and a peace-movement was gaining ground, led by John (scheming again), William d'Albini, Earl of Arundel and David Earl of Huntingdon (both Ranulf's brothers-in-law). Ranulf himself was in a difficult position since, while Richard through the summer campaigned south-eastwards into the Touraine and the Loire valley, he was left in charge of the army in Normandy. However, with the hard-pressed frontier liable to crumble he was on the defensive and he too may have been in favour of a peace settlement. The Earl of Leicester, hero of Richard's crusade, was captured at Rouen, where the city's Archbishop sought a truce with Philip. This was granted, and under its terms Richard received some of the castles back which Philip had taken or negotiated from John, such as Conches-en-Ouches, to the relief of the nearby Evreux and of the castle's owner Roger de Tosny who had lost it but had still remained at Richard's side, probably because his family also had considerable lands and castles in Leicestershire (Belvoir) and Staffordshire (Stafford).[3] Roger had fought with great distinction alongside Richard in the crusade and had sent his own son Ferdinand to be a hostage for Richard's ransom. However, the new peace was to be short-lived, largely because Richard was unconvinced of its benefits since overall he himself had the upper hand in the duchy. While he thought he could win, there seemed little mileage in truces and the lull was soon ended by Richard who returned to the offensive. Conches, like other castles whose strategic locations remained irrespective of ownership, would soon change hands once more.

Ranulf's home-life since his marriage had been almost non-existent. A mutual loathing growing between he and Constance made sure this was not a problem, however. Brittany's allegiance did concern Richard greatly, since it held the key to Normandy's western flank in any campaigns in either Normandy or the Touraine; in addition its rocky, wreck-strewn coasts had to be navigated by every English or Norman ship which headed for either Poitou or Gascony. To sail farther than St Malo was to require Breton agreement to safe-passage. Since Richard had been in the Holy Land he had held Eleanor, the young daughter of Constance and his late brother Geoffrey in regal custody, hostage for Breton peace and acquiescence. Ranulf, as her step-father, probably felt little for her.[4]

Conches-en-Ouches (Eure). A link in the chain of Angevin castles around which the frontier ebbed and flowed through the 1190s despite large sums expended on their defences. Conches was key to a successful encirclement of Evreux and changed hands three times between 1193 and 1202. (2006)

While imprisoned in Austria Richard had negotiated for his gaoler, Duke Leopold, to marry the young Eleanor to one of his sons, as part of his own ransom, with a dowry of 50,000 marks. She herself would have had no part in negotiations, nor would she have had any opportunity to object. To modern eyes this political marriage market (always to the advantage of the family or its estates rather than the individual) is harsh. It may have seemed so to contemporaries too, but little is said by them. Eleanor was not badly cared for. In fact she lived in comfort with the daughter of the Emperor of Cyprus (Isaac Dukas Comnenus, captured in 1191) and his family at Rouen. From 1190 Eleanor appears in records as the regular beneficiary of court expenses.[5] In 1195 Richard spent over £168 on clothing alone for his hostages as they were moved by their gaolers to Chinon.[6] Her impending marriage to Leopold's son occasioned the move and she was actually on her way, when news came of the death of the Duke after a riding accident. Since he was generally disliked, Brittany was unhappy with the proposed marriage and Richard was also loathed to honour such an agreement made under duress. Now everyone was happy, presumably apart from Leopold. Eleanor returned to custody by the end of January.[7] The remainder of the family was also a problem, however. Constance, backed by her mainly northern and western (Breton-speaking) barons, was agitating on behalf of her son, Arthur, himself still promised in marriage to the daughter of Tancred, King of Sicily.[8] Although Arthur was indeed the named heir to Richard – and had been since 1190, John's reconciliation with Richard had now put him back in the frame too. Since Constance and Ranulf seemed to loath each other, Ranulf could not be relied upon to back hers and Arthur's cause at court; the Earl was clearly the King's man.

In order to prise Arthur and Constance apart, Ranulf and King Richard hatched a plan which took some time to execute. It was planned from the outset that the wayward Constance needed to be brought to heel and Arthur be brought to court to end their machinations. They met 23 March 1195 at Ranulf's castle of St-James-de-Beuvron and planned the detail when Richard signed a charter of royal protection for one of Ranulf's sponsored monasteries, St Marie de Montmorel.[9] It was witnessed by Ranulf, his half-brother Roger of Chester, Roger de Lacy Constable of Chester and the knights Baldwin Wake (one of the hostages for Richard's ransom terms and not long released), William de Verdun (a family long associated with the earls of Chester) and others. All may have been party to the plan – to take Constance and Arthur captive.

Constance was stirring up elements of the Breton nobility against Richard and the Anglo-Norman cause, making the most of their simmering resentment of all things non-Breton. By no means all the Breton noble houses agreed either with her, or amongst themselves, since disunity had been a hallmark of their previous dealings both with England and France. The peninsula divided roughly along cultural lines. To the south and east lay broadly French-speaking Brittany, which would declare either for England or France, always seemingly on the basis of whichever was in the ascendant. To the west and north lay mainly Breton-speaking Brittany, a simmering pot of discontent. The Bretons here sought only independence under their Duke and dismissed his feudal obligations to either England or France as secondary at best, at worst irrelevant. Their cause was immensely personal and any attempt to play politics with the Breton succession (from Duke Geoffrey onwards) brought only anger and bitter resentment liable to spill a great deal of blood.

In order to spring the trap Constance was summoned with Arthur to Rouen.[10] The pretext is not known, but she may have been led to believe that the question of Arthur's succession to the English throne was to be formally discussed, or perhaps a rare family reunion with the hostage Eleanor. Little else may have been persuasive enough. In the meantime Ranulf headed for his lands in western Normandy, just behind Richard's messengers. Straightway he sent out spies to shadow the King's messengers and elicit from them Constance's movements and note the time of her departure. Watching her passage, they then rode to Ranulf who waited at his castle at St-James-de-Beuvron with a small force.

The progress of Constance and Arthur's entourage would have been a stately affair, probably a hundred horses or more in number, as befitted a ducal court, and it was probably well armed. She took the main road, probably from Dinan eastwards. A day or so east of Dol-de-Bretagne, a town still notable for a number of surviving Romanesque stone houses, the land suddenly drops from the last ridge of Brittany to the flood plain of the River Couësnon and the bustling market town of Pontorson. The road descends in full view of the plain, and anyone watching from below. This was familiar territory for Ranulf but was the border between Brittany and Normandy, the waterway from the interior to Mont St Michel visible in the distance. Pontorson itself was Breton, home territory and Constance had no reason to think twice (she was after all under the terms of the King's summons) and expected to pass into Normandy uneventfully. However, with a small force out of his castle at nearby St-James-de-Beuvron, Ranulf ambushed Constance and Arthur at the crossing of the Couësnon.[11] He had been following her progress all the way from deep inside Brittany and knew where she would cross and when, straight into his hands. While Arthur managed to escape to St Malo, whisked away by his tutor, Ranulf took his estranged wife to the castle at St-James-de-Beuvron. There she would remain his prisoner for over a year. Ranulf could now once more (and did) style himself Duke of Brittany, at least until Arthur, still barely ten years old, came of age.[12] The ability to style himself Duke was of particular value to Richard since Henry II had exempted parts of the Breton army (such as the forces of Pontorson) from service unless the Duke served with them. While Arthur was in the ascendant, Richard could not call them to arms; with Ranulf Duke in more than just name, he could. The King had just recruited perhaps a thousand more soldiers at a stroke, provided they would follow convention and desert Arthur for Ranulf.

For much of Brittany this was simply too much and rebellion, never far from the surface, turned into full-scale revolt as Arthur fled to the court of Philip Augustus. As ever, Richard wasted no time and early in 1197 Richard and Ranulf led an army into eastern Brittany and cowed the rebellious lords. They capitulated and reluctantly signed an alliance.[13] Arthur and his advisors continued to agitate from the safety of the French court. Normandy's western frontier was shored up once more, for the time-being. Richard could not afford for the Bretons to coalesce since under a good leader they were formidable in battle. The contemporary historian Geoffrey de Vinsauf noted that Richard himself had placed the Bretons in the second line at the battle of Arsuf (1191) in the Holy Land since, Vinsauf observed, at that time they were second only in discipline to the Knights Templar of the front rank; the Normans and English had been in the fourth rank, with the King's standard.

Conversely, it remains a possibility that the historian was affording them undue respect when in fact Richard had deployed them as more expendable than his own knights. In the Holy Land it was in fact normal for the Templars, as protectors of pilgrims, to be the shock-troops of the front rank – their casualties were often heavy as a result but everyone agreed on their ferocity in battle.

By the summer of 1196 Ranulf had been back in Normandy with Richard on active service for two years. He was then about twenty-six years old, younger than Richard, who was now approaching forty. The glory-days of his campaigning in England seemed to be over, replaced by the attrition of constant campaigning and a procession of sieges. It is worthwhile noting who his companions were during this time. Those nobles who held most of their lands in Normandy, Brittany, Poitou or the Touraine were already engaged in the campaigns. Richard wrote in April 1196 to the Archbishop of Canterbury to ensure that such men came to his aid quickly, with only a short delay of a month or two for those whose lands were principally in England, presumably to make arrangements for their lands and properties in their absence.[14] However, whereas in the England of 1191–3 the King's party was thrown together by their opposition to John and moved around as a single armed party, in the Normandy of 1194–6 they were spread along a volatile frontier. The bonds were looser. Ranulf's personal entourage and companions at this time was a group much more familial than it had been in England. He relied on men whose families had served his father before him, and his grandfather before that. He knew them all personally and they trusted each other. Most would remain with him for the next few years. Other than the visit to St-James-de-Beuvron in March 1195, Ranulf is known to have spent time in 1196–8 with his brother-in-law William d'Albini Earl of Arundel, Saher de Quincy, Earl of Winchester, Peter de Préaux, Hasculph de Soligny, and Hugh de Colonces, his noble knights from western Normandy.[15] He also renewed his acquaintance with William Earl Marshall, almost twice his age, with whom he was building a deep trust and bond which would stand the test of time.

In 1196 Ranulf was summoned with others to take a part in the most talked-about castle-building project of his generation.[16] Richard I was in flagrant breach of agreements with Philip Augustus, brokered by the Archbishop of Rouen, and began building a new castle on a precipitous rock above the River Seine at the town of Les Andelys, land that the Church declared to be neutral, so controversial would be its control by one side or another. So serious was the breach of the Church-sponsored truce that by way of punishment, eastern Normandy was placed under an episcopal interdict in November, a form of punishment which not only forbade the performance of church services, but even prevented the burial of the dead by the church. Roger of Hoveden records that in Rouen and other towns and villages the squares began to fill up with unburied bodies.[17] The interdict was only lifted by the Pope in 1198; it had been ineffectual since the building work carried on regardless and only ordinary civilians were suffering.

At Les Andelys the castle at the centrepiece of the fortifications came to be nicknamed Château-Gaillard (the 'bold' or 'brazen' castle) and formed the latest part of an existing fortified line which included the local towns of Tosny and Bernières on a large bend in the river. The nearby town of Great (then called Old) Andelys and its port, Little (or New) Andelys were fortified, while in the middle of the Seine itself was built a new castle on an island,

L'Isle d'Andelys, to which Ranulf was posted during 1196 and 1197. In 1198 he went on to the Rock itself (as Château-Gaillard was then properly known). From the island-fortress he was partly responsible for protecting the landing of raw materials brought up-river for the new castle-construction programme, looming high above, while also performing the function of fortified customs post, regulating the traffic which was bound for the French-held lands further upstream, with Paris and the Isle de France beyond. Once the castle was completed, the Seine as a waterway could be controlled at a stroke, with a defended boom or chain across its navigable channels. The single biggest artery to Paris could be blocked and the lifeblood of France cut off. The castle's construction was the boldest of blockading moves and an act of all-out war. Bold and brazen indeed.

The new castle was the very latest in military design and technology, superbly sited. Richard was rightly pleased with the result, which, finished in only two years, he soon referred to as his 'beautiful one year old daughter'. He swore he could hold it if its walls were made of butter; by way of retort, Philip Augustus swore he would take it even if its walls were made of iron. Units and commanders were rotated to garrison it and all were agreed on its amazing strength. Ranulf's posting there in 1198 may have been as commander of the garrison since he seems to have been there non-stop from June through September. Even today, as a ruin, its location is all-commanding, whether approached from the river, the bridge across the river, or from the town; its natural eyrie lends it every advantage. If assault was to come, it could only come from the north, and here the latest innovations in castle defences came into their own, presenting a daunting prospect. It is likely that Richard had been well impressed with the castles in which he had spent his captivity in Austria and Germany. Château-Gaillard's location and aspect is very reminiscent of Dürnstein on the Danube, the best-known of Richard's former prisons in 1192–3.

The period around 1195–8 was generally a time for refortifying existing castles under cover of truces, although none could compare with the efforts lavished on Château-Gaillard (£11,500). A sum £5,000 was spent on the fortification of Eu.[18] Another £90 was spent on new ditches at Verneuil, while expenditure on the garrison of Domfront cost £500, principally due to a rather expensive mercenary Welsh unit. £1425 was spent on artillery and weapons at Pont de l'Arch and Vaudreuil alone.[19] Such expenditure was a gamble, since other, equally notable castles, such as Gisors (£2600) and Neaufle-St-Martin (£195), Dangu (£208) and Châteauneuf-sur-Epte (£300) had had over £4000 spent on them by Henry II in 1184, with the garrisons costing over £800

Château-Gaillard, the Castle of the Rock (Eure). The keep and inner ward. Ranulf was called here during the construction programme to attend Richard the Lionheart. (2004)

a year, only to see them fall all too easily when put to the test.[20] It was a recipe for financial disaster across the duchy. Richard's coffers seemed inexhaustible but it was an illusion. He continued to make gains and he added the castles of Nonancourt (bloodless) and La Ferté-Bernard (by storm) to the list of his conquests and re-conquests. Responsibilities for each new castle would further drain the funds and stretch the manpower even more.

Demands which were routinely made upon the nobility to turn up to do battle and pay for their own men-at-arms, were becoming increasingly burdensome. Neglect of family homelands and a steady stream of casualties meant that knightly defections were regular, not out of any disloyalty, but at the end of feudal contracts many were unwilling to stay on. Richard barely paid lip-service to the custom of ending campaigns at harvest and striking truces through the winter. He just went on all year round. His answer to depleted ranks was to raise further units of mercenaries, never popular since they were unpredictable and uncaring of just who they turned upon. They comprised Welsh (as at Domfront), men of Brabant, Flanders and Poitou, loyal Bretons and even units of Saracens from the Holy Land. However, mercenaries had to be paid for; more outlay.

Payment for these huge outlays was effected by unpopular war taxes, known as a 'scutage' (from the Latin *scutum* = a shield). These were financial levies of knights in place of part of the service they owed and were used to equip and pay either mercenaries or landless or debt-ridden knights. In this way a 'scutage of a tenth' would demand every nine knights who did not wish to serve at that time to equip a tenth between them in place of their own appearance in the field. It could be popular so long as there was enough cash available. There were also appeals for 'aids' (one-off taxes) from the nobility and the clergy. One was levied across all England and Normandy in 1195 from which Ranulf was excused since he was serving in person.[21] Another was called when the coffers began to dry up in 1198. However, on the second occasion it was unsuccessful in England because of opposition from the Bishops of Lincoln and Salisbury who objected to its levy for foreign wars, when England itself was not threatened. Such objections still ring down through the politics of opposition in the early twenty-first century.

Four years of war were beginning to tell on the entire duchy of Normandy. To add to the pain, however, in the late summer of 1197 nature took a hand. Great storms lashed the coast and drove inland, destroying the crops, slow to be gathered on farms whose manpower had been siphoned off to the army.[22] Inevitably, famine and cattle plagues followed. Not for the last time, towns in Normandy had to import their foodstuffs, including ironically, English cheeses (63 alone to Evreux in 1198).[23] In order to eat, more were driven to the army, where foraging, military rations and a reliable food supply were the accepted fare, plus whatever was captured from the French as a bonus. Beyond the militarised frontier, brigandage was rife. Normandy was quickly becoming a difficult place for anyone to exist. Travelling around the duchy at this time, St Hugh, Bishop of Lincoln wrote that 'nothing is safe, neither the city to dwell in, nor the highway to travel'.[24]

It is not known what moneys Ranulf was forced to expend at this time on his own castles. They were undoubtedly proportionately less than the King's own, not least because Ranulf's castles lay well away from the embattled frontier for the time-being. Briquessard, administrative stronghold of the Bessin, was in a so-far peaceful area, as was the huge tower-keep of Avranches. On the western frontier with Brittany, St-James-de-Beuvron, (Ranulf's probable favourite – simply because he is recorded there more than any of the others), enjoyed a wonderfully defensible position. Commanding a major river crossing, it needed little additional defence. St Sauveur-le-Vicomte was even further removed from the frontier.

The modern St-James-de-Beuvron has lost nothing of its magnificent situation. Perched high above the River Beuvron, it stands guard on the border between Normandy and Brittany. The near ox-bow of the river is its first defence, once dammed to create a series of fishponds in the immensely fertile valley floor, which still sports well-tended gardens and lush greenery. While the castle-site, at the edge of a precipice, still commands a central position in the town, there is nothing left above ground, its place taken by a wide, open plaza and car park, regular scene of market trading. The nineteenth-century rebuilt parish church of St Jacques, beautifully painted with saints around the interior, together with an adjacent former monastery, are the largest buildings around. It is still possible to walk around the foot of the town walls, much repaired and rebuilt since Ranulf's day. The site still forces car and foot passengers alike to wind around the hairpin bends to get up to the town from the east. For an attacker in the thirteenth century it could only be approached from the west, site of the strongest man-made defences. Encirclement was pointless for such a naturally defended position.

Avranches today is bustling. Its castle is still one of the most prominent landmarks in the town, which was badly damaged in the Second World War. The castle keep Ranulf knew is long gone, reputed to have been in plan very similar to the White Tower (the core of the Tower of London). What remains of the castle is generally post-1204, but today it houses the new *Scriptorial d'Avranches*, a gripping repository in bold concrete for the fabulous medieval archives of the nearby Benedictine Abbey of Mont St Michel, itself a wonder to behold.

St Sauveur-le-Vicomte today, a more sedate place, is a modern-looking town of wide, bright streets which has recovered well from the dark days of the Second World War, during which it was pounded by the advancing US forces and those of the German defenders in full retreat. The castle came through relatively unscathed but is today a little-known tourist attraction. The castle *enceinte*, punctuated by mural towers, is dominated by the solid square keep at one corner. Some believe it was built in the fourteenth century but everything about its form shouts out a twelfth-century core, perhaps embellished later. It sits on a steep earth glacis which accentuates its height above the valley floor and a public park below. In a graveyard also below the castle walls are tombs of nineteenth- and twentieth-century descendants of Ranulf's knights from St Sauveur, Milo and Philip Barbe d'Averil, who themselves ended up in Coventry in later years.

During these years Ranulf was again styling himself '*Dux Brittaniae*', Duke of Brittany, despite total estrangement from Constance and his complete disinterest in Arthur, except as a pawn. Official documents were already suggesting that many now considered that John was tacitly acknowledged as the heir to the throne, Arthur sticking like glue once more to Philip of France.[25] In 1198 Ranulf became heir to the earldom of Lincoln to add to his Chester inheritance. Ranulf had been distantly related to the Earl through his mother.

As if matters in Normandy were not pressing enough, in early 1199 Ranulf was distracted by unrest back in England. The periodically volatile frontier between Cheshire and Wales came under pressure and the Welsh King Llewellyn ap Iorweth (Llewellyn the Great) laid siege to the town of Mold (known at the time as *Monte Alto* or just *Montalt* –literally 'High Mountain' but really relative, perhaps 'The Big Hill'). A short, bloody siege ended with the town being taken by the Welsh on 6 January. The Constable of Chester was killed along with the local baron (Ranulf's man), Ralph de Montalt.[26] Ranulf was forced briefly to remain in Normandy, so his fragile frontier of Cheshire, a buffer zone between England and Wales, would have to hold without his help for the time being. The men of Chester were exempt from conscripted feudal service in Normandy (unless they themselves wished to, and then at Ranulf's expense) so their service on their own border was assured. Mold was retaken, but the loss of de Montalt was a blow.

That year held some good news, however. Ranulf secured the very creditable marriage of his sister Hawise to Robert de Quincy, son and heir to the Earl of Winchester, Saher de Quincy.[27] It would be a good union and cemented a growing friendship between Ranulf and Saher which endured through war and peace until Saher died on campaign at Ranulf's side twenty years later. The wedding probably took place in England, as likely as not in Salisbury and Ranulf would have been in attendance. His return gave him the opportunity to attend to difficulties on the Welsh border and to make provisions for his new dominions in Lincolnshire, which were to be administered thenceforward by one of his trusted stewards, Walter of Coventry.

In 1199 the balance of royal power shifted dramatically. On 6 April, Richard the Lionheart died of wounds at Chalus, in a minor siege, a side-show, quarrelling over ownership rights to a hoard of excavated Roman treasure. It was an inglorious end to a great soldier's life. John was quickly proclaimed King of England and

Duke of Normandy. This had a great potential to put Ranulf's interests in jeopardy, both in England and France. For the moment a coronation was postponed, so pressing were matters in Normandy. Richard was buried in Fontevraud Abbey, at his father's feet, while pointedly his heart was interred in Rouen Cathedral.

With the change of administration, Arthur's fortunes picked up. John acknowledged him Duke of Brittany and Earl of Richmond in return for his allegiance. Thus ended Ranulf's tenure of the Dukedom and its dependent northern earldom (by right of his marriage), and once more his western frontier through Pontorson to the sea was under immediate pressure. Ranulf, for the second time in a decade, was faced with the question as to whether his face would fit under a new administration. This time, however, he had lost the lever of Brittany and Richmond.

The Abbey of Fontevraud (Deux-Sèvre). The tomb of Richard the Lionheart beside John's wife, Isabelle of Angoulême. Nearby Henry II lies beside Eleanor of Aquitaine. John almost certainly paid homage to his family when he passed by in June 1214. (1996)

Arthur, flexing his new muscles, straightway returned to his mother's independent and wholly embittered counsel. Under her and her brother's guidance he led a Breton army to Angers which the constable (Thomas of Furness) meekly handed over, probably harbouring pro-Breton feeling.[28] This was the principal castle of the Angevin royal house – from which they took their name – and a bitter blow. Quickly the nobles of Anjou, Maine and Touraine declared for Arthur, raising the very real prospect of a southern alliance separating Normandy from Poitou and tearing the Angevin Empire in two.[29] Constance moved on to Le Mans and, mindful of the sudden severity of the situation and the likely backlash, sent Arthur to Philip Augustus in Paris under the guard of the French heir (Dauphin), Prince Louis.[30] There, trumping John's earlier gesture towards Arthur, Philip recognised John as King of England and Duke of Normandy. In addition, he knighted the teenage Arthur and paid him homage for French possessions in Brittany, Angers, the Touraine and Normandy. Part of his recognition was to state that Arthur was to hold Brittany for John. The French court ratified it all.

In one fell swoop, France had sold Brittany out and had left the treacherous lords of the Touraine, Maine and Angers without the promise of French help. John was now free to vent his anger on them, lay waste the land of this own former allies – and make even more enemies. Philip was giving John enough rope to hang himself. His innate poor powers of judgement meant he could do little other than to oblige.

True to form, John marched on Le Mans (Maine), intent upon swift revenge against those who had broken their faith with him, sure in the knowledge they would not be able to seek French aid. We are given a brief insight into the siege in April 1199, since the aged St Hugh, Bishop of Lincoln, found himself on the wrong side of the lines. Trapped briefly in Le Mans, Constance was warned of a plot to sieze her and she slipped out under cover of darkness with a small armed escort.[31] She sent back a rescue party to get Hugh out the next day. John took both the town and the castle of Le Mans quickly and razed them to the ground. The fate of its citizens is unclear but a happy ending is unlikely.

Constance, who never sought any kind of reconciliation with Ranulf, now moved to sever all familial links in October 1199. Though she had sought a divorce from him on the grounds of consanguinity, judgement from Rome had never been given either way. She could wait no longer and bigamously married her lover, Guy de Thouars, brother of Hugh, Count of Thouars and a vehement ally against England.[32] Ranulf probably did not protest, tired of her Machiavellian scheming. Some have felt that Ranulf led the break, but evidence is equivocal. Constance quickly fell pregnant to her new husband with twin daughters, Alice and Catherine. Her maternal joy was short-lived, however, since she was soon diagnosed with leprosy.

In an attempt to side with all the other loyal Anglo-Norman lords, Ranulf wasted no time and swore fealty singly to John in a great council of nobles at Château-Gaillard on 18 August 1199 before moving on to Rouen with the new king.[33] Hemmed in to the west by a totally hostile Brittany and with war on his southern border with Maine, he had every reason to go over to Philip Augustus and John was unconvinced by Ranulf's show of allegiance. He was under suspicion and entering a period of great uncertainty. Later that year he was forced to re-state his allegiance at Northampton.[34]

4

NORMANDY IN TATTERS (1199–1204)

Beginning again under a new and distrustful King was going to be an uphill struggle. Suspicion of Ranulf's every move hung over his affairs. As the year 1200 wore on, it threatened to derail new plans for his increasingly happy personal life. At the fringes of his court, but well within the remit of his family alliances were the Barons de Fougères. Baron Ralph de Fougères had been Earl Hugh's greatest ally in the war with Henry II in 1173. He had been harshly treated in the aftermath although thereafter had been appointed Seneschal of Brittany by Prince Geoffrey during the 1180s. He had died in 1191 on crusade with Richard and the head of the family was now William de Fougères (his nephew) who, perhaps wary of the perfidious English crown – and as a Breton in difficult times, was reticent about old allegiances with Chester, especially given its recent relations with Brittany through the Duchess Constance. However Ranulf, long since estranged from the Duchess, had now formed an attachment to William's daughter Clemence. She had been widowed by the death of her first husband Alan, Baron of Dinan, lord of Becherel (between Dinan and Rennes) and sometime Seneschal of Brittany. Since their union was childless (Alan had children by a previous marriage), she had had to relinquish all land claims, except her original dowry, back to her late husband's family. Clemence was probably a little younger than Ranulf (who was nearing 30).

How Ranulf conceived a marriage to Clemence is not known. They had moved in the same circles for years so were surely well acquainted. It is unlikely that love was involved, an unusual basis for marriage between nobles at this time. That perhaps would come later. Whatever the reason, the political benefits to Ranulf were potentially great, since the natural inclination of the Fougères barony was to side with an independently-minded Brittany against all comers. An alliance between the Norman Avranchin and Fougères would create a buffer-zone, which could theoretically deal with either side at a personal level, enabling the politics of reason and personal contact to continue when war prevented the Norman and Breton courts from meeting officially across a table of truce. The Barons de Fougères also had interests in Lincolnshire, where Ranulf now held major lands, so there were mutual benefits on the other side of the Channel too – provided they would consent to talk to each other.

While Clemence's late father had been Baron of Fougères, her mother Agatha was even better-connected. She was the daughter of William de Humet, Constable of Normandy and one of John's right-hand men.[1] This made her uncle, now baron, William de Fougères very suspicious. He was also unwilling to agree to a dowry out of Breton lands, which would befit a lady of Clemence's position and breeding, which might benefit a Norman inheritance. His reticence led to a family row, Clemence's side being championed at Fougères by her brother Geoffrey, heir to the Fougères barony and already in Ranulf's circle.[2] He too was to benefit from the marriage arrangements which involved complex transfers of war-ravaged lands around Fougères, English manors (Twyford, Westkinton and Long Bennington) and annual payments over a five year period, but with numerous get-out clauses. In fact, nothing would induce William de Fougères to meet his obligations and the issue of the dowry would become a festering sore.

Plans were nearly scuppered by the King when rumours began to circulate that John himself was showing an inappropriate personal interest in Clemence, who must have been at court regularly for such a rumour to begin. This may have been a personal matter, but would have totally alienated Ranulf in the run-up to his proposed wedding. To settle this side of the marriage, William de Humet, who had been a signatory to the ill-fated dowry agreement with de Fougères, gave £200 to John to ensure his good will (and perhaps cease his own unwanted attentions) in the matter of his grand-daughter's marriage.[3]

John gave in but, now deeply resentful of Ranulf and suspicious of the level to which his marriage might divert his allegiance, he posted Ranulf back to his homelands in Normandy, in a sort of internal exile. His immediate destination was a castle in the remit of his new relatives, the de Humets, at St Pierre de Semilly, near St Lô. They only occupied it by virtue of marriage into the de Semilly family (William de Humet's son, Enguerrand was married to the Semilly heiress, Cecilia). John now promised it to Ranulf as part of his marriage settlement, replacing the Breton lands which he was clearly not going to receive.[4] Semilly was then a relative backwater which he was to hold at the King's pleasure. Still well connected, the Archbishop of Canterbury, the Bishop of Ely and his old ally John de Préaux stood surety for Ranulf's good behaviour.[5] While he was not under any compunction to stay there indefinitely, his new castle was an added responsibility and distraction, conferred partly because of his impending marriage, partly to bind him closer to the King if he wanted to keep it as a benefit. If John had cause to take it back, the de Humets would also lose it – so it placed considerable pressure upon William as a result of his faith in Ranulf. It was part carrot, part big stick.

Today St Pierre de Semilly is tucked away in a wooded river valley east of St Lô. The village itself is strung out, with the de Humet castle at one end. Now in private hands, it is not open to the public, but little survives from the early medieval period, having continued as the core of a working farm until modern times. The gatehouse, directly onto the main road out of the village, is mainly post-medieval around some nondescript earlier stonework and blocked Romanesque windows. It has a forbidding air for all that.

The year 1200 was a whirl of activity. Ranulf was at court throughout the summer months and travelled extensively across Normandy to the Touraine, from Bonneville-sur-Touque, via Rouen, Argentan, Chinon, Tours and Bordeaux, far south to St Sever (Gascony) and then back north to Condom and La Réole in the company of the King, who was touring his continental dominions.[6] Ranulf throughout was accompanied by Clemence's grandfather William de Humet, Constable of Normandy, William Marshall, Earl of Pembroke and William (nicknamed Longsword), Earl of Salisbury and John's half-brother. Ranulf seems to have left the court at La Réole in mid-August, probably to return to Normandy by boat for his wedding; his departure, in mid-progress, near Bordeaux cannot otherwise be explained. This may have been the point at which malicious rumours of John's philandering towards Ranulf's fiancée Clemence took their toll. His departure seems to have been at about the time of John's own sudden and controversial marriage on 24 August, to Isabelle of Angoulême. Ranulf seems to have been in a hurry to depart.

Ranulf and Clemence's wedding went ahead probably in the early autumn of 1200 (the family argument came to a head over the dowry in early October); where exactly the ceremony took place is not known for sure, but a principal candidate must be the church of St-Pierre du Château at Semilly. Here, the stately Romanesque south door sits comfortably within a well looked after building, surrounded by centuries of manicured gravestones which vie for dwindling space. Certainly at this time Ranulf is recorded as issuing charters at Semilly, his new castle, surrounded not by nobles and knights (most of the court attended John) but by senior churchmen and monks from his family-favoured churches, the Cathedral of Bayeux and the Abbey of St Sever (near Vire).[7] Gifts to Ranulf are recorded at this time, further suggestive of his wedding, including two greyhounds called Lym and Lybekar, given by Ranulf of Merton in Cheshire[8] Ranulf's interest in hunting with both dogs and hawks was well-attested, having his own favourite hunting parks in both Normandy (Trevières, near Bayeux) and Cheshire (Darnhall), among others.

At this time, despite the depradations suffered by Normandy, Ranulf was able to continue to augment his Norman dominions. In the second half of 1200 he gained rights to land at Creully and Saye near Caen, which had been disputed.[9] Although at the very edge of his normal ancestral lands, it brought him the service of additional knights at a time when new fighting men were becoming hard to acquire. He promised to pay the King £100 for the privilege and won the dispute since his old friend Peter des Préaux of the Channel Islands held it for him by 1203; in fact it is likely that lands such as this were frequently up for grabs since their knightly lords had become casualties of war or had gone over to the enemy and the King took control of them until they could be sold to raise revenue. He also found time to stand up for his friends who came under the King's suspicious gaze or who were under huge financial obligations to the crown. In a rare foray into the borderlands of the war-torn frontier, he stood as guarantor in the sum of £100 for repayment of the King's mortgage by Richard de Reivers on the forest of La Lande, near the castle of Vaudreuil.[10] Such forests were not only valuable for their game but also for their timber which provided the material to fortify or besiege castles. As will be seen, however, honouring debts in a war-torn land was not always possible.

Ranulf ended the year 1200 at St-James-de-Beuvron; he spent Christmas at the castle, surrounded by his family and knights. Here his Christmas court comprised (at least) William d'Albini, Earl of Arundel (Ranulf's brother-in-law) and his brother Ralph, Pierre de St Hilaire de Harcourt (of St-James-de-Beuvron), Hasculph de Soligny of Avranches, Thomas de Coulonces and Ralph de Praère (the Coulonces and the Praères were related by marriage and held lands in the Avranchin of the de Solignys. Ralph was Ranulf's steward (he also witnessed his dowry charter in October 1200), but this is the last time he is heard of in relation to the Earl. Also present were Bartélémé l'Abbé (probably a Knight-Templar and possibly the same man who soon became one of King John's principal clerks), Jean de Paynell, Baron of Hambye (north-west of St Sever), Pierre Roaud of Tallevende (near Vire), Juhel de Louvigny from near Caen, Juhel Berenger of St Pierre-de-Semilly, William Angevin of Barfleur, William de Serlant, Luca de St Leger, Geoffrey Force, Jean d'Escaiol and Philip Orreby of Lincolnshire, the only Englishman and a steward, like Ralph de Praère.[11]

This was a court which was full of experienced knights. Some were regular attendees at the royal court. Many had been with Ranulf for some time and are met with in documents from the start of the Norman campaign in 1194. Bartélémé l'Abbé was indebted to Ranulf for the gift of 100 acres of hunting land from his own park at Trévières in 1197, Pierre Roaud for lands at Tallevende near Vire and Juhel de Louvigny for lands at St Martin, also near Vire.[12] Here were loyal followers who held their lands by virtue of Ranulf's feudal generosity. The court was also marked by good stewardship. Philip Orreby's presence is notable. Having already looked after the Chester dominions in England for some time, in 1206 he would become Ranulf's chief *justiciar* (a sort of financial steward-cum-solicitor) in England. However that was some way off. His presence was probably connected with his native Lincolnshire. Not only did Ranulf have very new responsibilities in that county, his new wife's dowry had been settled (or so he thought) and she had received the Fougères family manors of Long Bennington, Westkinton and Foston in Lincolnshire, along with Rependon and Ticknall in Derbyshire, Ippleden in Devon and Twyford in Buckinghamshire.[13] It is likely that Orreby was present to have the necessary documents and deeds of transfer made up before a return to England. Crown ratification of the dowry would take a full two years to come through but the personal grants could be settled straightway. This is made all the more likely since soon after Christmas, Ranulf left Normandy in an unusual and hazardous midwinter-crossing and by 12 January was in Lincoln. In the spring he was at Broderton, Yorkshire, having joined the court again briefly as John went through that county, stopping at York and Conisborough. Ranulf must have been smarting in this part of the world, since he had so recently lost the earldom of Richmond, having held it by right of his errant first wife for a full decade. This would have depleted his coffers and robbed him of the services of numerous knights as well as the great castle of Richmond. The knights there now owed their allegiance to the wayward Arthur of Brittany.

His stay in England was short. He probably visited Chester and other centres of his dominions since he (or more usually his steward) was called to answer in land disputes and arguments over knight-service at Chester, Dereford and in Lincolnshire, the last being heard as late as June of that year in Lincoln.[14] Ranulf was probably one of a number of nobles and barons who now put their collective foot down and refused to return to France until they had been guaranteed their personal rights by John. A suspicious group met at Leicester to demand what was due to them, in a small, unwitting rehearsal of what would transpire at Runnymede in 1215.[15] Their demands were met and the King went out of his way to reassure them but he was forced to send an advance-guard for the new campaigning season in Normandy with the rest of the army following later. Ranulf had gone back by early July.[16] An unusual amount of documentation survives for the English domestic scene for 1201–2 since many mechanisms of local administration had been stalled by the continuous warring in Normandy.[17] The arrival of any of the great lords back in England for a few months was the sign for a re-emergence of all the old manorial disputes and for meetings of the assizes to resume. On Ranulf's return to Normandy he visited his mother's manor at Brècy. She had not been heard of in documents since Ranulf's convalescence from serious illness there some years before. He then moved back to the restive frontier.

The first two years of the new century saw Brittany return to the fore. The formidable lady Eleanor of Aquitaine, wife and mother of kings, was now over 80 and confined by infirmity to her quarters; yet she still managed to play politics. She had somehow managed to bring the firebrand Constance (she was, of course, her erstwhile daughter-in-law) back into the King's peace and reconciled Constance's third husband, the Poitevin Guy de Thouars, now Count of Brittany, to John.[18] The Breton and Poitevin interests appeared to be converging with those of the English throne. This became a problem for Arthur, who was being wrenched away from his liege-lord, Philip Augustus. In theory this should not have affected Ranulf, now that he and the Breton house had parted company, but events were to take a sinister turn. In August 1201, Constance succumbed to leprosy.[19] As a mark of his new respect, John allowed her will – details unknown – to be enacted unhindered (even, perhaps, if he did not fully agree with her wishes).[20] As if fate was intervening, that year saw the death too of Constance's mother, Margaret.

Without his mother's counsel, however inconsistent it had been in the past, Arthur was even more the loose cannon. He marched on the castle of Mirebeau and there imprisoned his own grandmother, the redoubtable Eleanor. She had sworn fealty to Philip Augustus for Aquitaine but was still the doyenne of the Angevin dynasty and commanded respect. An enraged John, in a lightning march reminiscent of his elder brother Richard, turned up at the castle and laid siege to it. The castle was taken and Arthur went into captivity.

Much has been written about the subsequent murder of Arthur at about Easter 1202, an act for which John was eventually held personally responsible by an opportunist Philip Augustus.[21] The sixteen year-old Arthur disappeared while in captivity in Falaise during the spring, was murdered and his body apparently dumped in the Seine although it is reputed that it was fished out by a peasant to be given proper burial. When challenged to prove Arthur's whereabouts under pressure, John could produce neither Arthur nor his dead body. One of Arthur's gaolers William de Braose (of Glamorgan), seems to have been the most likely perpetrator, but the connivance of King John is almost certain. Ranulf was never formally implicated by anyone, but it is doubtful if he felt any regret for his former step-son's passing. His reaction is not recorded, whatever his thoughts on the matter. One lingering instance of mistrust may suggest that Ranulf was suspected of complicity by some. After retrieval from the Seine, Arthur's body was reputedly buried secretly at the Priory of St Marie du Pré, a daughter-house of Bec. When, much later in 1220 Ranulf was involved in deciding the royal advowson of Earl's Barton in Northamptonshire, Delapré Abbey in Northampton (founded out of St Marie du Pré) objected, because it was 'opposed to the Earl of Chester'. It is by no means damning, but is a curious attitude at a time when Ranulf was at the height of his fame and in otherwise universal favour with the Church.[22]

The result of Arthur's death was predictable as Brittany rose in widespread revolt; for once its church and barony were united in their outrage, although the traditional view that they arose at a great council of bishops and nobles at Vannes only fifteen days after the murder seems far-fetched. Such news would take twice that long to reach every part of Brittany, let alone for the nobles to galvanise and head for a council on the south coast, inexplicably as far from the place of action as they could be. When they did meet, they did lay the blame squarely at John's door and there was no delay – all Brittany now threw in its lot with Philip Augustus. Even John's continued wardship (imprisonment) of Eleanor made little difference. She continued to stand hostage for a duchy which would simply not obey. Others rallied, seeing a battle alliance of France and Brittany unassailable. The Poitevin Viscount of Thouars and much of the Touraine went over to Philip's side, tearing John's dominions in two. Only Aquitaine remained unassailable, held, not by John, but by the dowager Eleanor in her own right. In Normandy, the Count Robert de Dreux of Evreux defected with his castle at Nonancourt. With him went Ranulf's mother's inheritance and her family's dowry lands in Normandy.

Philip Augustus' ranks were swelling and this was beginning to tell in the field as siege after siege yielded dividends.[23] Beaumont-le-Roger and Conches were besieged for the last time. Vaudreuil surrendered without a fight, giving rise to cries of treachery on the part of the two castellans, Saher de Quincy, Earl of Winchester and a knight with a vicious reputation, Robert FitzWalter, who were accused of lacking moral fibre. Little by little the eastern half of Normandy was neatly rolled up. The French King redoubled his efforts; there was no truce at the end of 1202 and war simply went on through the winter. For the first time Philip Augustus could sense the end-game was near.

John felt himself beset on every side and, not for the first time, he set upon his friends, some of whom he had been burdening for quite some time with an inconsistent and vindictive approach. On 11 April 1203 he turned upon Ranulf, charging him with treason while at Vire.[24] If the accusations were true, Ranulf and Fulk Paynell (Pagnel) had apparently conspired with others to change sides.

Certainly the opportunity and motive were now in place. While Ranulf was now married to Clemence, Fulk had recently married Agatha de Humet, Clemence's mother, who had been recently widowed.[25] This now made Fulk family as well as Ranulf's vassal. The new familial links also gave them both intelligence into two generational spheres of the de Humets and the de Fougères families. They were now both more pivotal than ever in the family politics of the Norman-Breton border.

He and Fulk were ordered to appear at court to give account of themselves before the assembled barony. It is not known what was said but Ranulf, as the most senior, was ordered to return the castle of Semilly to the King via Hugh de Chacombe and Robert de Tresgoz, who had orders to strengthen it.[26] A model of stoicism, Ranulf maintained his innocence and his supporters rallied around. William de Humet acted as his ultimate guarantor, while Roger de Lacy, Constable of Chester, came forward as hostage for his fidelity. In addition, Fulk Paynell sent his own son as hostage, while William de Humet, Ralph Tesson (Seneschal of all Normandy) John de Préaux and even Robert de Tresgoz (who took possession of Semilly) all gave hostages, so firmly convinced were they of Ranulf's innocence. After only a month John relented, satisfied of Ranulf's fidelity and at Falaise on the 8 May 1203 he reversed the confiscation, addressing Ranulf slightly obsequiously as 'our beloved and faithful earl of Chester'.[27] Although this term of address was relatively common in royal letters, it must have sounded hollow to Ranulf. As if to reinforce Ranulf's return to favour (and perhaps due to the de Fougères' increasing disaffection), John finally confirmed his new dowry holdings at Long Bennington and Foston.[28]

War was taking its toll on Ranulf's finances. When his accounts were rendered at the Norman exchequer that year, he was at the head of a dwindling number of loyal, but increasingly hard-pressed Norman barons. Due to the depredations of war, he had been unable to collect taxes and tolls due from most of his dominions for some time, and there seemed little hope of this trend being reversed. There was no escaping the fact that he was massively in debt within the Duchy. His accounts show just how much debt he carried: £2600 tax from his dominions, £1050 loans from King John, £700 loan from Gascony and £100 due to the King for having the King's support over the disputed land at Creully (this was a standard sum paid in settlement of such disputes). In addition there was £195 tax relating to relief from 14 knights' – service by the Bishop of Bayeux (scutage) and a massive £2250 of four and a half years tax arrears for revenue from St-James-de-Beuvron, as Viscount of the Bessin, from the Viscounty of Avranches, the district of Vire. In terms of provisions for the army, he owed 240 quarters of wheat (four years' crop-tax), owing from the district of Vire.[29] Naturally the annual dowry payments due from his wife's great-uncle, William de Fougères, had themselves not been paid (nor was there any hope of it). Ranulf's coffers were unlikely to be re-filled for some time.

Meanwhile the number of Philip Augustus' targets was dwindling. Rouen was the prize but was very strong in defence. However in August 1203 the French King brought his siege equipment to try to unlock the door to Rouen, Château-Gaillard. The castles there were well garrisoned under Ranulf's right-hand man, the doughty Roger de Lacy, Constable of Chester. They settled in for a long siege, despite the relatively rapid demise of the castle in the Isle and the port and town at Les Andelys. Refugees and beaten troops streamed up to the castle on the rock which admitted them for the time-being.

John, convinced of Château-Gaillard's impregnability, turned his attention to Philip's western allies and invaded Brittany; he still had Eleanor with whom to bargain when things went his way again. Angry but still disorganised, the Bretons could yet offer little resistance as John marched west into the Duchy. He quickly sacked Dol, destroying even the cathedral, an act for which he would later profess some remorse, offering to fund its rebuilding – which did indeed take place, but without his help. He then moved on to Tours and Le Mans, destroying both.[30] Ranulf was present in senior army command throughout but no one was disposed to stop some wanton destruction by John's mercenaries. However, unable to stretch his supply lines too far, John then retreated to Argentan, with his enemies closing in on all his borders.

Within Normandy too, John's support began to hemorrhage. In the more loyal areas men began to desert him in droves, leaving him increasingly isolated amongst his paid mercenaries and a band of cronies known as the King's 'bachelors', usually landless knights or uninvested young nobles. Their fawning and obvious lack of experience made them poor counsellors who were much reviled by the establishment whom John seemed so ready to distrust. Ranulf's own seemingly solid support of John cut no ice with his own barons and throughout the summer his own supporters began to waver. In February 1203 William de Fougères (and Ranulf's wife's family) went over to Philip Augustus. It was hardly surprising as Bretons, who had always been unwilling to back Ranulf in his marriage to Clemence. John's response that same month was to have William's sister, Margaret taken into custody and her lands confiscated.[31] The dowry lands followed within months. This probably served only to madden the Fougères contingent further.

Perhaps with this in mind, at the end of May 1203 the King assigned the massive royal castle of Avranches (known as 'the tower of Avranches') to Ranulf.[32] It was, after all, in the midst of his territory. This he probably delegated to Fulk Paynell, who was baron of Avranches by right of his late first wife (with whom he had no children). Ranulf now held a string of castles from St Sauveur-le-Vicomte down the coast to Mont St Michel, inland to St-James-de-Beuvron and across to Vire with local lands held for him by local lords. St Pierre de Semilly he held in his rear, along with his family interests around Bayeux. On his immediate right flank was the Earl of Salisbury, William Longsword (the King's half-brother). With Caen held for John, the Cotentin peninsula was still protected by a chain of strongpoints from west to east and right up the spine towards Barfleur. It remained to be seen whether John or his barons still had enough loyal knights for any of them to be defended successfully. Ranulf's principal castles soon comprised St Sauveur-le-Vicomte, St-James-de-Beuvron, Briquessard (all hereditary), Avranches (by gift of John), St Pierre-de-Semilly (by marriage). His closest supporters held St Hilaire (Harcourt), Hambye (Tesson) and Vire.

Near the end of 1203 John's hold on Normandy was becoming untenable and his adherents were so few that he was advised to abandon all hope of further military action. He was in danger of losing his last few friends. He made one last journey across all Normandy in November, taking a very circuitous route (Rouen – Bonneville-sur-Touque – Caen – Bayeux – Domfront – Vire – Gonneville – Barfleur) since the main roads were unsafe for him. His personal adherents were now only those whose principal lands lay in England and his closest, most senior Norman officials, most of whom had served Richard before him. They were now nothing even approaching an army and their effectiveness was reduced to that of little more than a personal bodyguard. In the parish church of St Mary, Montfarville, near Barfleur, the court held its last great Norman council on 26–28 November. Here they were joined by Ranulf and William Longsword who were formally given the task of holding the western frontier and the Cotentin. When, after a few days' stay at his Ducal Castle of Gonneville, the King suddenly left Barfleur at the beginning of December, no one was under any illusions about him returning any time soon. John was stupefied by events and their speed. All across the Duchy the best anyone could hope for was to hold until relieved. Aware of the deteriorating situation and despite his instructions to hold the western frontier, Ranulf followed John to England within a week.[33]

Today Montfarville hugs its oversized church and graveyard almost completely around. St Mary's Church has a somewhat forbidding grey stone on a rainy day, dominated by a typical slender Norman tower with pitched roof, but the interior, scene of Normandy's last great meeting, has a splendour none could guess. Although it is post-medieval, there being little Romanesque (or even Gothic) left, the magnificent painted panelled ceiling is a joy to behold. Tucked into a side chapel is a painted statue of the Virgin and Child from

The interior of the church of St Mary, Montfarville (Manche), scene of the last Great Council of Normandy, 26th – 28th November 1203. (2007)

Ranulf's day. It was saved from looters during the revolution by being buried, later to be dug up and restored to the church.

Just up the road to the west, Gonneville is even more forbidding in the rain. It is tucked away, a silent place, discreetly keeping its secrets of an English King racked with pain and angst as he signed his last documents as Duke of Normandy on 29 November 1203. Corner towers from John's day stand sentinel at the edges of the castle *enceinte*, with its parish church just beyond, but the age of enlightenment has replaced the bailey with a sweeping carriage drive and an extensive if rather severe domestic range greets visitors of a more recent age.

After so long the grey-brown granite of Barfleur nearby still looks resolutely back at the raging Channel, refusing to be budged by all that the sea continues to throw at it. The houses and other

Château de Gonneville (Manche). John signed his last document here as Duke of Normandy, 29th November 1203. Within days he fled out of nearby Barfleur. (2007)

buildings seem relatively low-built, hunkered down against the wind on this exposed tip of Normandy. The wide open harbour, which once welcomed (and when the sun shines it can welcome still) kings and nobles every month, is home to a myriad small yachts and dinghies. The narrow harbour entrance with its slipway, is marked with a stone commemorating the departure of Duke William of Normandy in 1066 on his way to become King of England. No such stone marks the cowed Angevin King John's departure at the end of 1203. The church of St Nicholas stands guard by the slipway, place of prayer and reflection for all those whose lives have been touched by the ravages of the deep. Here many a fleet of medieval sailors have prayed for safe passage to Portsmouth or Dover or given thanks for their arrival on dry land. Neither John nor Ranulf would have been any different.

Ranulf was with the court in England from January until August 1204, witnessing charters at Westminster, Lambeth, Bridgenorth, Wallingford, Farnham and Oxford.[34] Separated from his lands, he was powerless to have any effect on matters at home in Normandy although events across the Channel were gathering pace.

In March 1204 the worst news began to filter out of the Duchy, confirmed a few weeks later. Château-Gaillard had fallen.[35] They might have been only weeks from salvation as, unbeknown to the defenders, John was preparing an amphibious (river-borne) relief force on Seine barges. In charge of the castle, Roger de Lacy had held out steadfastly for six months against the French royal siege train. To conserve rations, he had even expelled civilian refugees into the ditches (where many met a miserable end, caught in crossfire or frozen through the winter). Nevertheless the castle had been taken piece by piece until only the innermost defences were left. After sneaking spies in, reputedly up through a garderobe (toilet) chute near the castle chapel, the French issued an ultimatum. The garrison, reduced to 20 knights and 1[illegible] men-at-arms, counted discretion the better part of valour and marched out into captivity. Philip quickly moved on towards Rouen but at the last moment (to reassure Rouen of his magnanimity in victory) he turned away and marched west into the heart of Normandy where lay Argentan, Falaise and Caen, the now-empty treasury of the Duchy. For over a year only English finances had kept the war going and the castellans were all paid in English coin. As most were now John's much-resented mercenaries, they could not be relied upon without it. Ranulf contributed a large part of Roger de Lacy's ransom of £1000, but had to borrow 200 marks of it from John.[36]

In the west the Bretons opened a second front.[37] William Longsword Earl of Salisbury, held the castle at Pontorson with a small force of mercenaries commanded by Ranulf's knight, Hugh de Colonces. William was a skilled enough soldier but his family ties were a problem. Although he was one of the few men to be on constant good terms with King John (his half-brother), he had married into a prominent Breton family. His sixteen-year-old, reputedly ravishing wife Ela, on whom he doted, was the daughter of William Earl of Salisbury and Eleanor de Vitré.[38] She was the sister of Andre de Vitré III, who held the eponymous border castle in Brittany. His loyalty had been suspect for some time and in summer 1204 he too went over to Philip as the borderlands opened up to the Breton armies. Unless William and Ela had children, the earldom of Salisbury would revert to his niece's gift in marriage and, for the time-being his sister's keeping. It is not perhaps surprising therefore to note that when the Breton army attacked, they bypassed Pontorson and William. In turn he left them

Mont St Michel (Manche), in 1203 the hinge to the door of western Normandy. Defended by treacherous tides and shifting sands, it was Breton knowledge of those same characteristics which 'unhinged the door'. (2006)

unmolested, seeking to protect his marriage-interests in England by keeping well out of it.

Ranulf's forces were totally compromised by this inaction, losing their entire right flank and the Bretons moved directly to cut the Couësnon and Rance river traffic by taking Mont St Michel, garrisoned since June 1203 by a grand total of five knights and fifteen men-at-arms. This huge island fortress was quickly infiltrated and taken with little difficulty by the only people who knew how, local Bretons. They knew well and exploited the patterns of the treacherous tides to gain access; they were at once both its strength to outsiders and its weakness to the locals.

Sensing that their own cause was lost, Ranulf's erstwhile loyal knights deserted his cause; he could not be consulted since he was still with John in England.[39] Avranches fell, almost certainly without a fight by Fulk Paynell who formally changed sides, taking with him Hambye, deep inside Ranulf's lands and splitting St Sever from Vire, which still held a small garrison until Whitsun. The de St Hilaire de Harcourts went, taking St-James-de-Beuvron. Peter des Préaux changed sides, robbing Ranulf of Creully and Saye near Bayeux; soon after Pierre de Roaut, Hugh de Colonces and Thomas de Colonces all went over to Philip. Their family ties and their landed responsibilities meant they could do little else and almost all their eggs were in a single Norman basket. Any English lands they held were too far away to worry about. Ralph Tesson the Seneschal defected, the last semblance of ducal administration gone. Lastly William de Humet went over to Philip. With him went St Pierre de Semilly and the last of Ranulf's Norman castles. Most had been witnesses, signatories and guarantors of Ranulf's dowry from the de Fougères. As a result no redress in that matter could now be found through them. The final documents of government were issued after the King had left Barfleur under the name of William Marshall, Earl of Pembroke. The last surviving lines concerning the Duchy come not even from Barfleur, but Southampton.[40] Rouen negotiated its own surrender with Philip Augustus, despairing of help ever coming from John. Further south in the Touraine, the great royal castle at Chinon held out until into 1205 but no one was in any doubt, Normandy was lost.

For Ranulf the loss of his hereditary continental dominions was dire. Being Viscount of Avranches, Viscount of the Vau-de-Vire, Viscount of Bayeux and of the Bessin and Baron of St Sever were hereditary titles and privileges. These were no mere sinecures but had brought immense wealth to generations of his family – who were all locals. The Viscounty of Avranches had brought £60 per year, the profits of St-James-de-Beuvron £100 per year, the Viscounty of the Vau de Vire £180 per year and the Viscounty of the Bessin £140 per year. His four years of uncollected debt would at least now be wiped out since the Anglo-Norman treasuries of Caen, Falaise, Rouen and Verneuil no longer even existed.[41]

Ranulf's power had been dispensed through the great castles of St-James-de-Beuvron, St Sauveur-le-Vicomte, Vire, Avranches and latterly St Pierre-de-Semilly. These were now to be redistributed by Philip Augustus in return for feudal service and allegiance. To the victors went the spoils, Brittany to Guy de Thouars, St-James-de-Beuvron to Simon de Dammartin, brother of the Count of Boulogne, St Pierre de Semilly back to de Humet, the Barony of St Sever to André de Vitré and St Sauveur-le-Vicomte to Richard de Harcourt (later to William Paynell).[42] The magnanimous Philip Augustus returned many of them to those who knew them best, Ranulf's old allies and one or two of his former personal enemies. Ranulf's personal feudal entourage had been one of 52 knights owing him service (from his Norman lands alone), with perhaps five times as many men-at-arms in their train.[43] In short he had enjoyed the following of a small army in the service of first Richard and then John. For each of them only the feudal head had changed, although it had taken ten years of war to arrive at that point. For Ranulf it was all gone and he had to look to his lands and titles in England alone. The transition was not going to be easy.

5

CONSOLIDATION (1204–09)

Just as England now had a king whose attention was supposedly undivided, the earldom of Chester might now have a fully focused earl, if only they could both draw a line under the loss of their Norman lands. Things did not begin auspiciously as the spectre of John's distrust reared up once more. He now suspected Ranulf of treating both with Philip Augustus in France and rebel princes in Wales. John was certainly under pressure, and throughout the latter half of 1204 and through 1205 England fully expected a French invasion, with the south coast on high alert. As early as February 1205 Philip Augustus was indeed considering an invasion under Reynald de Dammartin, Count of Boulogne, who had been his commander in chief throughout the Norman wars.[1] In Wales too there was indeed a plot against England by the Prince Gwenwynwyn (perhaps encouraged by the success of Wales' celtic Breton cousins), but there was nothing unusual in that; they rarely amounted to more than raiding in force, countered by the forces of the earls of Chester or marcher lords further south. Chester stood as a buffer zone, and for John this was part of its problem. It had long been held by its earls 'by right of their sword' because the first earl had conquered it himself just after 1066. This meant that the King's writ did not run in Ranulf's lands, putting severe limits on John's power there. Ranulf held the equivalent of royal authority in Cheshire and well beyond. What once might have seemed a buffer zone in defence might now look like a cover for fomenting dissension and discontent with the crown. John feared that Chester, instead of looking to protect itself from the west, would turn and face east.

With Normandy lost, John turned pointedly for support to the Earl of Chester in the autumn of 1204. Detained in England until August, Ranulf had finally been able to cross the Channel at the end of the summer, to salvage what he could from the rubble of his patrimony. Beset by enemies and deserted by former friends, he no doubt talked to agents of Philip Augustus, if not the French King himself. The wholesale redistribution of his lands would take some time and there was a breathing space (nominally a year and a day) during which Anglo-Norman nobles might approach Philip and do homage to him for their Norman dominions, while owing allegiance to John for lands in England. William Marshall Earl of Pembroke and Simon de Montfort, Earl of Leicester, both took advantage and bought time for their Norman lands, much to John's chagrin, who maintained that their divided loyalties were unacceptable. Marshall backed off but Leicester, already in debt to the King, was stripped of the honour of Leicester, which John temporarily took into his own hands. The year 1204–5 was marked by such bitter rivalries. England was on a knife-edge, the north was in almost open revolt.[2] Everything pointed to a French invasion and the baronage geared up to muster a royal field army at short notice.

For Ranulf the ensuing year was a roller-coaster. After finally making it too late to Normandy in August 1204, two months after Rouen had fallen and the duchy had collapsed, he was still there in December. In early September he had been with the entire English field army at La Suze (Sarthe), perhaps aiming to give aid to the Touraine, parts of which still held out against Philip.[3] However, through the autumn his continued absence from court brought more suspicion; indeed he may have been considering taking the same route as Pembroke and Leicester in Normandy, paying homage to Philip for his Norman lands, simply in order to retain them. He was clearly unsuccessful as their redistribution shows. On the other hand any serious collusion with the King's enemies in Wales seems unlikely, simply because he was too far away, for too long. However, John would take no chances and for some reason his suspicions were aroused in early December, on whose reports we do not know. On 14 December 1204 John ordered the seizure of all Ranulf's estates in England (a process which would actually take some months since they were so numerous and covered such a wide area).[4] Others advised against treating the Earl so shoddily again, so soon after the last debacle in 1200. Both the Archbishop of Canterbury and the Justiciar suggested that Ranulf be brought home speedily and on 20 December 1204 letters were issued at Reading to guarantee Ranulf safe-conduct for his appearance before the King before 6 January.[5] For this to take place (in a maximum of seventeen days), he cannot have been far inside Normandy by this time. It might take five days, including the midwinter channel crossing, for the letter to reach him (if news as to his exact whereabouts was up-to-date, otherwise it would need to catch up), a day to complete his business, another to gather his travelling court, pack their belongings and prepare the horses, another five days to return and get to the appointed place in England; twelve days in all. So long as ships' masters could be found, willing to chance the crossing, he could make it.

The letter must have stressed the urgency, since Ranulf made Dover before 6 January 1205, seemingly enough to allay fears (here he was back under John's jurisdiction) and then reached Lambeth where he formally appeared before the King, late but perhaps not breathless, on 16 January. His re-profession of allegiance to John, whether needed or not, was not only accepted but rewarded. In early March he received almost the whole of the honour of Richmond as his own.[6] Not the wealthiest of earldoms, it was pointedly sweet vengeance for the loss of his homeland to the Bretons since the Dukes of Brittany had also been earls of Richmond. Their treachery had caused the loss of their English dominions. Ranulf also now moved to secure those family possessions which had belonged to the de Fougères, Ippleden in Devon (which he held in his wife's name), Twyford and Witleford in Buckinghamshire, Long Bennington and numerous properties in Lincolnshire, tied to the Fougères family patronage of the Abbey of Savigny, now cut off from its English lands.[7] In view of the disastrous results of his dowry agreement of 1200, these estates Ranulf now took under his wing to protect their interests and reap the benefits as self-appointed de Fougères heir-apparent in England. Some at least had been gifts to the church by the families of both his wives.[8]

Ranulf was able to consolidate and expand his own dominions but his former family allies in Normandy could do no such thing. Irrespective of the state of their relationship with Ranulf, they had incurred John's wrath and their change of sides settled the issue of their own English lands which were confiscated by the Crown for redistribution to more loyal subjects (or much-reviled mercenaries in return for their continued loyalty).

The list of sequestrations is instructive since it indicates just how much these individuals had been prepared to lose, so much greater had been their families' hereditary stakes in Normandy and their lack of faith in John.[9] At the head was William de Humet, who, although he later returned to the King's peace, lost considerable lands in the east Midlands and home counties. The rest were Ranulf's own family of knights.[10]

Some at least of the wider confiscations would benefit Ranulf directly. Indeed it may be that some had been held by these Norman knights by original gift of Ranulf since he himself would later be intimately involved with aspects of these manors, for instance Great Tew (Oxfordshire) and Sileby (Leicestershire) or their location indicated a neighbourly feudal dependence mirroring their former relationships in Normandy (such as Rothley as neighbour to Ranulf's Mountsorrel, Leicestershire). In other parts of the country Ranulf also began to pick up lands and manors which had belonged to rebel nobles with whom he had previously had little apparent contact such as Great Brickhill (Buckinghamshire), formerly of Robert Bardolf (for which Ranulf paid £100), Newton (Nottinghamshire), formerly of Alured de Soligny (who returned to John's allegiance by 1207) and Broughton (Nottinghamshire), formerly of Ralph de Arques.[11]

In the spring of 1206 Ranulf became closely involved in carrying forward a major building project, most likely it was the construction of a fleet for John for a proposed punitive campaign on the continent (an earlier one having hardly got under way in 1205). Contemporary chroniclers reckon the numbers to have been 1500 ships. John enjoyed very lukewarm support for this expedition and some prominent barons (such as the Earl Marshall) actually refused to go, due to their personal arrangements with Philip Augustus over their own Norman lands, something which left John furious. Ranulf did accompany him on this occasion, a fact which probably scotches accusations that he too had enjoyed a 'special arrangement', the cause of royal accusation in 1204. In March the King ordered his chief forester to provide Ranulf with the entire timber quota for the year from the King's forest of Salcey (Northamptonshire) (the Latin states literally: *such as he could have prepared* [not cut] – suggesting this was the entire felled-stock being seasoned).[12] There is no mention of tree-types and numbers or of its purpose. Secrecy seems to have been the watchword. This was surely either ship-timber or timber for siege-engines, for which green, fresh oak was not suitable. Ranulf was to take delivery at Olney (Buckinghamshire). It was just one strand of an expedition which saw men and material gravitate towards the south coast in quantities said to have put even Richard's war preparations into the shade. Ranulf appears to have been instrumental in the logistical build-up for the expedition.

As the expedition got under way for Poitou in the summer of 1206, John gave Ranulph custody of the north-east Midlands properties of Robert Muschamp, probably because he was the close relative (possibly brother) of Geoffrey Muschamp, Bishop of Coventry and Lichfield (1198–1208) and a close confidante of Ranulf.[13] This year saw a clear policy emerge as the King ordained that Ranulf should have full receipt of all the confiscated Norman lands in his Lincoln earldom. That he took all those within the honour of Chester goes without saying, since he did not need the King's permission for that. If all this was not enough, however, John added in April 1207 the county and honour of Lancaster and in July all the lands which had formerly belonged to the rebel Earl Simon de Montfort, Ranulf's own relative.[14] He did, however, retain the title of Earl of Leicester in his own hands. With all these lands Ranulf was now the most powerful noble in England.

Meanwhile as things had settled down in Normandy and perhaps expecting John's return, some of the rebel Normans did petition for their lands back. Richard and Jean de St Hilaire de Harcourt, sons of Robert de Harcourt (d.1208) both made overtures to John in 1206 on their father's behalf but only Jean returned to England. He finally received back possession of his family's English lands seven years later when he also became baron of St Sauveur-le-Vicomte.[15] His petition was sincere since he died in battle, fighting alongside Ranulf in 1219. Thereafter Richard was able to re-acquire the Harcourt lands for a payment of £500.

It is possible that, despite their apparent disloyalty to Ranulf in 1204, some of his vassal lords simply went over to Philip Augustus because they could no longer hold any allegiance to John and stand a chance of retrieving anything from the mess. It does not necessarily imply that their life-long ties to the Earl of Chester were broken irreparably. After all they had been family friends and allies for generations. Such ties do not break easily. It may be that Ranulf would be of help in some recoveries if he was sure of the former owner's fidelity and he himself stood in good favour with the King. Thus he was instrumental in helping Peter de Préaux regain the Channel Islands after a short period of French rule.[16]

Throughout 1206 Ranulf was beset by minor but irksome lawsuits and representations, particularly at Bugbrooke in Northamptonshire, where land disputes threatened to undermine his authority in his manor there.[17] Five men, Humphrey de Roche, Walter Passavant, Robert de Pinkenni (Moreton Pinkney), Michael de Basevill and Robert de Bukebroc (Bugbrooke) were a combined nuisance throughout the year but the cases were ably handled by the Earl's attorney, Walter of Coventry, who had been Ranulf's seneschal in Lincolnshire since 1199. Ranulf put his own man, Robert Bickley, into the manor, although the King took some of the land into his own hands, presumably to enable a cooling off period and also to leave the way open for one of the usual fines to buy it back.[18] In the end this amounted to 400 marks for Ranulf to have the King's good will in the dispute. The sudden rash of litigation is largely due to the presence of Ranulf back in England for the first time in ages; there was much backlog to clear. This is true of all England's nobles and the King himself, who in the couple of years after his return from Normandy threw himself into the business of government and administration with a will. He proved himself very adept when it came to the mechanics of government and administration, taking a keen personal interest and keeping meticulous records (the first English king to do so); it was his judge of character and his innate distrust of anyone else who held great power which so often let him down.

At this time Ranulf too needed loyal and capable supporters. Not now necessarily in need of knights with fighting experience, he turned to a breed of men who had begun to serve him well while he was still in Normandy. He now held a small empire and could not be everywhere to run it. Just as Peter de Préaux had once looked after his interests in Normandy, he now gathered similarly sagacious men around him. Walter of Coventry and Warin Fitz William looked after Lincolnshire and outlying lands; Philip Orreby, a Lincolnshire man who had been with him now for at least five years now became his Chief Justiciar (remember he had been the only Englishman present at the great Christmas court at St-James-de-Beuvron); Richard Fitton was seneschal for the honour of Richmond, while at Chester itself was the long-serving Roger de Montalt and at Coventry Walter Fitz Terry. His relative Ralph Mainwaring, once his justiciar and chaplain, stepped down to make way for Orreby and retired to St Michael's Church, Coventry with Ranulf's blessing. A new chaplain (called simply Thomas) continued to attend him.

As befitted his rank Ranulf also travelled with a small bodyguard of minor knights and advisors. Their names occasionally appear: Nicholas Fitz Liulph, Milo Barbe d'Averil of St Sauveur-le-Vicomte (later to be given lands at Coventry), Hugh Fitz Martin and Geoffrey Goldsmith. The last-named Geoffrey would gradually become one of Ranulf's most trusted stewards and in the 1220s would manage much of the Earl's affairs over a vast swathe of his lands from Staffordshire to Gloucestershire.

Through 1205, 1206 and 1207 Ranulf was regularly travelling with the court and can be found witnessing the King's charters as they moved around the country, Winchester in May 1205, Northampton and Olney in March 1206, Clarendon in April and Tewkesbury and Woodstock in November 1207.[19] In each case he was probably able to visit his own base of operations to check on the smooth-running of his own dominions, such as Chipping Campden when he was at Tewkesbury. At some point he was able to visit his lands at Coventry, which he ran from his manor house at Cheylesmore, part of which was archaeologically excavated in 1992 and a later gatehouse of which still stands in the city centre. The archaeological excavations suggest he began to building a new, fortified hall-house at this time, the south range of the growing manor.[20] Elsewhere, he could now afford to spend time at Chester, Richmond, Leicester and Lincoln with all his outlying manors.

When during 1206 Ranulf accompanied John on the punitive expedition to Poitou and Gascony, he made use of the newly re-aligned Channel Islands as a staging post for the fleet on the way to La Rochelle.[21] This obviated the need to hop along the hostile coast of Normandy and brought him tantalizingly within a few hours sailing distance of his own former continental lands. Although the expedition had limited objectives, and had equally limited results, it did reinforce England's continuing commitments to its former Angevin heartland (Eleanor of Aquitaine's former power-base). For a few short weeks John actually held court at Angers (much to Philip Augustus' chagrin) and dispensed justice as he and his forebears had once done as a matter of birthright. It bolstered Angevin and Anglo-Norman claims and gave new hope to beleaguered Poitevin allies. The army ranged widely, reaching as far north as Le Lude in the Touraine. Numerous hostages were taken to further protect the Poitevin border; they were placed in Ranulf's safe-keeping: Hugh and Pagan de Torarce, Ivo de Laille, Amicus Borsarce, Jodewine de Doe, Hugh de Chaorces.[22] These were not familiar Norman or French, but regional nobles from the Touraine and Poitou. They would support John if they thought his help would be regular, concerted and focused. It would remain to be seen whether their captivity could buy allegiance once John returned home, which he and the army did after a few months.

Their status as prisoners-of-war or hostages, handed over to Ranulf, is the only indication that Ranulf was present in Poitou, since during the summer months of 1206 he never appears witnessing the King's charters there, such was the level of John's distrust.[23] For a short time he kept Ranulf at arms' length, judging his continued allegiance. Despite its limitations, the expedition did manage to convince John of the immense task ahead of him if he was to succeed in wresting Normandy back from France. It also had the effect of putting paid to Philip Augustus' plans to invade England. He realised, before it was too late, that he himself could be outflanked and was rattled. In fact, when little more than a year later, the Pope wrote to Philip asking for France's lead in tackling the heretic Count of Toulouse in what became the Albigensian Crusade, Philip protested that he could not until the Pope could guarantee that John would not attack from England while his back was turned. No such guarantee was made.

With the expedition back in England, interests up north took up more of Ranulf's attention. Now holding the earldom of Richmond, he was exercising increasing power across the Pennines and was being drawn into purely local disputes. In the Pipe Rolls of Lancashire is the 1206 case of the Lady Quenild, something of a firebrand, who asserted that she held her lands not of the King but of the Earl of Chester, by military service (she does not state that presumably, as a woman, she paid scutage for another to serve in the army in her stead!). She wanted to organise her own marriage (to secure her inheritance to whomever she chose, not the King). She succeeded, by the usual gift to the King, this time of sixty marks and two palfreys (good riding horses).[24] Her choice was Roger Gernet of Halton (in Cheshire, one of Ranulf's main Cheshire manors). Roger was chief royal forester of Lancashire, who would be called upon to send provisions to Ranulf's court.

Family matters continued to crop up. Although Ranulf may have had ideas that his own children might never come, he was ready to distribute fatherly generosity. In 1208 he became godfather to another Ranulf, clearly named after him. He was the son of Peter, one of his clerks, probably at Chester.[25] Other aspects of his erstwhile Breton family were more problematic. Indeed, it must have seemed that Brittany and the question of its allegiance would never go away. On 27 May 1208 Ranulf's former step-daughter, Eleanor, freed for a short while and now dangerously styling herself Countess of Brittany, wrote to the Bishop of Nantes, the capital and foremost see in her former homeland, to help her get to England to visit her uncle, the King.[26] Her visit, she felt, would be to both their advantages. Surely there was some regal scheming going on in the background since letters of safe conduct were issued for her messengers at the coast only two days later, on 29 May.[27] Surely she had been summoned as John would have had to be fully aware of such an issue. She was probably taken back into English custody at this point once more, her safe conduct pass apparently worthless when it suited the King.

The year 1208 was a bad one for all England. John had recently got into serious dispute with the Church. He argued with the Pope over the appointment of a new Archbishop of Canterbury. Behind this was a wish to see England free of Papal taxation, the destination of which could not be controlled. In the election, the monastic houses elected Reginald, Sub-Prior of Canterbury, without recourse to John and his bishops, who wanted John Gray, Bishop of Norwich to be elevated to the prime see. John tried to bribe the Papal officials. Both elections were declared null and void by the Pope, who thrust forward Stephen Langton, an English scholar as the Papal candidate. John refused and the Pope laid an interdict on England. The bishops, thus relieved of their duties, left their cathedrals and John, in characteristically avaricious fashion, seized their revenues. Lesser clergy were almost outlaws and monasteries were reduced to mere subsistence. Church services were not held, marriages could only be unofficial, held outside church porches, children went un-baptised, the dying un-confessed and the dead could not be buried in consecrated ground. Although John back-tracked a little to allow a fraction of income to the clergy to help supply the monasteries, the interdict would last until 1213, via John's own excommunication in 1211.

At this time Ranulf was trying to consolidate his English dominions, while also attempting to draw a line under his former Norman inheritance. He was now able to regularise his income from his lands and in 1208 paid off debts to the Jews of Lincoln, totalling 110 marks (£70), although this may have had something to do with the Papal interdict and the spiritual predicament in which all England now found itself.[28] By paying his debts to the Jews Ranulf distanced himself from the King's own vicious attitude to English Jewry. John could be magnanimous in providing moneys for converting Jews to Christianity, but he was disdainful of their faith and abused their wealth and money-lending occupations mercilessly through onerous taxation.

Ranulf had gone to war for Richard and then John with lands on both sides of the English Channel. He had lost everything he and his family had ever owned in Normandy, mostly through no fault of his own (although it did not help that when the blow fell he was on the wrong side of the Channel). Now he found himself at the head of a vast swathe of England, Earl of Chester, Earl of Lincoln, Earl of Richmond; also of Lancaster and Leicester in all but name. He had become the most powerful man in England other than the King. He would need all that power and a great deal of diplomacy if he was to see out the difficult reign of John.

6

WALES, FRANCE AND THE RIGHT OF KINGS (1209–15)

Ranulf's power came at a price. As the most powerful baron in all England, he was expected to give of his time and considerable energies in good measure. An England without Normandy was now a relatively peaceful kingdom (although records show it was a very violent society on an individual level). The royal gaze might be considered relatively focused for the first time in generations on the kingdom alone; no distraction from Normandy. However the business of keeping the strict feudal order in line involved a constant reassessment of the *status quo* by minor adjustments in a variety of courts to ensure that the Church, the laity and the nobility all worked, broadly in unison, towards the King's good and, by inference, that of his kingdom.

Although no longer particularly distracted by events across the Channel, England's borders were by no means secure. True, Scotland was at relative peace, although its king, William the Lion, was ever seeking to regain disputed border-lands in Northumbria. Much of Ireland was an Anglo-Norman fiefdom, where the rulers were at best tolerated, at worst beleaguered by a constant state of ill-feeling and near-rebellion, a trait held in common with those who shared their Celtic culture in north-western Brittany. Independent Wales, however, never ceased to be a problem and war was never far away.

John had on his western frontier two of his most trustworthy nobles, both great friends to each other. In the south was William Marshall, Earl of Pembroke and Striguil, now in his sixties and very much the elder statesman at court. He was known simply as the Earl Marshall. In the north was Ranulf, aged 40 in 1210, whose lands stretched from Shropshire north through Cheshire and the Wirral, past the River Mersey and up to the River Ribble. To the west his power extended via his own trusted barons across into North Wales as far as Rothlent (Rhuddlan) and the edge of Snowdonia, beyond which lay the influence of Llewellyn ap Iorweth, Llewellyn the Great, King of Wales.

During the reign of Henry II the power of the earldom of Chester had acted as an English buffer to Welsh incursions; the raids, although common enough, rarely penetrated as far as Chester, and almost never beyond Cheshire. This situation had continued even when Ranulf was in Normandy. He had been accused by John in 1204 of conspiring with the Welsh to overthrow the English crown. They certainly had the power to wreak a little havoc now and then but any serious threat to the security of all England was purely in the minds of those few who in the long run sought Welsh destruction. That, however, did not now stop wider English attitudes turning to all-out war with Wales.

Despite his protestations of innocence concerning earlier conspiracy with Wales, it is probable that John began to see Ranulf's power as a growing threat if it ever combined with a broadly hostile Wales. Therefore, while in the years 1205–8 John had been instrumental in Ranulf's power-base widening to north and east, the very geography of these new lands had the effect of drawing Ranulf's administrative attentions further and further from the flashpoints of the Welsh frontier. This instead was left largely to his lieutenants, such as the lords of Mold (de Montalt) and the ever-youthful Roger de Lacy, hereditary Constable of Chester and Baron of Halton, in the long term none the worse for his dogged but fruitless defence of Château-Gaillard.

Some degree of diplomacy with the Welsh, well-meant or not, may be inferred from payments out of the exchequer to a single messenger in 1210 who had gone to both Llewellyn and Ranulf (suggesting their coeval residence somewhere near to each other – or separate messengers would have made more sense).[1] Impossible to prove, but they may have addressed the same matter, impending war. That year saw numerous messengers paid to go to the Earl of Chester. In fact in 1208–10 Ranulf rarely appeared as formal witness in the King's business, implying that during these years he might have spent more time based in his own lands. Sadly Ranulf's own charters are rarely dated and their place of presentation is only occasionally given; his movements during these difficult years involve a greater degree of conjecture than most. His temporary move westward can be further inferred by the promotion at this time of his old friend Philip Orreby as Justiciar of Chester, a post he held for a further twenty years. It took him out of the Lincolnshire sphere totally; this was henceforth fully administered by his colleague (since 1199) Walter of Coventry, who acquired something of a roving commission as the Earl's representative across the entire central and eastern Midlands.

Meanwhile Llewellyn was becoming too problematic and a fresh campaign, with the King's support was called for. In 1210 Ranulf went on the offensive on his western frontier alongside the

Earl of Salisbury,[2] ostensibly supported by the levy of a national war tax, a levy on the Jews, which raised £43,560 and another on the regular clergy, which raised £100,000. In time-honoured fashion, Ranulf probably received little of this, which was often siphoned off to support the lavish lifestyle of John and his court. Sources state that the army was of considerable size and that they carried out a scorched-earth policy across Wales, also killing many Welsh.[3] Independent sources put Ranulf building Holywell and Degannwy Castles in that year, while in 1211 he was at Chester and Rhuddlan's old castle, familiarly-known as 'Twt Hill'. All these lay just within his own lands, although deep inside what is now Wales. His companions at this time include a new generation of knights, plus a few older heads, such as Robert de Roos, a veteran of Normandy and lord of Braunston (Northamptonshire), members of the Verdun family (loyal retainers from Normandy) and the intriguingly-named Robert and Ralph Saracen.[4] The

Twt Hill, Rhuddlan (Flintshire): the castle motte. Here in 1210 Ranulf was caught napping by Llewellyn. He was relieved by Roger de Lacy leading a rabble from Chester itself. (2007)

name 'Saracen' does not necessarily imply that they were from Palestine, merely that they were foreigners; often it was used to describe Welsh, Brabançons or Flemings. Given Ranulf's ongoing associations, it is possible they were even Bretons.

The North Wales coast was, however, disputed territory and never very safe as events at Rhuddlan show. While at Twt Hill, Ranulf was taken by surprise by a Welsh army under Llewellyn. They laid siege to the castle, with Ranulf and the garrison shut up inside. The blockade cannot have been very tight since a messenger was able to slip though and reached Chester where the constable Roger de Lacy quickly set out at the head of a rag-tag mob of militia and men-at-arms, at best; anything but a stout relief force. They were reputed to have comprised those gathered at the annual Chester fair at the feast of St John the Baptist. Some days later, with no sentries posted and unaware that their blockade had been breached, Llewellyn's men took fright at the cacophony of the approaching rabble in their rear and fled.[5] A relieved Ranulf rewarded Roger with the privileges of magistracy in Chester and, in a personal joke between the two – hereditary command of the circus-folk of Cheshire. Had the Welsh realised the relief force was little more than a mob, they might not have departed at all. Unfortunately the old constable, heroic defender of Château-Gaillard, lived only a short while longer, to be succeeded in post by his son John.

Ranulf probably remained under arms, mostly on the Cheshire border well into 1212 when in August of that year he took delivery of eight hogsheads of wine from the King, with a further four going to the Justiciar of Chester.[6] They would have been the best quality, since they were actually gifts to John from the citizens of Dublin, presumably more than even the King's household could handle in addition to their normal, somewhat heavy, consumption. John had planned to take an expedition to Poitou in the summer of 1212 in a pincer movement on France with Otto IV, the German emperor. A great deal of supplies had already been put by, with huge sums of money sent on ahead. However, a sudden escalation of Llewellyn's attacks in Wales diverted his attention and forced the project to be put on hold. John switched his attention to Wales and was all ready to begin a campaign with the largest force ever mustered against the western frontier.[7] John's contribution to the campaign was supposed to have been considerable and preparations were laid for a well-armed force to campaign in Wales. They were to be ready for a forty-day campaign out of Chester (the summer of 1212). Although provisioned with 400 pigs and 100 cows, 3-hundred-weight of cheese and 2000 fishing nets (amongst other things), the force never set out. Beset by rumour concerning his own safety and increasing opposition at court, particularly from Robert FitzWalter, John changed his mind and backed out of the campaign. There followed some months of deliberately sensitive (but not necessarily sincere) manoeuvring to mollify his restive barons.

Ranulf must have felt somewhat let down. John actually spent some time campaigning in Ireland through 1210, largely against rebellious earls, members of the de Lacy family. Ranulf may well have joined him for a short time, although the evidence is equivocal. The source is the Anglo-French 'Legend of Fulk Fitz Warin', a rather unreliable apocryphal source, written about 90 years later in the time of Edward I.[8] Fulk was a somewhat disreputable baron whose father, also called Fulk, had quarrelled violently with the young Prince John in the last days of the reign of Henry II. The quarrel had re-surfaced many years later and Ranulf is said in the 'legend' to have championed the King's cause (who was now supposedly above it all by virtue of his kingship) against Fulk the younger. The 'legend' states that the Earl (Ranulf) conquered all the lands and castles in Ireland. When he had done this he returned to England. It also states that he did this to defend his rights there. These precious few lines give us few clues, exaggerating a rôle which was in fact the King's, but they do suggest that Ranulf spent a season fighting in Ireland, perhaps as an offshoot of the campaign in Wales. It may be the reason for the gifts of Dublin which John passed on. His part there is otherwise unreported. There are no details as to which of his rights had been affronted (although it is a believable hallmark of John's reign) or which lands and castles he took in order to restore them. It has all the hallmarks of literary license which was less concerned with historical accuracy (with a hindsight view of John's reign) and more given to the romantic ideals of chivalry.

In 1212, Roger of Wendover's embittered view of the years of John's Papal interdict includes a long list of the 'evil counsellors' who poorly advised John, whose own low-point had been his excommunication before the shocked baronage at Northampton in 1211.[9] Ranulf's name is not on Roger's blacklist. Unable to continue his stalling and opposition to Rome's policies, in the following year John negotiated an end to the affair and upon agreement, issued a charter which had the interdict lifted, on the basis that England should become a Papal fief of Pope Innocent III, who immediately sent his legate, Pandulf, to represent his interests. Ranulf witnessed the document along with his fellow relatives and earls and his close friends Arundel, Winchester, Derby and Salisbury.[10] Ranulf returned for another season's campaign against Llewellyn, aided by the Normandy veterans, Robert de Vipont (formerly Sheriff of Nottingham and Derby), the mercenary captain Engelard de

Cigogné and an up-and-coming firebrand Faulkes de Breauté, whose military prowess was beginning to turn heads.[11] However, the campaign was ended prematurely by the Papal imposition of a truce between England and Wales, an expedient of Rome's new involvement in England's politics.

Ranulf seems to have enjoyed some brief interludes of rest at this time, probably during the winter months when not campaigning. Although he was still required to attend court and undertook the custody of Welsh hostages, he also found time to hunt, one of his favourite pastimes, which he shared with many an Anglo-Norman ancestor, and the King himself. While at Gillingham, Kent, in August 1213 the King instructed Brian de L'Isle to select 100 bucks and does to stock one of his hunting parks at 'Royng' (probably a scribal quirk for Rockingham, Northamptonshire).[12] Soon afterwards, the King granted him another gift – a variety of fine claret and other French wines from the port of Southampton.[13]

The end of the Papal interdict saw Ranulf rejoin the court on some (probably most) of its many travels. In May he was at Wingham (Kent), June at Bere Regis (Dorset) where John had one of his favourite hunting lodges, September in York, October in London (where Ranulf witnessed the ending of the Papal Interdict as John signed England over to the Pope[14]) and November from Winchester across to Hereford.[15] Some time at least was spent in organizing the men and stores necessary for the postponed expedition to Poitou, which was now planned for the spring of 1214.

In fact the year 1214 would bring both personal and national milestones for Ranulf. Very early in this year (almost certainly January) he took his grandfather's favourite Cistercian monastery at Poulton in Cheshire and re-founded it on a new site near Leek,

Staffordshire.[16] The official Church view was that he had seen a vision of his grandfather (the soldier-earl Ranulf de Gernons) soon after his wedding to Clemence (1200); his dead grandfather (whom he had never met, of course) had bidden him move the monastery to a site he showed him in the dream. Ranulf awoke, told his new wife, who exclaimed '*Dieux encrés*' (may God grant it increase). Thus it was named. Clemence was probably now in her mid-forties and still childless after two marriages. She may have felt some great spiritual gesture might change matters before it was too late. It has been suggested that the foundation was required by the church as penance since Ranulf's estrangement without divorce from Constance in *c.* 1199 and his re-marriage to Clemence in 1200 was technically bigamous for a short while. Certainly such a state of affairs would be felt by many to be quite enough to incur heavenly wrath and deny them children. However, in 1200 it had been Constance who had been the principal antagonist. She it was who left Ranulf and quickly married Guy of Thouars; the whole matter had surely been fully settled by Constance's leprous death. The re-foundation of Poulton at Dieulacres is probably far more mundane and its timing came in a lull after three full years of campaigning in Wales. It is also likely, as some have suggested, that the monastery at Poulton was simply too vulnerable to Welsh attacks, isolated out on the Wirral. Although he had received the manor of Leek (where the site of Dieulacres lay) in 1207, Ranulf had had little opportunity in the following years to make the move, since the spiritual isolation of the interdict years 1208–13 would have made foundation at that time inadvisable. In 1214 came the first good opportunity. Their vulnerability at Poulton cannot have been helped by a tax levied by John specifically on the Cistercians in 1210, which yielded 33,000 marks (£21,780). There is probably no single reason for the move, but a number of contributing causes, not least the potentially disastrous mid-twelfth century habit of the Cistercians of accepting any gift of land (such as Poulton), whatever its quality or vulnerability, a serious misjudgement on a number of their sites across the country, where some degree of movement was later required, to new, more commodious or safer lodgings.

The new abbey at Dieulacres, as he duly named it from his wife's supposed exclamation, was only one of a number of foundations with which Ranulf was associated, and his largesse was distributed to many more foundations of different monastic orders throughout his life (see Appendix). It was, however, his favourite and, when he died, he would make that abundantly clear. Ranulf may have been around to see the first moves to build at his new foundation but events quickly required his presence elsewhere by the end of January. He had little time to fuss over his Cistercians who had to look after themselves for the time being.

Across the water in France, events were taking place which would also affect Ranulf in years to come. Brittany remained intriguing to all who had former Norman interests. In 1212 Philip Augustus as overlord gave the eleven-year-old Alice, daughter of the late Constance of Brittany and Guy de Thouars (and half-sister to the murdered Arthur), to one Pierre de Dreux, also known as Pierre Mauclerc, who on the death of de Thouars in April 1213 was created Duke of Brittany by right of his wife. Although he was cousin to Philip Augustus, Peter would in time become an ally of England and a celebrated crusader, who fought bravely and ably at Ranulf's side. But for a while longer he would remain unknown to most. Further north, the French had for some time been amassing an invasion fleet to attack England. Almost by chance in May they had been surprised by an English force under the Earl Marshall when at anchor in the estuary off Bruges (Flanders), their troops disembarked for foraging. The small English force fell upon the French fleet of perhaps 1700 ships (in a contemporary French account) and destroyed or cut adrift some 400, removing entirely the threat of invasion for the time being.

Buoyed up, in early February 1214 John finally undertook in person his postponed expedition to Poitou, backed up by another national *scutage*; Ranulf was placed in command of one wing of the army – his own contribution for the honour of Lancaster alone was just short of 80 knights'. He may have been contributing well over 250 in all, plus as many as five times that number in men-at-arms and retainers. He was very nearly the only English baron present, most of the rest being left in England in a climate of increasing disquiet at John's persistently autocratic and inconsistent style of rule. At the same time an army in Flanders under the King's half-brother William Longsword, Earl of Salisbury, drew the attention of Philip Augustus away from John's thrust into Poitou. While the army in Flanders manoeuvred towards a pitched battle, Philip Augustus' gaze was held. The English and their Flemish allies eventually met the French at Bouvines and suffered a crushing defeat after a bitter struggle. Many English were captured, including the Earl of Salisbury; although they were later exchanged for French captives. The defeat shook the northern army and that part of the expedition was finished as a viable force. Hostages were given in the aftermath. Ranulf was said by Matthew Paris to have offered himself, but was passed over for Hubert de Burgh, Earl of Kent, a preferment which Paris said rankled with Ranulf for years after and was said to be at the root of a growing dislike that the two men began to feel for each other.[17] We may never know; Hubert was patron to Paris' monastery so his view was necessarily coloured by the politics of patronage. In any case, Hubert's star was waxing and he was making enemies in many quarters. He was much disliked in some quarters and was elsewhere branded 'an evil treacherous earl ... a degenerate and wicked man'.[18]

Meanwhile in the south, Ranulf was faring better at the King's side. They left Yarmouth (Isle of Wight) on 8 February and proceeded via the Channel Islands and around the Breton coast to La Rochelle where the fleet docked eight days later. The passenger-list itself is interesting since John took his queen and also Eleanor of Brittany, still his captive (as she had been since 1208 after her brief respite in her homeland). It is possible that John planned to set up a puppet regime in Brittany. Later chroniclers note the King's overall indifference to his niece's lonely plight; John apparently determined that she should never have children.[19]

The area around La Rochelle was generally friendly, the town itself being very pro-English as a result of its strong trading links. Most of the surrounding magates quickly swore fealty to John except the notable lord of Mileçu, whose castle was overwhelmed in a quick siege (they had brought a siege train and engines with them).[20] The expedition proceeded, probably via St Jean d'Angely and one of the late Eleanor of Aquitaine's favourite abbeys, the Benedictine Fontdouce, to Angoulême where Ranulf witnessed official documents on 14 March.[21] The army then split in two in a move which would knowingly cause the maximum economic disruption to the mid-section of the pilgrimage route to Santiago de Compostela, where thousands of pilgrims would converge for St James' day (25 July). Through the spring and early summer, the roads of Poitou would be heaving with pilgrims who would have to move over for an entire invasion-force, losing out in the need for food, forage and lodgings. While John himself went south, down into Gascony, Ranulf was left in the Saintonge region (Poitou-Charentes and Charentes Maritime). His job was to persuade the local magnates to swear fealty to John, or subdue the area by force if necessary. After a short stay in Angoulême, which declared for John, it was back north, partly retracing steps to Fontenay-le-Comte where Ranulf again appears as a witness to official documents on 2 May, once more in the King's presence. That month saw a couple of brief moves, first to Niort and then St Leger. From there the army moved to Mervant where, amongst some of the finest hunting forests of the region, they took its castle which stood against them after only two days (to the shock and disbelief of the locals), carrying the walls in a sustained assault which lasted from daybreak to early afternoon.

They then moved on to nearby Vouvent where a local lord, Geoffrey de Lusignan, a hugely unpopular knight and a bitter opponent of John and the English crown, refused to admit them. Ranulf laid siege to the castle and town and began a barrage of the stronghold. They kept it up for three whole days, until an opportunity for a truce and a parley arose. Geoffrey, it seemed, was also on poor terms with Philip Augustus and had discovered another of his castles was besieged by the French. At this moment he found discretion the better part of valour and admitted Ranulf and John, who had returned from Gascony, promising to cement his new alliance by agreeing to plans to marry his own son to John's daughter. While this suited John to make an ally in Poitou-Charentes who might be a thorn in Philip Augustus' southern side, the de Lusignans had few friends in England and the alliance disquieted many in the English baronage.

Ranulf was the most senior noble present as he and a large group of Poitevin Barons attended the signing of the royal

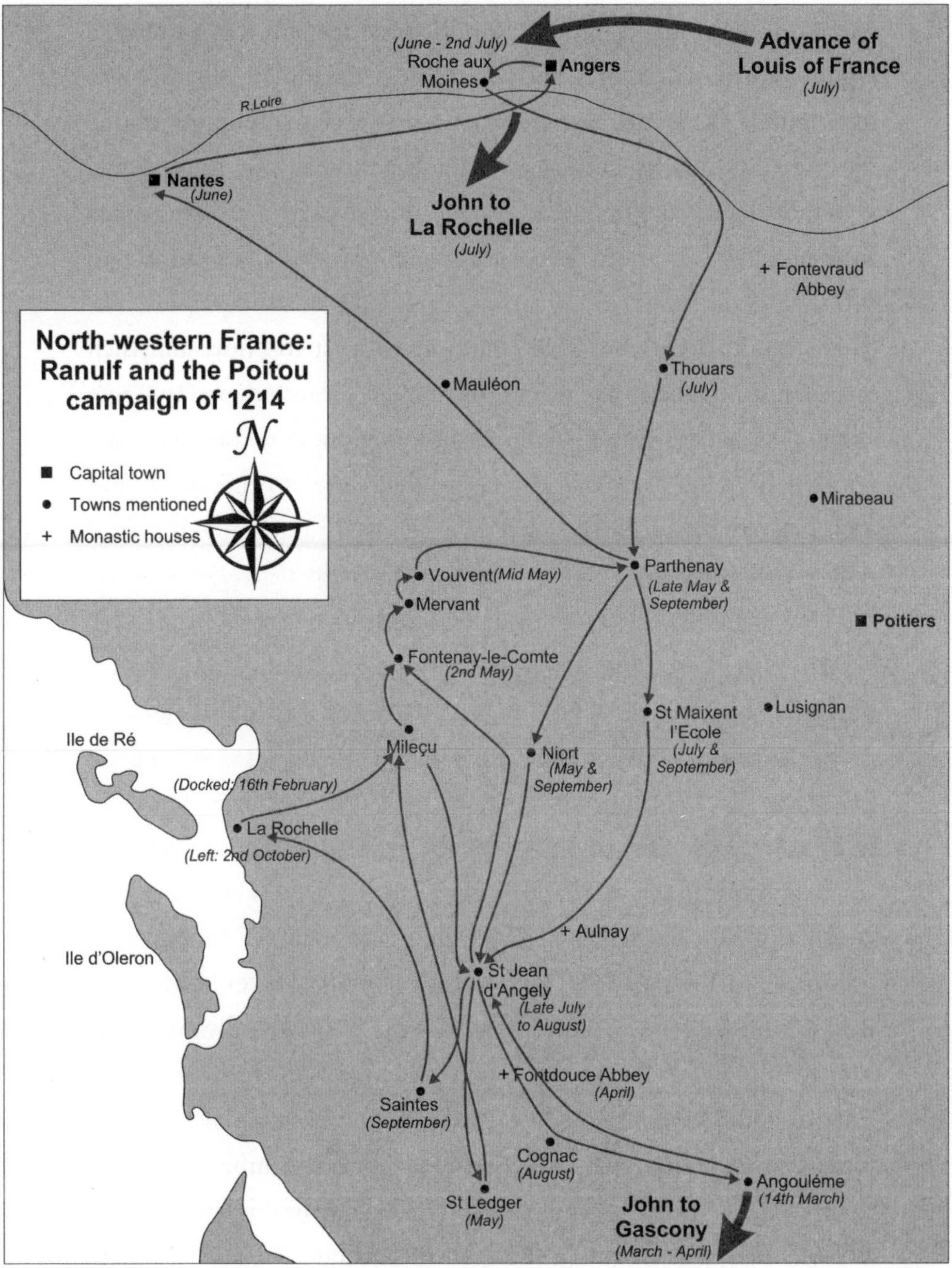

North-western France: Ranulf and the Poitou campaign of 1214. *Drawn by Jacqueline Harding.*

betrothal which took place at Parthenay in late May. He was also actively seeking to advance the cause of some of his former vassals and allies. On 25 June this would come to fruition for Fulk Paynel when John formally forgave him for his treachery of 1203–4 and re-admitted him to his English lands.[22] Meanwhile the army moved north-west to southern Brittany, where they launched an attack on the Breton capital, Nantes. In a brief but bloody encounter the English were successful, overcoming a mixed Breton and French garrison in some scrappy street-fighting on the bridge-approach to the ducal castle. Some prominent prisoners were taken, including the new Duke of Brittany, Pierre Mauclerc. John must have been well pleased with the day's battle.

It is tempting to wonder what John thought he might now do with hapless Brittany as he looked across his tent. In his presence he now had Ranulf, his staunchest ally and former Duke, Pierre – current Duke, and the stifled claimant Eleanor – his niece, hostage and daughter of another former Duke and Duchess, the late Prince Geoffrey and Constance. The ghost of Constance was doubtless there too as she was the link to each and every one of them! At news of the Nantes débâcle, nearby Angers opened its gates and warmed to its Angevin son. Although it was guarded by arguably the strongest castle in the region (and would grow even stronger in the years to come), it was now almost surrounded by allies of England. John settled down to survey his growing dominions. For only the second time since he lost Normandy in 1204 (and not since 1206), he sat in the castle of Angers, dispensing justice (of his own sort), with good reason to believe that the first few months of the expedition had been very successful indeed.

The detail of just how he negotiated the future of Brittany is unclear, but evidently the release of Pierre Mauclerc was relatively swift; Ranulf we might assume was sick and tired of all the competing claims to Brittany. However, within three years Mauclerc would come to John's aid, Ranulf would be at his side in England and give up his custody of Richmond to him, and the foundations of a brief but very successful military partnership between Ranulf and Mauclerc were born in these few short weeks. Poor Eleanor remained a hostage; she probably simply knew too much – about everything, from her brother, Prince Arthur's death onwards.

However, the growing confidence in the English camp was undone in a brief period in June and July. A short distance west of Angers lies the small town of Savennières in the Loire valley. Here lay the castle of Roche-aux-Moines, held by William des Roches, a minor castellan of Philip Augustus. With a temerity John did not expect only a stone's throw from Angers, William closed his castle, his stance threatening both river and road traffic to and from Angers west to Nantes and the coast. John was compelled to attack him and the whole army decamped to encircle the castle. There began a two-week siege with a full siege train. With the castle teetering, John's success seemed assured. However, an appeal sent out by William des Roches reached the Dauphin, Prince Louis, whose army had hitherto dithered in the Chinon region, waiting for his father's word from Flanders. With an unusual turn of speed he moved on Roche-aux-Moines, leap-frogging the English and bypassing Angers. John and Ranulf were in fact ready for him and had consolidated their positions but in one of those switches of allegiance which characterise the period, John's new-found Poitevin allies, happy to take part in a siege but unwilling to risk the financial uncertainties of ransoms after a pitched battle, simply deserted the English ranks, depleting the army by half. Thus reduced, the lines could not be properly manned and the siege fell apart.

Enraged he may have been, but John was now also powerless to resist. Angers was cut off from him by the advancing Louis after all too brief a stay. He had no time to dismantle the siege works at Roche-aux-Moines and in order to save the army, he and Ranulf had to abandon the siege engines and part of the war chest on 2 July, which fell disastrously into French hands, almost without a fight. Now impoverished and with insufficient allied cover so far from base, John fell back with the court directly to La Rochelle, while Ranulf took the majority of the remaining, now predominantly English, army back south into the Saintonge to shore up the castle-garrisons and try to ensure lasting allegiance. In late July he was at St Jean d'Angely, August at Cognac, where news arrived of the equally disastrous defeat of William Earl of Salisbury and Emperor Otto at Bouvines in Flanders (27 July). For Ranulf it was on to St Maixent l'Ecole, once more causing traffic chaos amongst pilgrims along the route to and from Santiago, while in September he was back in Parthenay, for the first time since the fateful meeting earlier in the summer, then on to Niort and Saintes, other major centres of the pilgrimage routes. By the end of September the whole expedition had clearly run its course and if ever the Poitevin Church had supported the English, they surely no longer did. The invasion's high water-mark was now four months gone and with funds running out a return to England was the only possible course of action. On 2 October the fleet sailed from the ever-faithful La Rochelle. John would never set foot in France again. Ranulf, however, was not quite finished with it; not just yet. The new alliance forged in 1214 with Pierre Mauclerc would leave a lasting impression and their paths would cross regularly. Within a short time Mauclerc would come to John's aid in England. Ranulf might appear at first sight to lose out in their negotiations (giving up the confiscated Breton inheritance of the honour of Richmond and its riches) but he would in return (with the help of Mauclerc) eventually regain something even more precious to him personally, his castle at St-James-de-Beuvron. Its position had become more precarious when its castellan, the previously loyal French baron Simon de Dammartin, together with his brother Reynaud Count of Boulogne, had changed sides and gone over (however briefly) to John in Poitou. Philip-Augustus, although he had declared the Dammartins traitors and had supposedly taken St James and Mortain into his own royal lands, had in practice seemingly been able to do very little about it, preoccupied as he was with the campaigns in Poitou and Flanders. It is most likely that St James, Richmond and the Dammartins' own rewards were bargaining chips in a diplomatic land-swap which would see Brittany re-emerge as a threat to France, just as it had been to the Anglo-Norman cause. John even had cause to believe that in his own former county of Mortain and Ranulf's barony at St James might lie the seeds of revolt in Normandy.

On his return from Poitou, Ranulf spent a large portion of the winter not back at home, but at the Temple Church complex in London where the court met on occasions.[23] This was the monastic centre of the Knights Templar. Although he made other visits there, this was an unusually long stay, probably from mid-November 1214 to mid-January 1215. It may be that while there Ranulf learnt that the Pope (Innocent III) was planning shortly to preach a crusade against Islam. Ranulf began to be actively canvassed to take part as his military prowess had become very well known and his spiritual credentials as the recent re-founder of Dieulacres were in order. The recent disruption of the pilgrimage route through Poitou must have put him in the Church's debt. Here began an interest in the coming crusade and an affinity with the Knights Templar, those fearsome knight-monks of the Holy Land. On Ash Wednesday 1215 he took a vow of crusade.[24] However, events would delay his fulfilling it for some while.

If the well-planned but ill-starred Poitou expedition had the effect of distracting minds from difficulties in England, it did so only for a short time. As 1215 dawned, old enmities and long-held grievances re-emerged across an English baronage which had long since tired of John's autocratic methods of government and his unpredictable actions, all too often based upon distrust of those who held any form of lasting power, independent of his own modes of management. The newly ransomed Earl of Salisbury was imprisoned on one of the King's more ridiculous whims, apparently because the ever-philandering John took more than a liking to his wife (and let us not forget that John and William were half-brothers). The advances of a king, however impolitic to resist, were unwelcome since the Countess Ela, although the noted society beauty of her day, was also a good Christian woman whose monastic patronage of both Cistercians and Carthusians would soon become well known.[25] Such was John's unpredictability, even to his closest friends and relatives. Ranulf's own bad experiences, in 1200 and 1203 had long since seen some recompense and he stood at the head of a small number of loyal earls (with the Earl Marshall, Ferrers, Arundel), but others, for so long supporters of the crown (such as Ranulf's great friend Saher de Quincy, Earl of Winchester) were drawn inexorably towards a group of rebellious barons who manouevred John into the great meeting which took place over a week in the summer of 1215 at Runnymede, Kent.

Stephen Langton, Archbishop of Canterbury was instrumental in pushing it forward, knowing that the Pope was on the point of preaching the crusade at the Fourth Lateran Council. England would be expected to take a part and internal strife was an unwelcome distraction for this Papal fief. The meeting's demands were for a guarantee of baronial rights; the consequence of failure, civil war. The result, Magna Carta, or 'the Great Charter', rings down the centuries with a resonance heard by much of modern western democracy, and latterly the overarching United Nations. However at the time, the document, which enshrined the rights of individuals (actually only a few in practice) and purported to curtail the more excessive tendencies of the King, towards its end tails off into a tirade of proscriptions against a few 'foreign' individuals who, as mercenary lieutenants of John, had bypassed the hereditary power and influence of the English nobility to hold high office and wield John's authority in (as they saw it) a high-handed and brutal manner. At the head of the rebels making their demands at Runnymede was Robert FitzWalter, a baron with a fearsome reputation for brutality whose wife, Matilda 'the Fair' was reputed to be yet another of John's recent sexual conquests. FitzWalter's motive as a cuckold was hardly that of a fledgeling democrat. He was just the latest in a long list whose wives had had to protest the advances of a blatantly amorous and totally immoral John who seemed to have no grasp of the sexual mores expected of him.

The rebels declared that some of the proscribed individuals were outside the law and their ejection *en masse* from England (all were from the same area of Poitou and the Touraine) was sought by the charter, which sadly closed as little more than an embittered tirade. Many of the proscribed were related to each other (the Athée, Martigny and Marc families), although nepotism was an accepted part of all politics of the day. Ironically, some were fearsome soldiers (such as their nominal head, Gerard d'Athée) who had served John with great distinction during the rearguard for Normandy in 1204, when others had turned tail. Others had subsequently held a number of administrative offices (such as sheriffs) with great distinction. At least one had become a trusted fellow combatant of Ranulf (Engelard de Cigogné) in the recent fighting in Poitou. Nevertheless the jealousies of the English nobility won through and their names glare out of the last sentences of what seems an ill-directed and ill-conceived codicil to Magna Carta, each one *persona non grata*.

Ranulf was one of a small number who put their collective foot down and refused to endorse Magna Carta, holding back, not least probably because of the proscriptions themselves. He may have been somewhat aloof, unaware of the growing pressure without, since he had been with John through much of January, parts of February April and May.[26] Eventually brought around by the healing which Magna Carta was designed to promote (its wider-ranging implications unanticipated) and the persuasion of the Earl Marshall, he endorsed the document a year later (under different circumstances) and went so far as to issue a parallel charter which guaranteed similar rights to the inhabitants of the honour of Chester, where the King's writ did not run. It must be remembered that Ranulf himself had been slow to swear fealty to John back in 1199, ironically unsure that his own rights were safe and secure under the then new regime, which Ranulf must have viewed with suspicion after years of fighting alongside Richard while dealing with John as his awkward neighbour as Count of

Mortain in Normandy. It was that same reticence he now saw in his fellow nobles, whose own experience was bitterly felt after fifteen years of John's reign. Ranulf must have wondered whether his own adherence to John over so many years was about to be wasted by such vehement and widespread opposition. Had he been a lackey or a mere puppet? Was he all too pliable in the King's hands, too easily bought off with an earldom or a barony?

The healing which Magna Carta was designed to promote was all too short and any time for, or inclination towards, introspection came to an abrupt end. Parties left Runnymede un-mollified by the King's apparently sincere undertakings (probably because he was almost forced to stay and repeat his promises to uphold his barons' rights) and he, in his turn, was unconvinced of the rebel barons' sincerity, so vehement was their opposition. It found no favour with the Church (whose fief England remained) and in August Pope Innocent III declared it null and void.[27] The King was right to be suspicious of his restive barons. Numerous individuals left Runnymede early and straightway began to prepare for war. In response John also began quietly to muster his earls (and in the circumstances he never really entertained the idea of expelling his mercenary lieutenants who would now become instrumental in his undertakings).

Ranulf travelled with the court for the summer, at the centre of preparations for war. He now held most of north-west England, the far north and much of the Midlands. He was the strongest link amongst John's loyal supporters and, as a prize the rebels needed, had at least once been contacted in an attempt to get him to switch allegiance. If he did not, the rebels said, he might consider himself their enemy. He stood firm. To his south lay the equally loyal Earl Marshall's lands, twin bastions against Wales, which was thankfully by now under a treaty of peace. Across the Midlands and the South lay the scattered offices of the hated mercenaries (such as Engelard de Cigogné, who was Sheriff of Hereford and Gloucester, and Warden of Gloucester, Odiham and Windsor Castles). While John set up his base at Oxford, he knew that his rear was secure. England braced itself for a bloody civil war, the likes of which had not been seen for more than 150 years. Across the Channel the voracious French King bided his time, fomenting discord.

7

THE DEFENCE OF ENGLAND (1215–18)[1]

Philip Augustus of France had never given up hope of wresting control of England from a hapless John. Long experience had shown him that whenever and wherever he met John in battle, France won in the end. Normandy, Poitou, why not now England itself? After all he could press excellent claims of his right to the English crown. The English rebels were quite prepared to countenance a French ruler and so Philip, now getting on in years, was well pleased when the rebels offered the crown of England to his son and heir, Prince Louis. He, of course, accepted (actually married to John's niece, Blanche of Castille, he felt he had legitimate claim through her) but would need to take the field in person against John to realise his claim. Preparations for an invasion, previously foiled in 1214 by the naval battle off Bruges, were put quickly in hand once more.

In England Ranulf soon began to benefit from the politics of secession, just as he had in 1205. This time he was aided by the very fact that he stood at the head of a very small number of loyal earls and barons indeed. Therefore John had little option but to begin to distribute his own royal castles as evenly as he could amongst those prepared to hold them. Ranulf quickly gained the castles of Newcastle-under-Lyme (Staffordshire), in August 1215 'The Peak' (Derbyshire) and in early 1216 Lancaster.[2] In addition the King put in train a series of land-transfers to Ranulf which would dispossess rebels of any of their lands which lay beyond the rebel-held areas of the eastern counties.[3] These included the castle at Bridgenorth (Shropshire), to which the custody of Staffordshire and Shropshire was appended.[4] Here Ranulf set to work building a new barbican to the castle, in the process knocking down homes.[5] Then in June 1216 the King added Richmond Castle to the list, with orders that, once taken, Ranulf should hold it or destroy the fortifications. It is believed that he took Middleham at about the same time.[6] The Earl of Chester, of course, could not be everywhere at once and we must assume that most of these castles would be commanded by able lieutenants. Neither could he personally win or take delivery of all these castles. Evidence suggests that The Peak, held previously by Brian de L'Isle, castellan at Knaresborough in Yorkshire, was not actually handed over for many months; and only then to the Earl Ferrers of Derby, perhaps as a familial intermediary.

Meanwhile Ranulf was also instructed to take wardship of lands which were due to young barons-in-waiting, still minors, or not yet considered trustworthy. These lay in a variety of counties, both within Ranulf's jurisdiction (such as Ranulph Fitz-Pagan in Richmond) and without (Robert Sancta Monica in Yorkshire).[7] In October 1215, in an almost despairing move, but one designed to give him huge incentive, John granted to Ranulf all rebel-owned lands in Lincolnshire, Staffordshire, Warwickshire, Leicestershire, Northampton, Norfolk and Suffolk, to be handed over by the respective sheriffs on demand.[8] Some of these, being in the east of the country, well behind rebel lines, must have seemed fanciful, but he now had a very great deal to fight for. In his own right he also became the beneficiary of some of his friends' misfortune. The best example is the hapless William Earl of Salisbury. Although no longer in prison to persuade his wife to comply with John's lecherous advances, the Earl was clearly still incensed and, for the moment, alienated enough to join the rebels. This cost him his lands. To Ranulph went his Newport Pagnell inheritance (perhaps unsurprisingly since it had been a de Paynel (de Pagnell) manor until 1204. With de Paynell's new allegiance from 1214, giving it to Ranulf was only one step away from restoration to its former owners).[9]

At such a difficult time Ranulf must have been uncertain of some of his own followers' loyalty. After all, some of his so-called friends may have deserted his ancestral cause all too readily in 1204. What was to stop others doing so now? It is for this reason that he issued his own Magna Carta to take effect within his own lands.[10] One hopes that it had more effect than that of John and that its effect was less easily obliterated within weeks than the King's own Runnymede prototype. It is not thought that Ranulf's own style of government and administration was overly high-handed (his style and methodology is seen to have been innovative and intuitive in later years). Most of his business was carried out through very able and even-handed stewards who were well respected in their own regions, so it is likely that the issue of his Chester charter, guaranteeing his subjects rights, was a reaction to the predicament in which his king found himself, seeking to fend off ill-aimed but damaging accusations which might tar him with the same brush as John.

Ranulf's friends do seem to have rallied round for the most part. His business, now spread over so many areas was conducted by new officials, as well as old, and we now see the addition of new names, signing on his behalf the length and breadth of the country: Adam de Staveley, Simon de L'Isle, Alan de Hereford, Roauld and Brian fitz Alan, Gilbert fitz Reinfrey.[11] Ranulf seems to have been more sure of his old retainers than was John. In July 1215 Ranulf was forced by the King to give a hostage (William de Wootton) for the good behavior of Nicholas de Verdun, whose family had followed the Earl all the way from Normandy.[12] The de Verdun family remained loyal and steadfast. With whole households accompanying their lords into the rebel camp, stewards and administrators were now also in short supply and we learn that on at least one occasion Ranulf had to second a secretary of his own to the King's service, one Hugh de Morton.[13]

Civil war, however, always strikes at the heart of the family – and not everyone remained loyal. Now was no exception. While Ranulf's brother-in-law William Ferrers, Earl of Derby (his sister Alice's husband) was unwavering in his support of John at this time, the same cannot be said of either his old friend Saher de Quincy, Earl of Winchester (father-in-law to his sister Hawise) or his sister Mabel's husband William d'Albini, Earl of Arundel. De Quincy was a valuable catch for the rebels. He took with him intimate knowledge of the parlous state of John's finances since he had recently been baron of the exchequer, while Albini held Belvoir Castle against John.[14] Their early defections to the rebel camp must have hurt Ranulf as they took two of his younger sisters with them. He must have hoped and prayed that, having found them such illustrious husbands, he would not now become the instrument in battle of their joint bereavement.

New friends must have been hard to come by in such times. However, a new and perhaps unexpected player entered stage-right.

In August 1215 the King wrote to Pierre Mauclerc, Duke of Brittany, to come to his aid in the war. In return he would receive back for Brittany the hereditary earldom and honour of Richmond, lost to them since Normandy had fallen.[15] The latter had been in Ranulf's hands now since 1206 and he had benefited greatly from it. Some commentators have suggested that Ranulf would have been affronted at having to give it back.[16] Seemingly far from it since he now gained the castle of Richmond at its heart (at least for the time being). As has been seen, political strategy as regards Brittany had seemingly been addressed following the successful storming of Nantes in the Poitou expedition of 1214 and, with the unlucky Eleanor of Brittany still John's prisoner at Corfe Castle, Mauclerc had everything to gain. Eleanor's claims, instead of being championed to Mauclerc's detriment, were now stifled by her interminable house arrest. John's threat of her claim being pressed at some inopportune and embarrassing date could cause him some discomfort as Pierre only held his own position by right of his wife.[17] With Mauclerc under pressure and diplomatically compromised, it was probably now that Ranulf gained Mauclerc's support in recovering his hereditary castle of St-James-de-Beuvron, aided by the support of Simon de Dammartin, in John's pay now for over a year. In the meantime Ranulf continued to administer Richmond and all its lands north of the Humber, firstly through his existing staff, but soon in conjunction with a Breton, named Jolland, Mauclerc's seneschal.[18] This would ensure a smooth handover. Although, because of a French naval blockade, it was not possible for Mauclerc to come in person until 1218 (despite letters of safe-conduct at English ports) his tacit support would be invaluable and worry the French at home. They could no more afford a restive Brittany then than England had in the long decade of strife 1194–1204.

Campaigns against the rebels were long and drawn-out. A long list of loyal castles surrendered to them in the eastern counties, unable to hold out and surrounded by rebel-held land. A safe exit was negotiated for their garrisons, living to fight another day as Ranulf and his fellow loyal earls (chiefly William Earl Marshal and William Ferrers) husbanded their resources and concentrated their forces. A vicious royal progress in force took Ranulf along the frontier of the rebellion from Kent up through the east Midlands as far north as Berwick-upon-Tweed and Durham in January 1216.[19] His part in a dozen nasty and bloodthirsty encounters is inferred (although history generally lays them at John's door).

Seven thousand French reinforcements helped to galvanise the rebel cause, although many were cowed by the sheer ferocity of the royalist campaigns which had spread back from the north down into the east Midlands and East Anglia.[20] John was acting with an unusual vehemence no one had seen in him since his sackings of Dol and Le Mans years before. Aided principally by his loyal three lords, Chester, Marshall and Ferrers, he had everything to lose but everything to gain. Buoyed up by Papal support for his cause (England remained a Papal fief), he had the holy mother church as his support. Anyone who opposed him was an enemy of the Church – and that included the King of France. Philip and Louis were publicly disdainful of John's support from Rome, branding the English King a murderer (Arthur again). Despite English attempts at sea to foil them, French reinforcements landed in May 1216 and marched to besiege Dover. John, now reverting to type, was long gone. Louis marched on London and took castle after castle (although Dover and a handful of royal castles held out).

Winchester fell in late June, battered by a full-scale siege. Louis then turned north-east and ravaged East Anglia which had barely recovered from its vicious visitation by John only months before.

As summer approached Ranulf himself was recalled south where revolt threatened in the west Midlands. More particularly, the city of Worcester, informed of the French invasion, had declared for Louis. William, rebel son of the Earl Marshall (and newly-appointed marshall of the French army) had garrisoned it for the French, a huge thorn in the royalist rear. On 17 July Ranulf, aided by Earl Ferrers of Derby and the energetic Faulkes de Bréauté, descended on the city and, finding the castle insufficiently guarded, took it in a lightning strike, causing many casualties; however, complete victory was hampered when many of their prisoners, taken in the castle for ransom, broke out.[21] The royal forces then sacked the city (perhaps to flush out the fugitives) and plundered John's favourite cathedral church, an act which must have rankled with him. In this somewhat unrestrained attack we even learn the names of some of Ranulf's soldiers. While some are Midland men (John de Arden, a Warwickshire man), plundering their own back yard, others are clearly Normans, French or of French extraction (Robert de Teuray) and may be deserters from the French cause (there were many).[22] During a process of pacification, Ranulf remained in the west Midlands, visiting nearby Hereford on 25 July (probably to hear mass in the cathedral – Worcester obviously being despoiled – as 25 July is the feast of St James the Great, a particularly well-respected feast day). He probably then moved north.

In the far north the royalist cause was further hampered by the rebellion of Alexander III, King of Scotland (awkward for Ranulf as the King was nephew to Ranulf's brother-in-law David, Earl of Huntingdon). After achieving limited success, John pursued him as his army moved through the east Midlands, but the young Scottish King escaped his clutches. A dispirited John was at his wit's end when rumours reached him of Dover Castle's plight – still secure but on the brink of starvation. Although the French army was hemorrhaging deserters at a rapid rate and won no friends amongst the overburdened populace, Dover was 'the key to England' and without it John's cause would be lost. Wearily a truce was agreed with the French and the castle re-supplied (but not relieved). John meanwhile stopped at Lynn (Norfolk) where the town feasted him royally. The corpulent King, who, like his father had grown fat on his wanton lifestyle, developed intestinal problems and took a fever. Nevertheless, he pressed on, only to lose part of his baggage train, including the crown jewels, apparently while traversing the quicksands and cross-currents of the Wash. The chroniclers seem quite consistent on this. However, if ever there was a case for suggesting that John had been both poisoned and then deliberately stripped of his regalia in favour of Louis, it is surely now. History leads us to believe in John's incompetence, but surely the reek of a lost cause (in rebel eyes) has as much to do with it. It is not inconceivable that the jewels were spirited away by rebel elements at court to be used on Louis when his time came.

The King's final journey became ever more painful. He could no longer ride and a purpose-made pallet made little difference to his pain and discomfort. He continued to eat inappropriate foodstuffs and his journey became increasingly painful. Eventually he gave up trying at Newark Castle, where he was administered the last rights and dictated a surprisingly dignified last will and testament, shot through with apparent regret and contrition for some of his excesses. There was, however, no forgiveness for the rebels.

John named his son Henry as his heir and appointed the aged William Marshall to look after both him and Richard, his younger son. A small group of nobles were appointed the 'ordainers and disposers' of his will. After the senior churchmen, Ranulf was one of the first nobles on this list, although, like the Earl Marshall, he was still in the west. John died on 16 October 1216 in Newark Castle. His last wish was to be buried in Worcester Cathedral, so recently despoiled by his own troops under Ranulf. The Abbot of nearby Croxton begged to be given his body, but instead had to make do with his heart and entrails, which were removed to retard decomposition in preparation for the cross-country journey of the funeral cortège. Worcester's Cathedral would receive a handsome burial fee, small recompense for the depredations wrought on it so recently.

Worcester Cathedral (Worcestershire): the Purbeck marble tomb of King John. Ranulf stormed and sacked the rebel town in summer 1216 and attended John's funeral here in October. (2008)

There was said to be little sorrow in the late King's bedchamber. Indeed it was reported that his household concerned themselves with what they could take in the confusion; it is possible that the crown jewels really disappeared at this time, destined for Louis, and the Wash incident was a contemporary (although widely reported) fabrication to cover up the embarrassment. For his executors, however, there were other concerns, principally the succession. John had been the focus of all the rebel demands which had given rise to the rebellion. Some (including Ranulf's brother-in-law, Earl of Arundel) had rejoined the King's camp during the nasty campaign in the eastern counties. Others held out while still more stood in confident opposition. If the vehemence of their rebellion was to be diluted, they either had to be placated or cornered; but whichever it was to be, it had to be quickly. There was no precedent for the situation in which the royal supporters now found themselves.

When news of the King's death reached William Marshall at Gloucester, where he was with the Papal legate, Gualo, he quickly sent envoys to Devizes in Wiltshire where the child-prince Henry had been under protection at the castle for some time. He had him brought to Gloucester where he could benefit from the Earl's greater power and influence. Meanwhile he moved to meet the funeral cortège at Worcester, where John was buried in the choir of the cathedral with all due ceremony. They then moved back to Gloucester where the company wrung their hands over their next move. Clearly they had to crown the young Prince Henry but there were certain formalities to be met and a full consensus was needed.

All John's executors were sent for. Ranulf seems to have been some way off, perhaps still unaware of John's death. Either that or his exact whereabouts were unknown and messengers took some time to reach him. Until everyone's arrival at Gloucester it would be unclear which messages had got through and which had not. The Earl Marshall was particularly under pressure to wait for the arrival of Ranulf, whose support and whose forces would make every difference to the new regime, whether they were given or withheld.[23] However, matters were urgent and the Earl Marshall was under pressure to act. On 27 October a council met under Gualo to make arrangements for Henry's coronation at Gloucester. He was first of all knighted by the Earl Marshall on 28 and then on 29 October he was crowned in Gloucester Abbey in the presence of Gualo, the Queen Mother, six bishops and the Earl Marshall, together with William Earl Ferrers of Derby (Ranulf's brother-in-law), Philip d'Albini (William d'Albini's son and Ranulf's nephew) and others. Therefore with Papal authority and with the residue of the English Church present (more bishops were absent abroad, sick or the sees were vacant), England had a new king, a nine-year-old boy, probably crowned with his mother's tiara in the absence of the crown jewels. It was perhaps an inauspicious beginning to the reign of Henry III.

A coronation banquet took place, probably a somewhat subdued affair, not helped by the rumour during proceedings that a force under Louis had laid siege to nearby Goodrich Castle. Since this was so close to Gloucester, Louis had clearly got news of the impending coronation and its whereabouts and was seeking to halt proceedings. He was said to be furious at the prospect. His spies also informed him that the bulk of the royal forces under Ranulf had still not arrived. England now badly needed good leadership. The assembled company turned to the Earl Marshall to take on the mantle of Regent. His reaction, mindful of both the current situation and his own advancing years (he was 72 but, exaggerating, declared himself over 80) was politic, as his long experience dictated: 'Leave the decision until the earl of Chester comes', suggesting that without Ranulf's support, no one could make a decision stick. He dismissed the angst-ridden group and went to bed.

On the morning of 29 October, as the assembled nobles were about to do homage to the new King on the first day of his reign, Ranulf arrived in Gloucester. There is no inkling as to why he was late.[24] It is possible that he held back, waiting to see who would be in the ascendant, Louis or a coalescent royalist party. This is perhaps a cynical interpretation, but one which would fit well the politics of the day, especially if his tardy appearance was planned in conjunction with Gualo and the Earl Marshall. If unanimity could be achieved amongst the royalist nobles *without* his power, then the addition of that power would add the seal of the nation's military might to firm political resolve. Louis' prospects and options would be diminishing fast. Ranulf expressed his agreement with all that had happened and joined the company to kneel in homage before the new King.

During the rest of that day the business turned to the prospect and choice of a regent to rule for the young Henry.[25] Everyone wanted to have their say. The Bishop of Winchester, Peter des Roches, chairing the council, bade Alan Bassett, a prominent baron from Staffordshire, speak first. He adjudged no one better suited than either the Earl Marshall or the Earl of Chester. No one else seemed to disagree; no other candidates are heard of although Hubert de Burgh, despised by Ranulf, is felt to have had designs – but was still shut up in Dover Castle, surrounded by Louis' besieging army. However, the Earl Marshall genuinely protested his age and increasing infirmity and encouraged Ranulf to take it on instead, promising his full support and obedience. At 46 Ranulf was a better prospect for longevity in the post than the 72-year-old Earl Marshall, and his already unparallelled power was still growing, thanks to John's lavish grants through 1215 and 1216. He was also in close touch with Brittany, negotiations with which were perennially delicate but, given time and patience, might yet turn the French flank through Pierre Mauclerc.

Ranulf backed off quickly and pointed out the singular respect which the Earl Marshall enjoyed and to whom Ranulf offered his own unstinting support. Although the conversation was reported by the Earl Marshall's biographer and eulogist soon after his death, Ranulf's modesty does ring true. However, whether he quite realised the implications or not in that moment, he had just passed up the Regency of all England. It was perhaps the most immense choice of all his 46 years so far.

The discussion seems to have been genuine and the chamber divided in their choice of the two candidates, who were, of course, friends and colleagues of many years' standing. As the day wore on Gualo took charge and called together a small group of nobles behind closed doors. They comprised Ranulf, the Earl Marshall, Peter des Roches and one or two others. Private discussions ensued and their re-emergence signalled that a new government had been formed. The aged Earl Marshall, pressed by Gualo, who held out the astounding prospect of Papal intercession for all his sins, had agreed to become Regent under the authority of the Pope, bringing to bear his administrative experience under three Angevin kings. Peter des Roches would become tutor to the young King, while Philip d'Albini would be his deputy. Ranulf, as befitted his own unique experience, would command the King's army. In the midst of a civil war he now held the required military support for the fledgeling administration and the boy-King. In one fateful afternoon the inner council of nobles had given England a fighting chance.

The first move was to send letters under the Regent's seal to all the sheriffs and wardens of England, bidding them attend a great council and meet the new King at Bristol on 11 November. How many messages could be delivered and how many delegates could actually travel in ten days across a desperately hostile and rebellious land is a moot point. The chroniclers only mention the names of those attendees whose nobility merits attention. In practice it is likely that many lesser barons were forgiven their absence in the circumstances and their more senior colleagues, already present at court, spoke for them in the hope of their loyalty. Much of England lay under rebel control so the summons doubtless fell on many deaf ears.

At Bristol Gualo swore the assembled company to fealty to the Pope and the new King. He then laid an interdict on Wales for siding with Louis. The French prince, encamped at the siege of Dover since October was already incandescent with rage at the affront of the English royalists. He now took the counter-step of asking his own rebel barons to reaffirm their allegiance to him, which they did. As soon as he heard of this, Gualo used his Papal authority to lay an interdict upon their lands which had not been recaptured. This sobered everyone up and a truce was declared, to last until Easter 1217. An embittered Louis withdrew to London, letting a beleaguered Dover Castle off the hook.

The lines were drawn with the truce. The French held London, and all of England from Surrey to Yorkshire and in places as far west as Wiltshire, with a host of strong castles. They had much of the east Midlands under intolerable pressure. They had pressed hard all along their north-south frontier, driving up the Thames

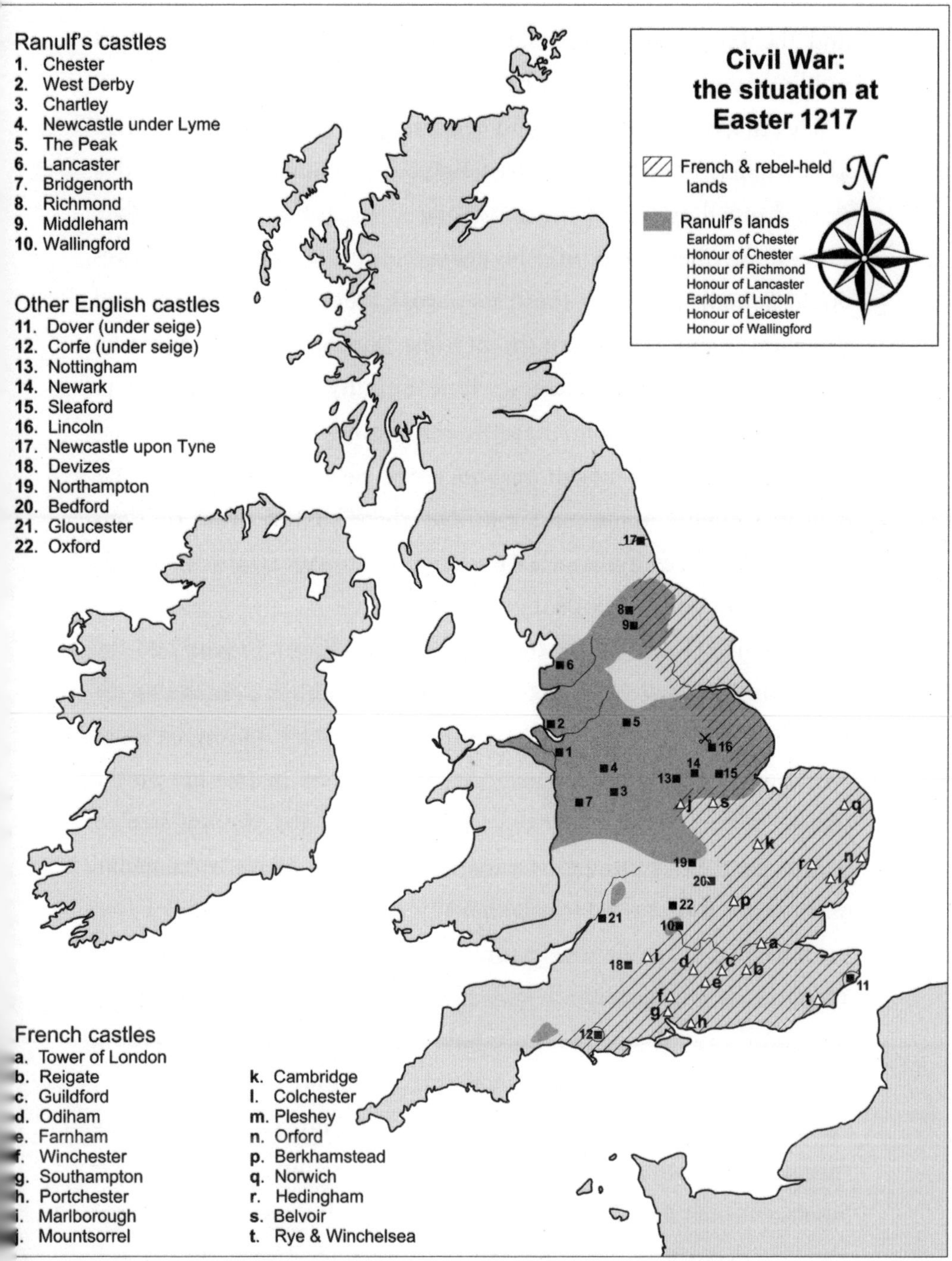

ivil War: the situation at Easter 1217. *Drawn by Jacqueline Harding.*

valley into Oxfordshire, to drive on Oxford and Northampton from the south, creating a salient in their rapid advance.

For the King there remained a smattering of castles behind enemy lines, such as Lincoln and Nottingham, Newark and Norwich, Orford and Sleaford (the last soon to come under the recalcitrant William d'Albini). The west remained almost totally loyal under the Earl Marshall and Ranulf, who together commanded a strong chain of castles which stretched from Dorset to Richmond and formed an impromptu frontier. It was probably about now that Ranulf gained Wallingford castle, traditionally a royal castle but which now needed a firm grip as it lay on one shoulder of the rebels' Thames salient and guarded the Thames river-crossing, within easy striking distance of rebel-held strongholds of Bedford, Buckingham and Marlborough.

Through the winter – and despite the truce – many of the remaining castles in the east, including Cambridge, Berkhamstead and Norwich fell to Louis, leaving their rear secure. This must have hurt Ranulf considerably since as part of the truce, he agreed to stand surety on 14 January 1217 for any defenders of royal castles who should be captured by rebels.[26] This was surely a financial millstone. An isolated Hedingham (Norfolk) was bargained away to save the garrison and retrieve them from French captivity. Things looked bleak but a plan for consolidation was unfolding. By Easter 1217 Louis certainly held almost the whole of eastern and southern England but the proverbial line had been drawn in the sand. The frontier followed the Jurassic ridge from Dorset, up through Hampshire and Wiltshire, Berkshire, Buckinghamshire, Northamptonshire, Leicestershire and Lincolnshire. One or two royal castles still held out behind French lines, notably Dover and Corfe; both remained thorns in Louis' side.

Louis, unwilling to openly break the truce and incur Papal wrath, had allowed himself to become surrounded in Sussex (nominally well behind his own lines) where his forces were running dangerously low on supplies. He was cornered and became blockaded in Rye and Winchelsea with his court. No attack had yet come since the royalists too were observing the truce. However, he was panicked at the news of Ranulf and the army's approach and on 27 February slipped aboard ship and sailed for France.

With Louis' departure (albeit temporary), the Papal Legate Gualo could enjoy a freer hand, with the opportunity to wage war without being seen to set king against king. He now declared the struggle against the rebels a crusade, bypassing the secular truce. Many who were on the point of departing to the Holy Land were persuaded to stay, wearing the white cross of the English crusaders in the present struggle. To many this would be preferable, still gaining the spiritual benefits while avoiding the difficult and dangerous land and sea journey to the east.

Following Louis' departure a constant trickle of defections from the rebel camp became a stream, as many did not believe he would return. Ranulf's brother-in-law William d'Albini, rejoined the royalists, as did the Earl of Aumale. Albini, who had held Belvoir Castle against John in 1216, barely escaping with his freedom and his life, was now given Sleaford Castle (Lincolnshire) to hold on pain of a heavy fine. The tide was now turning and the southern counties began to capitulate with castle after castle opening their gates. William Marshall was blockading the last of the rebel forces at Winchester, itself half burnt-down. From there late in March he dispatched Ranulf, together with the Earls of Aumale and Ferrers, Robert de Vipont and Brian de L'Isle, Faulkes de Bréauté and William de Canteloupe to Leicestershire, where Ranulf's old friend Saher de

Quincy was holding the castle of Mountsorrel (Leicestershire).[27] This was a very tough group of senior soldiers, amongst the best the royalists had to offer. Mountsorrel covered the crossing of the River Soar on the road north to Nottingham and Lincoln and also controlled river traffic. Only a bowshot from the river-crossing, it was (and remains) perched high above the plain on an eyrie of the hardest pink granite. Its height left little possibility of direct escalade and its granite base gave no opportunity for undermining; it would be a horrendously tough nut to crack. For this reason the royalists took a full siege train to batter the castle into submission.

Ironically, the castle of Mountsorrel had been built by Ranulf's great-great grandfather Hugh Lupus, Earl of Chester but it had become alienated from the family and their adherents thanks to the rebellion of 1173. Saher de Quincy had only received the castle in right of his wife's inheritance in 1215 shortly before Magna Carta, but, perhaps already knowing the way he would turn in the coming conflict had put in a small but trustworthy garrison. Revising his earlier decision, John had re-conferred the castle on the young William de Canteloupe – a somewhat empty gift up to that point. With the onset of the Civil War the rebel garrison regularly harried the surrounding lands, which included some of Ranulf's own in and around the town; they even routed a small royalist force sent from the garrison of Nottingham to relieve the pressure. It was into this awkward situation that Ranulf and the siege train now stepped.[28]

Saher de Quincy was present at Mountsorrel in person, aided by his very competent but brutal lieutenant Robert FitzWalter, one of the prime-movers of Magna Carta. The royalist army blockaded the castle and quickly set about bombarding the place, probably from the only side possible, an undulating expanse to its front, otherwise surrounded by a horseshoe of precipitous rock faces of roseate granite. Today these are softened by trees and brambles, but at the height of the Civil War they would have been scrupulously cleared of undergrowth to present a clear field of fire for the defenders. An engraving of 1757 and a photograph from the 1920s both show that a similarly bare rock-face survived until recent times.[29] Today houses and gardens nestle at the foot of the slopes, deceiving the eye into seeing a site apparently not as defensible as it once was. In fact such was the natural defence of the place that de Quincy's garrison numbered only ten knights and about fifty men-at-arms, commanded by a trusted rebel knight from Northamptonshire, Robert de Braybrook.

Mountsorrel Castle (Leicestershire). The commanding view of the crossing of the River Soar. The castle sustained a full artillery barrage by Ranulf in 1217 but the siege was lifted. Within weeks Ranulf returned and destroyed it. (2007)

Before the trap could close fully, de Quincy was able to slip out in person with a few retainers to seek Louis, who had landed at Dover at Easter with reinforcements of 140 fresh French knights and their retinues, led by the Count de Perche, who had a fine reputation in battle. Attended by their men-at-arms the new force probably numbered close to a thousand, adding fresh impetus to the remaining rebel troops. Louis had also brought a large, new and particularly notable trebuchet for the coming sieges. It might yet be needed. The Mountsorrel garrison had already held out for over a month when de Quincy found Louis at Farnham in Surrey. He had come up through Kent, shocked to find his forces were suffering reverses everywhere and keen to stop the rot. William Marshall ordered a scorched-earth policy; all the re-taken English castles were to be torched – except for Farnham, which was actually still under siege (Louis had taken the bailey but was being stalled by a dogged defence of the keep). He was alarmed at the news de Quincy brought and immediately dispatched a relief force north, to both aid Mountsorrel and reinforce a rebel army laying siege to Lincoln, which was said to be about to give in.

Perhaps mindful of earlier experiences at the siege of Roche-aux-Moines in 1214, Ranulf had been careful to place scouts a long way south of Mountsorrel. They did their work well and the approach of the French force was noticed well in advance, buying sufficient time for the royalist forces to crate-up their siege engines and move off in good order. One presumes they were disappointed to be almost-victorious but any besieger always knew they had to take a castle before relief arrived or they would be disadvantaged themselves. In addition it was rumoured (falsely) that Louis was leading the relief force in person.[30]

The besiegers took themselves to the far stronger royal castle of Nottingham, re-fortified and strengthened since its own fateful siege in 1194. Ironically of course, Ranulf had led that siege, so knew just how best to defend the castle should it come to that and where its weak points lay. However, it was not to be and once Mountsorrel had been relieved the rebel reinforcements moved to Lincoln where they piled on the pressure on the walled town, which quickly fell, leaving only the castle holding out for the young King. This was then invested by the full weight of the rebels.

News of Lincoln's worsening plight brought matters to a head and William Marshall summoned the royalist forces to muster at Newark on 15 May.[31] Contemporary chroniclers note that they numbered 400 knights, 250 crossbowmen and an unknown number of men-at-arms, perhaps bringing the whole force to about 2500, with large numbers of servants, squires, grooms, ostlers, farriers and others following behind with the baggage and provisions. As they congregated at Newark a council was held to draw up the battle strategy. Scouts informed them that the castle was holding out but the walled city all around it was now in rebel hands. An unknown number of rebels under Gilbert of Ghent and the French force of 611 knights and 2000 men-at-arms under Count of Perche now held the city but they could not very effectively besiege the castle in front of them and defend the city walls behind them. The rebels and their allies now found themselves in a uniquely difficult position and stood to be soundly out-manoeuvred.

They may have lacked a suitable numerical superiority but the royalists lacked nothing in courage. Ranulf, perhaps echoing his grandfather's part in an earlier siege of Lincoln (1141), apparently declared that, as was Norman privilege, unless he could stand in the vanguard and strike the first blow, he would not fight. This is pure theatre on the part of William Marshall's eulogist but does ring true since it gave the writer no particular opportunity to make the Earl Marshall look better. As it was, the battle order was decided. Ranulf would take the first division, the Earl Marshall the second, William Earl of Salisbury (recently returned to the royal cause) the third, and a fourth would be led by Peter des Roches, Bishop of Winchester. A body of crossbowmen as skirmishers would lead the way, led probably by Faulkes de Bréauté. The army heard mass at Torksey before moving off. They then divided and approached Lincoln from different directions, a manoeuvre which took a few days and required some coordination, in order to throw a tight cordon around the city. At the first approach of royalist skirmishers, Saher de Quincy and Robert FitzWalter reconnoitred and quickly realised a major force was approaching. Envoys for the royalists tried to open negotiations but found the rebel backs firmly shut up. They had good reason to fight hard since Gualo had excommunicated the whole rebel camp and the city of Lincoln. The gates were closed.

Gradually the net closed. Those who came from the south arrived first, others wrapping around the city. This took all day, prompting the French leader, the Count of Perche, to demand aggressively from the walls why the royalists were holding off. The reply came back that they were waiting for the Earl of Chester (whose own division was to attack at the north gate, the toughest). Towards evening Ranulf's division made its appearance. Peering down at the Earl of Chester, the tall and handsome figure of Perche snorted, exclaiming loudly and with intended derision, his astonishment that the army had waited at all for 'THAT DWARF of a man'. We must assume that, having pursued Ranulf up from Mountsorrel and having been given the slip by him, he had formed an unseen opinion of him and was surprised by his diminutive stature.

However, this was medieval battle-taunting at its best. Ranulf, who of course understood every word of his enemy's French, since they shared their mother-tongue, made a swift and angry reply, noting that before sundown the following day the Count of Perche would think him taller than the nearby cathedral tower, shortly before meeting his own death.

At dawn on 19 or 20 May the royalists attacked. They appeared not to have brought the Mountsorrel siege equipment from Nottingham. Each of the four divisions took on a different gate, Ranulf at the north gate, and did it the old-fashioned way – battering their way in without the aid of siege equipment. Ranulf seems to have been first to force an entry although other royalists almost simultaneously managed to get in by an old sally-port, known only to a few of them. Once the royalists were inside, the rebel cause was effectively lost, especially as the castle garrison, emboldened by events outside, now took up their cause once more at the rebels' rear.

The royalists poured in and the main street of Lincoln seethed with a heaving morass of pushing, shoving bodies of men and horses, so tightly packed that few could even swing a sword and bowmen could not string an arrow. For seven hours this melée flowed along the street, spewing the exhausted and the battered into the side-streets and alleys. Little by little the French were forced back, their numerical superiority lost in the confined space as they were disadvantaged with the slope behind them. Trying to rally their troops, first Saher de Quincy and then Robert FitzWalter were captured, along with the sons of David Earl of Huntingdon, Ranulf's own nephews. Seeing their kinsman in the forefront, they may have thrown themselves on his personal mercy at the first opportunity, since otherwise, the moment of capture is the most dangerous moment in battle. Better to be sure it was one's uncle or brother-in-law, than a bloodthirsty nameless man-at-arms. Certainly Ranulf himself captured the rebel garrison commander Gilbert of Ghent and his kinsman Maurice. Shortly after, the Count of Perche was killed. Since he was one of only a very few deaths in this melée, it may be surmised that Ranulf had him singled out and dispatched for his previous effrontery. Out of 611 rebel knights, 400 were captured, including 25 signatories to Magna Carta. So much for visionary democrats – they were rebels, plain and simple.

Only two rebel Englishmen of note escaped, William de Mandeville, Earl of Essex and John de Lacy, Constable of Chester, whose part in rebel proceedings must have galled Ranulf no end. It is possible that Ranulf let him go as his ransom would have been to his own financial disadvantage. Only three French nobles made their way out, fleeing to London. Despite the low body count, few rebels of any description evaded eventual capture. Some were probably apprehended and killed as they fled through the fields of Lincolnshire in the ensuing days. Some would languish in prison for quite some time to come.

The royalists had won a famous victory, known within a few months as 'The Fair of Lincoln', since so few noble deaths had ensued in the bruising and overcrowded melée and the winning side had never seen so much treasure, which they liberated from the French. They rather spoilt the victory, however, by then going on a brutal killing spree in the town, also plundering the churches and the cathedral. The whole place was excommunicate and therefore fair game for pillaging.

Within days the army marched south to relieve the siege of Dover. On the way the Earl Marshall received news that Mountsorrel had been deserted. The rebel cause was collapsing like a house of cards. The Earl of Salisbury was dispatched to secure the castle for the King. On 23 May the King's council confirmed Ranulf as hereditary Earl of Lincoln (he had lost it to a French-backed usurper during the troubles).[32] His first act as earl was to have the Earl of Salisbury's instructions rescinded and the castle handed over to him instead. He promptly razed it to the ground, perhaps piqued that it was the only castle he had never been able to take.[33] It was never rebuilt.

Success followed success. Lynn fell to Faulkes de Bréauté, becoming known for his battle prowess as 'the rod of the Lord's fury', an epithet his brutal actions confirmed as the excommunicate rebels fell back before him. He then sacked Bury St Edmunds, another town branded by the Church for its rebel sympathies. At the beginning of June the mother church came to the fore once more as the endgame of the Civil War was being played out. The Archbishop of Tyre arrived in England to preach a crusade, accompanied by the Cistercian Abbots of Citeaux, Clairvaux and Pontigny. A less hostile English Channel also now enabled letters of safe conduct to be issued on 8 June to Pierre Mauclerc, Duke of Brittany, whose help for his kinsman Louis must have been painfully noticeable by its absence. He now made his way to England as negotiations for peace accompanied the last desperate throes of the war. It was meanwhile confirmed that Ranulf still held Richmond for him, despite the recent threats in the North.[34]

On 8 July the Pope (Honorius) wrote to Gualo, particularly concerning Ranulf. The Pope had received a petition from someone, un-named, urgently asking him to consider making Ranulf joint regent of England, since the Earl Marshall was becoming infirm and increasingly too old to fulfil his duties – and after all Ranulf had been the other candidate. The Pope neither agreed nor disagreed, simply delegating the decision to Gualo, whose counsel was pivotal in the original appointments anyway. Who the original petitioner was remains unclear; it may even have been the Earl Marshall himself, whose final illness was in fact not far off. There is no real evidence of dissension or discord in the royalist camp, just genuine concern for the much-respected Earl Marshall and widespread support for Ranulf. The Pope's reply, while delegating to Gualo the decision, is nevertheless politic, to avoid any possible dissent, stating that 'As far as is possible and especially in these (difficult) times, we must be at pains and take care to engage the noble Earl of Chester as our ally'.[35]

Rebel and French operations were now increasingly confined to the south-east of the country and in the middle of August Peter des Roches and Philip d'Albini commanded an English fleet which soundly defeated the French off Sandwich (Kent), effectively ending all possibility of their success. Left with insufficient means either to reinforce or to evacuate, they took the only course left to them and sued for peace. On 12 September 1217 a peace treaty was signed at Kingston-upon-Thames, on an island in the river. For the English Ranulf was the fifth signatory, after Gualo, the young King, the Earl Marshall as Regent and the Chief Justice (Hubert de Burgh). Fourteen others followed. For the French, after Louis, one of their chief signatories was Pierre Mauclerc. One wonders whether his inaction on their behalf in the war and the growing esteem with which first John and now the Royal Council regarded him, made for a very willing signature, hastening his own cause, which was rapidly converging with that of England. Under the terms of the peace, beaten French nobles would not be allowed to claim their English lands until the defeated party, Louis included, promised to intercede at court with Philip Augustus, in order to once more secure for England possession of her former Norman lands. Some hope. Mauclerc and Brittany, however, were tacitly excepted (no such exception was written down of course) since their negotiations were already well under way.

The recriminations of civil war were many. Some, including Ranulf, who had been on the verge of losing a great deal, had made a huge amount of money and land from ransoming prisoners. Two full years after the Battle (Fair) of Lincoln, Maurice of Ghent brought a writ against Ranulf, who could not attend in person. Ranulf's men, he said, had seized his manors of Leeds and Bingley (Yorkshire) – and he wanted them back.[36] He stated that Ranulf had taken him prisoner at Lincoln and that in order to buy his freedom, he had promised a ransom of £2,250, five horses, each worth £22 and five hawks at Easter of 1218 (once more Ranulf's love of hunting was catered for). The agreement was that if he defaulted his manors were considered forfeit, to be held by Ranulf free of service, for the fee of one sparrowhawk a year. The deal was signed in the presence of (so-called) independent witnesses, the Abbot of Chester and the Prior of Tutbury (who would hardly find against their earl and patron!) Sure enough Maurice defaulted and, although the case went to the King's Bench, the court found in Ranulf's favour. In fact Maurice continued to crop up for the next ten years, always agitating against England, and always licked into shape by Ranulf and his court for his bitterness. Elsewhere Ranulf showed forgiveness for his enemies and those of the young King.[37] Henry wrote to him and extended his royal forgiveness through the Earl to a rebel, Alexander of Moulton, who was to receive back his confiscated lands in Yorkshire. Ranulf evidently held them by conquest and was apparently refusing entry to the sheriff! It was now time to let bygones be bygones. They were also part of

Pierre Mauclerc's earldom of Richmond, now reconstituted as the hereditary right of Brittany. Mauclerc remained in England into May 1218 to take delivery of Brittany's rights and claims. Ranulf had already been working with Pierre's seneschal, Jolland and the handover was a smooth one.[38] On his western frontier, even Wales thought discretion the better part of valour and Llewellyn did homage to the young King Henry and concluded a truce with Ranulf, ending decades of warring. Ranulf had never known a peaceful western border with Wales!

No doubt other scores would yet be settled, and bitterness and rancour would remain within hearts hardened by more than two years of brutal civil war. Ranulf was not alone; numerous barons, such as Robert de Vipont, tried to hold on to lands and castles they had taken, not altogether willing to return them to newly-forgiven rebels.[39] But for the moment the country could afford itself a forgotten luxury – thinking of the future. Government and administration could begin to build once more, although it would be more than four years before some courts began to sit again, hearing backlog cases shot through with the anger and bitterness of civil strife. However, for the moment, with hostilities at an end and the Breton negotiations concluded to his satisfaction, Ranulf's own thoughts could turn more fully to overseas plans he had been harbouring for some time.

8

DAMIETTA (1218–20)

Although Ranulf had been eager for the coming crusade and had taken the sign of the cross as long ago as Ash Wednesday (4 March) 1215, he had been prevented from fulfilling his vow to the Church by the war at home.[1] Once a vow of crusade was taken, it was sacrosanct. In fact the Church might hound one who did not fulfil it. King John had felt the cold shoulder of spiritual reproach during his reign for refusing a crusade (reputedly offering to send 100 knights in his place) and one such as he might be considered a spiritual outcast for such a refusal. Ironically, it was the Pope himself, via a letter to the Legate, Gualo, who had persuaded Ranulf in April 1217 (and just before the battle of Lincoln), to delay his departure.[2] However, from that moment the Waverley Annalist says Ranulf decided to wear in public the surcoat of the crusader, a white cross on a black background, in order to 'pursue the enemies of God and the Church, the opponents of his Lord, the King of England'.[3] He must have been dressed in this way at the Battle of Lincoln a month later. Free now to resume his chosen course, preparations once begun but put on hold, were restored and through the early summer of 1218 his stores, weapons, horses and men-at-arms were readied.

To help Ranulf's cause the government of the young King Henry, chiefly in the persons of the new legate Pandulf (Gualo resigned and was recalled in early 1218) and William Marshall, wrote off his existing war-debts to the Exchequer, which must have been considerable.[4] Ranulf now gathered around him his companions in arms, not forgetting his chaplain, probably a man deliberately chosen for this difficult period, whose name we know as Jocius, who served Ranulf between 1217 and 1222. In Whit week (3–9 June) 1218 they left Chester, in the company of the Constable, John de Lacy, making amends for his brief opposition to John and Henry (he was captured at Rochester, escaped, evaded capture at Lincoln; and even then his lands had been restored).[5] Ranulf had placed his Cheshire and Staffordshire interests in the hands of a trusted knight, Henry de Audley. They probably proceeded via Ranulf's castles and manors, the expedition gaining numbers as they went: firstly Dieulacres (to hear mass and receive a blessing), Chartley (Staffs), Coventry (Warks), Bugbrooke (Northants) and thence to the south coast, probably Ranulf's manor at Chalton, Hants and on to Portsmouth (since a crossing from the Cinque ports to Barfleur would entail passage through a hostile Normandy).

On the way their ranks were swelled: from Winchester came a rehabilitated Saher de Quincy, father-in-law to Ranulf's sister Hawise, perhaps trying to put his drastic opposition under Prince Louis behind him; many others were both friends and relatives whose companionship in war – and occasional opposition – tied bonds as strong as blood. William d'Albini, Earl of Arundel came, husband to Ranulf's sister Mabel now for twenty years and another former rebel; the ever-loyal Earl Ferrers of Derby (Ranulf's sister Alice's husband) came too. With these came Oliver, illegitimate son of the late King John and elder half-brother to Henry III.[6] Unable to inherit, he might make a name for himself on crusade. These alone would have been formidable enough, but with each of them came scores of knights owing service to their lords and hundreds of men-at-arms. With Saher de Quincy rode his long-time lieutenant since the fight for Normandy, the disreputable rebel firebrand Robert FitzWalter, another Mountsorrel rebel, helping make redress for his allegiance to Louis. Brian de l'Isle came, a man now supremely skilled in siege-craft who left his castle at Knaresborough in the hands of his deputy. On his return he would become the King's chief forester for his keen eye for the finest timber. Perhaps most poignant was William de St Hilaire du Harcourt, one of Ranulf's trusted knights, once of St-James-de-Beuvron, proof, if any were needed, that old bonds had been re-tied. Gathered to cross to Normandy, the army probably now numbered in excess of three thousand troops, of which probably at least some 100 were mounted knights (with two or more spare horses each) and a huge baggage train to match.

In later years, with the benefit of hindsight, others were claimed to have sailed with the army. The Count of Eu was said to have gone, but records show that he died at home in Poitou before the crusade really got going. Matthew Paris named Ranulf's old friend William Earl of Salisbury as another of his companions, but contemporary records show that, even with Ranulf half way across the Mediterranean, William was angling to hold a tournament on 8 August at Northampton, postponed at the last minute by William Marshall as being liable to cause a breach of the King's newly-won peace. Only a year before, William had been very unwilling to give up booty and castles taken in the Civil War. He would hardly change his tone so completely to leave them to chance within the year. In the absence of its great magnates, England would remain restive. Some feel that Matthew Paris (writing at St Albans Abbey after 1236) merely miswrote the Earl's name, mixing him up with the Count of Saarbrucken (who was there).[7] It is perhaps just as likely that the stories of the Fifth Crusade which circulated after 1220 produced a longing felt by many that they or their relatives too had sailed with the fleet, just to be able to say 'I was there'.

We can only guess the emotional farewells which would have been said. It is too easy with so great a length of hindsight to see all knights at this time as hard-bitten fighters who felt little regret or sentiment. However, each knew they were embarking on the most dangerous journey of their lives, with no guarantee of ever returning. A generation later, on the verge of the Sixth Crusade in 1249, the literary knight Jean de Joinville wrote of being unable to look up as his boat, journeying down the Rhône on its way to Aigues-Mortes passed his family home on the river bank.[8] He was compelled to think only of his wife and children and the pain of their mutual loss. In the event Joinville did return after many adventures. The same cannot be said of Ranulf's party, which, all told, is said to have numbered around 100 knights with perhaps ten times that number of men-at-arms.[9] Many would not return; for those who did, life would never be the same.

The journey to the Italian port of Genoa took about eight weeks. Their route is not known for sure but at this stage they would have to go west and then south, given safe conduct by the newly allied Pierre Mauclerc, Duke of Brittany. South around the treacherous Atlantic and Biscay coasts of Brittany, between its sheltered harbours of St Malo, Roscoff, Concarneau, Vannes or St Gildas, Guerande, then down to La Rochelle and inland across Poitou and down through the Saintonge, where English interests remained strong and then east from Bordeaux, crossing the lands of the Count of Toulouse, whose independence guaranteed he would not interfere on behalf of Philip Augustus. It was considered a terrible crime to make war on a crusader whose vow to God and His church overwrote all earthly allegiances. However they could not be complacent, since exceptions had been common and history had proved that kings and princes did not always obey such rules, as Richard the Lionheart had once found to his cost. They would have approached Genoa through a southern France wasted by ten years of the Albigensian Crusade, where the dispossessed Simon de Montfort, once Earl of Leicester and Ranulf's own uncle (and Saher de Quincy's brother-in-law), had carved out a name for himself as a master of siege-craft until his death that year, his head smashed in by a missile in a siege at Toulouse.

At Genoa Ranulf and his army met their spiritual advisor, the Anglo-Poitevin Cardinal Robert Curzon, a prominent Church academic sent from Rome. Here too they linked up with a clutch of other senior churchmen and numbers of the French nobility who had organised passage. Here no doubt they held mass for the army which must now have been many thousands strong. Their supreme spiritual leader-in-waiting, Cardinal Pelagius Galvani, Bishop of Albano, proceeded to Brindisi, where another great fleet had waited for over a year (paid for by the Pope) to take many more troops to their crusade. This self-important man, the Pope's legate in the whole enterprise, would prove himself able but unreasonable and time would show he was anything but a sensible leader. Together they took ship for their ultimate destination, Damietta, on the Nile Delta.

Damietta had been a scene of inter-faith strife before when besieged by the Franks in 1169. Furthermore, as long ago as the Third Crusade, Richard the Lionheart had identified that an attack on Egypt might divert Muslim forces from the defence of Jerusalem, although previous strikes by the Kings of Jerusalem in this direction had only served to unite the forces of Syria and Egypt under one Caliphate. Richard seems to have made some preliminary plans, but like so much else, his return to England via irksome and costly German captivity meant his plans came to nothing. However, in the first decades of the thirteenth century, an attack on Egypt, with the city of Babylon (the contemporary name for Cairo) at its core, became the accepted strategy to win a bargaining chip with which to wrest control of Jerusalem away from the Muslims.

Damietta was the prize, and what a prize! Old Damietta was a strongly fortified city of up to 80 000 inhabitants (perhaps an exaggeration of the time), close to the modern container port which today bears the same name (Dumyat). It lay only two miles from the sea, thus enabling the crusaders to maximise their own ease of supply, painfully stretched from southern Europe on the one hand or via the Christian strongholds of the Levantine coast on the other.

The immediate key strategic importance of Damietta however, was that it commanded one of the two main branches of the Nile and all its traffic to and from the interior. As so often before, Château-Gaillard on the Seine, Pontorson on the Couësnon, Mountsorrel on the Soar, a river crossing and its abilities to control both river and road traffic was a focal strong-point and the key to Cairo, the capital. Such strong-points were usually fortified and in war they had to be taken to gain the upper hand. No beachhead on the Delta would be secure without taking Damietta and only with Damietta, controlling Nile traffic to and from Cairo, could the Muslims be brought to the table to negotiate over the future of Jerusalem.

The journey from Genoa to Damietta took about a further four weeks, with a probable stop at Cyprus, before hugging the coast of Palestine with a landing for supplies at Acre. Roger of Hoveden states that the comparable return journey from Acre to Marseille could be completed with a fair wind in as little as fifteen days. Ranulf and the fleet out of Genoa anchored off the Nile Delta in September 1218.[10] The main fleet from Brindisi would arrive a short while after, probably having come a roundabout way via Acre in Palestine. On shore a struggle had already begun and the vanguard of the Christian army, which had arrived in late May from Palestine under Count Simon von Saarbrucken, was already embroiled in its first bitter struggle for the outworks of Damietta.

The commander of the Muslim forces, Malik-al-Adil Seif ed Din, (Saphadin to the crusaders, and brother of the late, great Saladin who had died in 1193) was now 65 years old and beleaguered in his own land, beset by conspiracies and in-fighting. Once upon a time Richard the Lionheart had ridden three magnificent Arab horses given him by Saphadin and had even proposed that Saphadin should marry his sister Joan, the widowed Queen of Sicily. However, this astounding and far-sighted union was abandoned since she (not he) was enraged at the need to convert to the other's faith. Since 1193 Saphadin had carefully kept his late brother's legacy together, but only just. He was worn down by decades of tough politics and the fact that his own leadership had only come about at the cost of dispossessing the two sons of Saladin.

Previous experience had shown that Damietta could not be taken from the landward side alone (where a broad sweep of marshland covered any approach). It could be re-supplied from the water. Consequently, Saphadin had greatly strengthened the Nile defences of Damietta with a strong fort or tower on an island in mid-stream, not dissimilar to the effect of the fortified Isle d'Andeli at Château-Gaillard where Ranulf had spent the summer of 1198. To one side, blocking the main navigable channel, was a huge chain; to the other, linking tower to shore, was a bridge of boats, together creating a heavily fortified toll-house which ensured no craft slipped by unannounced or untaxed, again just as at Château-Gaillard. If these fell into the hands of the crusaders, they would not only control the Nile traffic, they could cut it. It also covered the flank of the crusaders, who could not cross the Nile at Damietta unseen or in safety.

Realising that the island and its Nile boom would free up their flank and give them a huge tactical advantage, preventing re-supply to the enemy in the city, the vanguard of the crusader army attacked the tower in mid-August 1218, backed up by other ships with deck-mounted catapults. The scene was later graphically painted by the Dutch master Cornelis van Claesz (1562–1638) who merely seems to have updated the naval ships to his own seventeenth-century experience. There was apparently virtually no shore around the tower and access was by boats supporting scaling ladders against its walls, bobbing about wildly in mid-stream. The press of battle and the currents ensured no one got far and the attackers were routed to howls of derision and a cacophony of drums and trumpets.

Beaten off, the crusaders resorted to an artillery barrage, from mangonels and trebuchets for days on end. This at least could keep up the pressure from the far bank of the Nile while the besiegers regrouped. Discouraged, but keen for any innovative suggestion, they turned to Thomas Oliverus, Bishop of Paderborn.[11] Previously unknown for any engineering skills (unsurprisingly for the average Bishop), he designed a pre-fabricated timber siege tower or belfry which was mounted upon two assault ships fixed gunwale to gunwale.[12] Its corner frame was made of ships' masts, braced by sailyards, with sailcloth stretched around the whole. Thick hides strengthened the sailcloth against missiles and the whole was soaked through to prevent the spread of fire.

Within a few days the pontoon-bridge of boats linking Damietta with its tower had been destroyed by the ongoing barrage. The tower could no longer be reinforced. While this was the encouragement the besiegers needed, it was offset by the observation that the water level of the Nile was rising alarmingly, producing unexpected eddies and cross-currents. The annual inundation of the Nile was approaching. The crusaders chose this moment to strike before it passed. The impromptu siege tower was anchored against the fort and a bitter struggle ensued to gain a foothold on the ramparts, under cover of unremitting artillery fire. Counter-barrages flew from the walls but, little by little, the attacking crusaders inched forward, watched by nervous churchmen at prayer on the far shore. The defenders withdrew to an inner defensive ring and allowed their own engines to re-engage, 'dismasting' the siege tower. However its lower portions continued to give protection and at the shoreline the attackers pounded at the fort gate for over a day. Seeing there was no hope, a number of defenders threw down their weapons and escaped by diving into the swollen Nile; a few drowned. The rest, given assurances of humane treatment, chose to surrender the tower. About a hundred thus survived and went into captivity. The chain-tower was taken on 25 August, after which came a period of regrouping; Oliver of Paderborn called it idleness.[13]

Ranulf and the two fleets arrived soon after this initial success.[14] The army was now swelled to its greatest strength, headed by

Princes, nobles and churchmen from all over Europe and Outremer.[15] Pelagius took spiritual command, as the Pope had intended, although the nominal war-leader was John de Brienne, King of Jerusalem; the head of the crusade was King Andrew of Hungary. Pelagius then formed a high-council of respected senior advisors and experienced soldiers from the assembled nobility. Ranulf was amongst them as the leader of the large English contingent. The enterprise could not have had a more auspicious start now as, soon after the capture of the chain-tower, came news of the death of Saphadin, probably to a heart-attack. He was succeeded by his two sons, Malik-al-Kamil Mohamed, who became Sultan of Egypt (known as Kamil), and Malik-al-Moadden Isa, Sultan of Damascus (known as Coradin). Coradin was a cultured man who commanded great respect. Ironically he is said to have been knighted by Richard the Lionheart when he came of age (presumably during 1190–92), although what this meant for a Muslim is difficult to understand since chivalry dictated that knighthood was an office designed to a peculiarly Christian end. One of Coradin's first acts was to begin raising a northern army to go to his brother's aid in Damietta.

Not content with just waiting for the inevitable siege, the inhabitants of Damietta began adding new fortifications to the city, often under assault from artillery and even ventured to send out raiding parties in strength, in amphibious landings across the river. Unavoidably exposed, they took heavy casualties, despite infiltrating parts of the Crusader camp.

With the numbers of the crusader army now at an all-time high, the question of the conditions in camp and the welfare of troops arose as never before. The camp, we are told was surrounded by a deep ditch, and presumably a rampart on the inside, formed from the up-cast of the ditch. In fact a description by Jacques de Vitry, a contemporary historian who was present at Damietta, indicates that the Christian defences on the west bank of the Nile were gathered around a typical motte and bailey castle of the sort which characterised the contemporary landscapes of Western Europe. Here, however, riverine silt and desert sand were unsuitable for building purposes so a huge motte, flat-topped to support a high, wooden tower, was revetted on the outside with a mud-brick wall.[16] Such apparently improvised construction methods were to meet local conditions; particularly, Vitry said, due to a lack of building stone in the Nile Delta. This was surely far from a restriction, however, as in fact such a motte already possessed tried and tested examples as far away as leafy Surrey (South Mimms) where the set-up had worked well for some time, and not for any lack of suitable building stone. Around this focus the crusaders seem to have formed national and cultural camps within the camp as a whole, each man (and women) living cheek-by-jowl with his countrymen for companionship, mutual help and simply ease of language. English, Welsh, Breton, Norman, French, Italian, German, Flemish and Magyar would all have been heard. Only Latin was understood and spoken by large numbers of men of every camp.

While major supply drops could take place from the sea (and a number of supply-fleets arrived from time to time, bringing replacement horses, reinforcements and all manner of materiel), everyday supply became difficult, not least because the normal agricultural regime of the Nile Delta was wholly disrupted by having to supply (presumably against the will of many ordinary Egyptians and Bedouin) food and fodder in enormous quantities. While Egypt had once been the grain bin of the Hellenistic and Roman world, it was no longer the producer it had been.

The land in which the crusaders found themselves was a place of fantasy to most of them. They would have known it only from those Bible stories which their churchmen had shared with them, associated so closely with the sufferings and captivity of the children of Israel under the Pharaohs. It was not a place of cultural excellence in the popular Christian imagination of the day. However, the early thirteenth century was an inquisitive time and the wonders of the natural world attracted both Muslim and Christian alike. While Oliver of Paderborn himself was not particularly forthcoming about such things, normally being a man of uncompromising religious zeal and very little cultural understanding, thirty years later (1249) the far more worldly and tolerant Jean de Joinville made a considerable digression to relate details of a major expedition which had become known to him. The following is an extract:

> I should say something here of the Nile which runs through Egypt, and which comes from the earthly paradise (Eden, the African interior). While all other rivers are fed by numerous tributaries, the Nile is different and seems always the same. As it crosses Egypt, it floods across the countryside. At around St Remy's day it expands to fill seven branches and flows across the plains. When the waters have receded, the farmers reappear and till the ground with wheel-less ploughs, and then sow wheat, barley, rice and cumin, which make fine crops.
>
> No one knows the origin of this annual inundation, except from God's mercy. If it did not take place, Egypt would produce nothing, due to its hot climate; it is near to the rising sun (the Equator) and it scarcely ever rains.
>
> The river is quite muddy from the crowds who come out in

the evening to draw drinking water. They place into their water jugs four almonds or beans, which they shake well, and next day the water is clear and fit to drink. The local fishermen come each evening and cast their nets into the river, and in the mornings frequently find spices in them, which they sell at a profit, such as cinnamon, ginger, rhubarb, cloves, lignum-aloes etc. They are said to come from the earthly paradise* and that the wind blows them from the trees. What falls into the river is carried downstream, collected by merchants, who sell it to us.

* '*Paradeisos*' is an ancient Greek word – borrowed from Persian – for 'park' or 'garden' and from the New Testament onwards, was also used of the garden of Eden, in Greek and Latin. Both contemporary Christian Europe and the Muslim East seem to have thought this lay in the African interior.

Joinville went on to describe what was possibly the first expedition into the African Interior since Roman times, and certainly the first by the Arab rulers since their conquest of Egypt in the seventh century AD.

I heard in the region of Cairo that the sultan had frequently attempted to find out the source of this river by sending experienced travellers to follow its course. They carried with them a bread called biscuit, for there was no bread on their route, and on their return reported that they had reached a large mountain of cliffs over which fell the river. On top of this cliff they saw forest and many strange animals such as lions, snakes, elephants which came to gaze at them. The travellers dared venture no further and returned to the Sultan.

> The Nile, on entering Egypt, divides (at the Delta) into branches across the plain: one of them flows to Damietta, another to Alexandria, another to Tanis and another to Rexi.

The explorers had seemingly followed what became known as the Blue Nile across the flatlands of Sudan to Lake Tana and a huge horseshoe-shaped gorge in the (largely Christian) Ethiopian highlands, since called 'Africa's water tower'. Their journey presaged those of Burton, Speke, Livingston and Stanley in the nineteenth century.

Methods of purifying drinking water and the bounteous flotsam of spices drawn from the current might well have been marvellous news for 10,000 crusaders camped on the Nile Delta whose daily hard-tack was probably very poor, but the river could also be the bringer of destruction for the unwary. Camped as they were so close to the coast, they were taken unawares in the middle of the night, on 29 November 1218. An unusually high Mediterranean tide, driven by a storm, overwhelmed the low dunes fringing the delta shore and flooded the camp. To the south, the flow of the Nile, briefly held back by the storm-surge, spread out rapidly and swept over the camp.[17] Tents floated away, ships dragged their anchors and drifted to the enemy bank (where they were torched from the ramparts using Greek Fire). The storm lasted three days and, crucially, it had swept the crusaders' food supply away, although everyone dined well in the short term on thousands of fish; a heady mix of marine and freshwater species, left flapping in the shallows of the flooded camp.

The loss of the food stores was a dire blow as it was not long before terrible sickness swept through the camp. Oliver of Paderborn describes hideous symptoms: excruciating pains in the

The keep at Domfront (Orne). Ranulf probably spent much of his childhood here, ward of Henry II for his father's good behaviour. (2004)

St Sauveur-le-Vicomte (Manche). The keep of the Earls of Chester. (2007)

St-James-de-Beuvron (Manche) looking west across the valley of the River Beuvron to the hill-top site of Ranulf's castle. The large building is the adjacent former Priory of St James. (2007)

Above: Château-Gaillard (Eure). The view north from the castle shows the fortified Isle d'Andelys in the River Seine where Ranulf was stationed. The town of Petit Andelys is to the right. (2004)

Left: St Pierre-de-Semilly (Manche). The much-altered gatehouse to the castle, Ranulf's wedding gift from John in 1200. (2006)

The parish church of St Pierre-du-Château, Semilly (Manche) probably where Ranulf and Clémence married in 1200: Romanesque south doorway. (2006)

The multi-period urban castle at Fougères (Ille et Villaine). Ranulf should have received much of what surrounded the town in his marriage settlement in 1200. (2004)

Château du Lude (Loire), most northerly point reached by the punitive expedition of 1206 which turned out a damp squib. Ranulf was kept close but denied top command by a suspicious John; he seems to have been in charge of POWs. (2003)

The Abbey of Fontdouce (Charentes Maritime): the chapter-house. One of the few stops along Ranulf's route in summer of 1214 which could put up a royal army with the roads packed with pilgrims. Fontdouce had been a favourite of Eleanor of Aquitaine. (2004)

Nantes (Loire Atlantique): the later castle. Here a scrappy melée across the earlier drawbridge approach in 1214 left all the claimants to the Duchy of Brittany languishing in John's custody. (2007)

Above: Angers (Maine et Loire): the castle, heart of the eponymous Angevin Empire, recaptured briefly by John in 1214. (2003)

Left: Corfe Castle (Dorset). Although entirely surrounded by the French in 1216-17, it held out for John, whose favourite castle it was. Later it became a prison for Ranulf's erstwhile stepdaughter, the hapless Eleanor of Brittany. (2006)

Richmond Castle (North Yorkshire): the keep. Traditionally held by the Dukes of Brittany (as Earls of Richmond), Ranulf was told by John in June 1216 to hold it from the rebels or destroy it. (1988)

Gloucester Cathedral (Gloucestershire): the nave, where Henry III's coronation proceeded without Ranulf, who arrived next day to profess his allegiance. (2008)

'The capture of Damietta' by Cornelis Claesz van Wieringen (c.1580-1633). An imaginative painting showing the cutting of the chain across the Nile as the fleet arrived in 1218. *By courtesy of the Frans Hals Museum, Haarlem*

St Mary's Benedictine Cathedral, Coventry (Warwickshire) during excavations in 2000. Completed *c.*1224 at the heart of Ranulf's dominions, the church was the burial place of Richard, his uncle. *Photo by Bob Fielding.* (2000)

Cheylesmore Manor, Coventry (Warwickshire) during excavations. Ranulf probably built the fortified south range in the 1220s. (1992)

Beeston Castle (Cheshire), chief amongst Ranulf's new castles of 1225. Like Château Gaillard, it was officially known as 'The Castle of the Rock', from its commanding location. Inner ward. (2009)

Bolingbroke Castle (Lincolnshire), a polygonal castle, without keep, but with D-shaped towers. Built by Ranulf as a new chief residence for his Earldom of Lincoln from 1225. (2008)

St Gildas-de-Rhuys (Morbihan). The Poitou invasion, led by Ranulf and Richard Earl of Cornwall, disembarked in the bay, May 1230. (2007)

St Gildas-de-Rhuys (Morbihan). The abbey, burial place of the father of British history, Gildas. Here the invasion force would have heard Mass for their safe arrival. (2007)

The castle of Suscinio (Morbihan) surrounded on three sides by forests, lagoons, marshes and a hunting park. Begun by its owner Pierre Mauclerc in 1218, and unfinished, it would have been the army's first stop along the coast-road in May 1230. (2006)

The castle at Vitré (Ille et Villaine). In 1231 too tough a prospect, even with 500 knights and 1500 men-at-arms in tow and a string of victories behind them. Plans with Pierre Mauclerc for a siege were shelved. (2005)

The castle at St Aubin-du-Cormier (Ille et Villaine). Here on 4 July 1231 Ranulf and Pierre Mauclerc forced a humiliating three-year truce on the besieged King Louis IX of France, his forces already defeated and the royal baggage train captured. (2007)

Above: Wallingford Castle (Oxfordshire): apartments. Already ill for some months, Ranulf died here on 26 October 1232. Henry III rushed to his bedside from nearby Reading to pay his last respects. (2008)

Left: The chapter-house of the former Abbey (now Cathedral) of St Werburgh, Chester (Cheshire), burial place of Ranulf, his father and his grandfather. (2006)

legs and feet and lower legs turning black.[18] The inside of the mouth swelled so that sufferers could not chew, gobbets of extraneous flesh grew on the gums. Modern medical opinion suggests that Oliver was describing acute scurvy, the dreadful results of a lack of vitamin C in the diet. Trench-foot and Vincent's infection have both also been suggested.[19] Many may have been ill-prepared after as much as six months on campaign, but for everyone the loss of stores may have robbed them of what little dried fruits and vegetables they had. They would have to forage for what they could get through the winter, until the following spring with its new sailing season and the next supply fleet.

With no safe home to retreat to, the crusaders abandoned the usual rules of war and did away with any idea of a campaigning season. Battle continued unabated through the winter and Oliver of Paderborn relates amphibious attempts by both sides to mount raids on each other. The besieged built new outworks up to a mile out from the city.[20] Ranged downstream along the bank, these were seemingly of mud-brick and timber and on them were set up banks of stone-throwing engines; they would cover the flank of any Christian crossing. In front of Damietta, they sank some of their own ships as obstacles and drove piles into the river bed to rip out the hulls of approaching vessels (just as German defenders later did in the shallows of the Normandy beaches in 1940–44). When the Christians made to cross further upstream instead, the Saracens simply sent their field army to defend the bank and deployed three ranks deep to repel anyone who tried to land.

Despite the obstacles and expecting heavy losses, a date of 6 February 1219 was nevertheless set for a crossing in force. However, the night before a spy noted that the defenders had withdrawn from their positions under cover of darkness, presumably since it could be seen that the Christians were amassing a force they could not repel without their artillery (which was now committed on their outworks downstream and well out of range).

Despite deep water and a very muddy shoreline brought about by poor weather, the crusaders crossed unopposed. A blockade was swiftly established around the city. The outworks downstream were useless since they now faced the wrong way. The crusaders built a bridge of boats to link their forces on both banks and the envelopment was completed. It was now a siege in every sense.

If Damietta was discouraged by these events, the city's hopes rose considerably with the arrival of Coradin and his relief force from Syria.[21] His approach took the Christian army by surprise and a counter-siege was mounted adjacent to the bridge of boats. The siege was briefly broken, allowing river-traffic to get to the city once more, and threatening the crusaders' original camp and port facilities. In order to demoralise the Christian army, Coradin now chose to attack on Palm Sunday (31 March 1219) when religious observance held their attention. Facing Saracens on both sides, German and Frisian elements of the Christian army, led by the Duke of Austria, held off the attack for some four hours until, its momentum spent, the Muslim force retreated with heavy losses.[22] It would never be strong enough to mount such an attack again.

The arrival of spring brought a new danger, complacency. With the new sailing season, hundreds of crusaders, their vow of service fulfilled, chose to sail home, led by the Duke of Austria. As a soldier of note, he had impressed the Earl of Chester, and Ranulf took his departure as an opportunity to show his appreciation. The Duke was particularly supportive of the Templars' new castle at Athlit in the Holy Land (Just south of Haifa, it was known as the Pilgrims' Castle as it commanded the principal pilgrim roads of the Levantine coast, for Muslims that from Damascus to Mecca and for Christians that from Acre to Jerusalem). It thus had both offensive and protective potential. While the Duke gave a small fortune towards the Templars' building costs, Ranulf chipped in with fifty silver marks towards the strengthening of its walls and towers.[23] Ranulf's interest is of note since Oliver mentions no others making any such contributions. It is possible that Ranulf was particularly interested in the design of the castle.

For a few weeks the Christian ranks looked as though they would be dangerously depleted by those departing for home. However, as luck would have it, their passage home was with the first fleet to dock that year, which had just arrived carrying reinforcements, food and horses early in May 1219. A renewal of hostilities greeted the new arrivals.[24] With the sea-lanes clearly open once more, the besiegers could only grow stronger with every day that went by, while the defenders' reserves dwindled. The siege had to be broken either by force or by the Christian army becoming demoralised by a mixture of casualties, disease and the knowledge that they were a very long way from either home or anything they even recognised, let alone their wives and girlfriends (although there were many women in the camp). On 16 May, again choosing a Christian festival (Ascension), the defenders sallied out both on land and river to test the besiegers' resolve and probe the siege-works. Clearly a test, they were laying plans for a major break-out which finally took place on 31 July. Leaving no reserves, the Muslim defenders sallied out against the Templar contingent who, unusually, broke under the pressure, exposing the flank of their co-besiegers to either side. The siege-lines were abandoned but the Franks poured into the yawning gap. Although their efforts faltered, they gave the Templars time to regroup and the Saracens, whose initial impetus was now faltering, found themselves exposed and a long way from their own lines. They were quickly forced to retreat, which they did in good order, but not without sustaining heavy casualties as their flanks came under attack from the Germans and the Franks. In the end, the speed with which the Templars had broken prevented similarly heavy losses.

If the defenders of Damietta had learnt anything, it was that, although their own strength was waning, the attackers could still be taken by surprise. Their probing continued and in the blistering heat of mid-summer 1219, they sought to confuse the besiegers' chain of command by sallying out at a number of points simultaneously. Ranged in such a wide ring around the city, the various Christian commanders could not easily communicate and each sector had to fight its own battle independently, hidden from those further around the ring by the dust raised by 10,000 hooves and deafened by the noise of battle at half a dozen different points. This tactic proved devastatingly successful; although most may have been diversionary feints, one in particular reached what must have been the only real target, the Christian artillery. Oliver of Paderborn gives this Muslim success only one line in his history, so great was the embarrassment and difficulty it caused. He states that almost all the machines prepared against the city were destroyed.[25] Despite their growing numerical superiority, without engines a siege could never be carried against the walls of Damietta. Could they build more? Perhaps, but it is likely that after more than a year camped around the city, there was not a suitable tree standing within twenty miles. New siege engines were just one more thing which had to be brought by sea from Acre or Malta, Cyprus or Sicily – and word had to be sent first, also by sea.

The round trip and subsequent construction time would probably delay their arrival until the following spring.

Attempts were renewed to enter the city by escalade but to no avail; the knowledge of a Christian absence of artillery simply enabled the defenders to trust their strengthened defences all the more. Without artillery support the Christian army began to get concerned and a period of inactivity followed.

The stalemate was broken on 29 August when a poorly-directed mass of largely unsupported infantry, impatient for something to happen, turned their attention to a relatively lightly fortified camp held by a mixture of Damietta's garrison and Coradin's chastened relief army, laagered some way off near the coast, apparently out of harm's way.[26] Still too small to assault the Christian lines, this army was presumably awaiting further reinforcements. However, they were now presented with an opportunity. The Christian army had left its siege-works, was out in the open and lacked a clear objective; all these efforts distracted it from Damietta. The Muslim relief force had just enough time to abandon its camp, taking the time to appear to quit the scene by packing up tents. The Christian army's advance reached the abandoned camp, but here its impetus faltered. They themselves now made an impromptu camp and many scattered into their national groupings, bewildered and annoyed that the enemy would not give battle. Suddenly they were roused by an attack by Coradin from the right. The Cypriot knights, about a hundred strong, were overwhelmed and the Muslims were in amongst the infantry. The Italians broke and fled, followed by a rag-tag of horsemen of sundry units and some of the Knights Hospitaller.

Beset by heat and thirst (they carried no additional water), the rest of the army broke and a rout ensued, threatening huge casualties.

Small bands which turned and faced the enemy were overwhelmed and fell where they stood. The rot was stopped by a small band of prominent knights fighting for their lives, which wheeled their horses and turned to face their pursuers. Led by the doughty King of Jerusalem, John de Brienne, they comprised elements of Templars, Hospitallers, Teuton Knights and the cream of the military nobility of France, Flanders and Germany. There in their midst, Oliver of Paderborn singled out and named one Englishman – Ranulf, Earl of Chester.[27]

In such a rout, or at best a fighting retreat, with backs turned, casualties are always at their highest. A generation after, similar engagements were recounted by Jean de Joinville who, unusually amongst contemporary chroniclers, described wounds sustained by French knights, again at Damietta, in 1249:

> Sir Hugh d'Escosse was desperately hurt by three great wounds in the face and elsewhere. Sir Raoul de Wanon and Sir Ferrers de Loppei were also badly wounded in their shoulders, so that the blood spouted out just like a barrel of wine when tapped. Sir Errart d'Esmeray was so severely wounded in the face by a sword, the stroke of which cut off his nose, so that it hung down over his mouth.[28]

Even in such distress knights might find courage. Pierre Mauclerc, (by then the former Duke of Britanny), was badly wounded in the same engagement in 1249.[29] Joinville relates:

> the count came to us … having had a most furious skirmish. He was so badly wounded in the face that the blood came out of his mouth, as if it had been full of water, and he vomited it forth. He

> was mounted ... and his reins and the pommel of his saddle were cut and destroyed so he was forced to hold on to the horse's neck. He ... frequently turned around and shouted abuse at his pursuers.

Although Mauclerc died of disease, ignominiously in the hold of a galley later in that campaign, this is an interesting insight into this particular man, a close ally of Ranulf, and his character as a soldier, given that his middle years were caught up in military service alongside the Earl of Chester (see particularly Chapter 11).

Archaeology from time to time records grievous battle wounds on skeletal material. The hacked-up, dismembered body of (probably) Sir William de Audley was excavated at his family's own Hulton Abbey, a Cistercian house in Staffordshire; he was amongst a group of knights ambushed and killed in battle on Anglesey in 1282. A medieval skull excavated from the church of Coventry's Benedictine Cathedral Priory, bears two horrific partly healed battlefield wounds which may have left the victim suffering from epilepsy for the rest of his life.[30] In state records relating to the same Priory, is an entry of one Roger de Chester (not Ranulf's half-brother, but possibly a descendant), a Sergeant-at-Arms under Edward I, sent there in 1301 'who has long and faithfully served the King and was maimed in his service, so that he is unable to serve longer, and whom the King has caused to be sent to them and that they will find him for life all the necessaries of life in food and clothing according to the requirements of his estate'. Both the injuries on excavated bones and the unrelated document attest the brutal reality of the need for the wounded to be cared for, often long after their wounds were received. Nothing changes today.

Ranulf however, mounting a rearguard in the midst of what was becoming a rout, became a pivotal figure as the Christian forces began to rally and with others he began to instill some order into the retreat.[31] They checked the Saracen advance, skirmished and, when on the point of being overrun, turned and retreated once more; formed up, fought and retreated. In this way they covered the flight of their own army and took the brunt of the repeated Muslim attacks. Casualties mounted up but the tactic continued until they reached the Christian siege-lines. There, in front of their own defences Ranulf and the rearguard of knights, now much depleted, held the Saracen attacks until all the remaining Christian troops had found their way back: as many as 4,300 had been killed.[32] Forced to endure repeated attacks, Ranulf and his band were the last to re-enter the siege-lines. On this single engagement turned the whole enterprise, for the impetus of the defending army was now spent.

Pelagius now received a strange request from a young man who had recently arrived and had watched the recent disastrous engagement. This grubby figure, dressed in rags, was named Francis and he wished to convert the Sultan to Christianity, or die in the attempt. Pelagius reluctantly granted him permission to seek audience with Al-Kamil, who was rather amused at his antics and the demeanor of one who seemed deranged by his simple faith. He was certainly leading a strengthening peace-party but this was not the way to make any headway, when delicate negotiations were needed.[33] It is probable that both sides were considering negotiations as neither side really had the upper hand any more, but equally, neither side had given up hope of winning. Al-Kamil was polite but firm in his rebuttal and Francis was given safe conduct to his own lines. He had impressed many with his selfless devotion to the cause of God's peace. As time would tell, he may have impressed Ranulf in particular.[34] He is today known as St Francis of Assisi.

Matters worsened for the defenders when it became clear that the annual inundation of the Nile had failed. Crops could not be sown and the whole of Egypt was faced with the threat of starvation, not just the garrison under siege. Peace negotiations were opened and a short truce concluded. Perhaps true to form, both sides spent the time strengthening their defences. Although the crusaders were losing more time-served members of their army, the last fleet of the sailing season brought reinforcements on 21 September, led by the Anglo-Poitevin knight, Savaric de Mauléon.[35] They were carried on ten galleys so may have numbered perhaps only twenty knights and 100 or so men-at-arms with all their horses; nevertheless they were fresh. When Al-Kamil broke the truce on 26 September, de Mauléon and his new force were in the front rank. Their part was decisive and the Muslim attack failed.

Al-Kamil faced a brutal reality. He could give in and save Damietta by offering Jerusalem, thereby also saving Egypt from famine, or hold out longer but risk losing Damietta anyway to further siege and risk losing Egypt also. It was a lose-lose situation. He preferred the former option and offered the Christian army what they sought, Jerusalem and the lands up to the Jordan if they would lift the siege and go home. Astoundingly, this represented total Christian victory. It is therefore perhaps surprising that the camp was split on its possible reply. For acceptance stood a strong party comprising John de Brienne, King of Jerusalem (who stood to regain his kingdom), the French and Ranulf Earl of Chester.[36] However they were outvoted (if ever anything so democratic was possible). Those who wished to refuse were led by the senior churchmen, the Templars, Hospitallers and, significantly, the Italian contingent whose part in the enterprise had been to seek a mercantile base in a captured Damietta, for exploitation by the men of Pisa, Genoa and Venice, the great traders of the medieval Mediterranean. For them *carte blanche* to begin trading in a captured city was their only option – to hand it back was unthinkable, whatever the prize. Greed dictated they could contemplate nothing less than total mastery of the city. The siege would go on and Al-Kamil's terms were rejected.

Another month proved decisive and on 3 November 1219 the Christians attacked the three concentric walls of the city's fortifications and its 28 towers in force, a brief engagement in which Saher de Quincy was killed. Gaining easy entry, they were briefly shocked by what they found.[37] Out of a city of perhaps 80,000, less than 3,000 inhabitants were left alive, most now incapable of bearing arms. Everywhere were corpses, wasted by festering wounds and disease (ironically the grain stocks were still holding up). Initial gratitude for the crusaders' success led to the consecration of the central Mosque of Damietta as a church, dedicated to St Mary. Ranulf and the English knights themselves consecrated two other mosques as churches with very English dedications, one to St Edmund the Martyr, the other to St Thomas Becket.[38] Each nation's knights were assigned at least one of the captured towers in which to set up their headquarters.[39] However, the whole army now reverted to type and the pillaging began, not just of the city of Damietta, but of numerous outlying towns and villages. Finery of every description was wrested from the inhabitants and the Nile Delta witnessed the unbridled arrogance of a victorious army. Further castles of the Delta defences fell one after another like a house of cards.[40] Victory appeared to be complete, but appearances can be deceptive.

Early in 1220, as soon as the sea lanes were open, time-served crusaders went home, among them John de Brienne (whose hope for his own kingdom was surely now gone). The senior council could not agree on a suitable replacement and inactivity ensued.[41] New crusaders continued to arrive, and Pelagius used the reinforcement to argue for a conquest of all Egypt. Ranulf's brother-in-law, William d'Albini, Earl of Arundel was said to have been vociferous in opposition to this foolhardy idea.[42] The crusade had run out of impetus, its prime objective supplanted by greed.

Pelagius' refusal of Al-Kamil's offer had robbed him of his one bargaining chip to win Jerusalem and Palestine and now the crusaders held a fortified town at the end of a huge (and seasonal) supply chain, in a famine-ravaged country. Without its use as a bargaining chip, they could no longer rely on a constant flow of fresh new crusaders. It was only a matter of time before they either had to abandon the foothold or have it besieged by Muslim forces massing at Cairo and reinforcements landing at Alexandria or crossing the coast of the Negev. They had been hoisted on their own pétard.

In early summer, Ranulf and the time-served English knights petitioned Pelagius for leave to depart. Although probably reluctant to lose this wealth of experience, he could hardly refuse, since they had now been under arms and away from their homes for two full years, much more than most.[43] The English ranks were badly depleted. Robert FitzWalter had died in battle. Oliver, the young King's half-brother had been killed. So too had Ranulf's great friend Saher de Quincy, Earl of Winchester. He and Robert may have died side by side given their previous close association. Ranulf had much to regret. Even more, Savaric de Mauléon's arrival in early summer 1220 had probably brought worrying news of events unfolding in England. William Earl Marshall, aged regent of England and Ranulf's great ally, had died 12 June 1219, leaving the fractious Hubert de

Burgh as vice-Regent to the Papal legate, Pandulph. On that same day died Ranulf's eldest brother-in-law, David, Earl of Huntingdon.[44] Another friend at court, William Earl of Salisbury was gravely ill through the spring of 1220.[45] While he had been away, Ranulph had seen old friends and relatives killed in battle before his eyes, but his family was also bereaved at home and his allies were losing their grip in his absence. His world had changed and he had been able to do nothing. It was all rather reminiscent of his powerlessness in the first half of 1204 when he had been separated from events in Normandy.

Amongst the army and the crusader council, Ranulf's departure in July 1220 was greeted with universal acclamation, in gratitude for the magnificent part he had played when the crusade had hung in the balance in front of Damietta. The Dunstable Annalist summed it up perfectly when he commented 'At Damietta's capture, the entire church pointed to the example of the Earl of Chester'.[46]

With him returned John de Lacy, now probably closer to Ranulf than anyone, William d'Albini, Earl of Arundel, William Ferrers Earl of Derby, Brian de L'Isle and the other survivors.[47] If the casualties amongst the high command at Damietta are a guide to the army as a whole, then the English contingent had probably suffered at least twenty-five per cent losses, amongst knights and men-at-arms alike to a mix of wounds and disease. An English contingent continued to serve at Damietta, such as the fresh unit with Savaric de Mauléon and even later arrivals such as Ranulf's nephew, Philip d'Albini. However, the Fifth Crusade was stuttering to a disagreeable conclusion, its force spent.

Contemporary historians agree that Pelagius and the army gave Ranulf a rousing send-off.[48] However, if he thought that after two years under arms, his return journey would be an anti-climax, he was mistaken. Crossing the Mediterranean, his fleet was caught in a vicious storm.[49] Ensconced below deck, Ranulf was said to have sat impassive (in all probability terrified and cursing his helplessness) as his ship was tossed about. He was rooted to the spot until exactly midnight, when he started and exclaimed that all would be well now, since that was the time when his monks at Dieulacres were bound by agreement to pray for him. The storm blew itself out and the fleet made land safely, perhaps indeed aided by the Cistercians' prayers at Dieulacres. There was no doubting his faith. While Ranulf headed directly home, some took a diversion. William d'Albini, Earl of Arundel probably put in at Brindisi, followed by a land journey through Italy, via Rome, where he would have been de-briefed in the Papal See, delivering the latest dispatches from Pelagius and the command at Damietta, while also recounting his own recent opposition to Pelagius. While staying at Cainell, near Rome, the Earl of Arundel fell ill. He languished, unable to continue his journey and there he died on 1 February 1221.[50] Given his vociferous opposition to Pelagius, his death might be viewed with suspicion. His body was eviscerated, boiled to de-flesh it (the so-called 'German custom'), and his bones reverently brought home by his companion and chaplain, Thomas, a Benedictine monk of St Albans Abbey. They were buried at Wymondham Abbey (Norfolk) where his family was hereditary patron. Ranulf had lost a long-standing friend and another brother-in-law. His closest circle (his so-called *familiares*) was much depleted.

By contrast Ranulf made good speed, arriving back in England at the beginning of August 1220, perhaps in the end driven in the right direction by the storm.[51] In fact so fast was his journey back that it seems possible that he was deliberately trying to break all records, and possibly not a few horses in the process. Contemporary historians note that he arrived back in Chester with John de Lacy the day after the assumption of the Blessed Virgin Mary, 16 August 1220.[52] His reception at home was no less rapturous than his departure from Damietta. The Chester Annalist stated that he was received 'with the greatest veneration by both clergy and laity'. News of his approach must have been widely known days in advance, since he received Llewellyn, Prince of Wales and an embassy the very same day.

9

A QUESTION OF CASTLES (1220–24)

Ranulf returned to an England much changed from his departure. A mere two years had made a great difference to the balance of power. For the Church, Gualo had resigned, to be replaced by a new legate, Pandulf, a rather nepotistic and self-seeking cleric. His new assistant in government (the Earl Marshall having died a year since) was Ranulf's detested political opponent, the Justiciar Hubert de Burgh, who was now Regent in all but name (actually Pandulf now held that office, as directed by the Earl Marshall on his deathbed).[1] In addition Ranulf had returned without so many former allies at court, casualties of the crusade. Although in the case of some (particularly Saher de Quincy and William d'Albini), their sons were of age and slotted into the family role – eventually with great success (particularly Philip d'Albini) – for the time being they lacked the experience and time-served confidence of their fathers, who died in the prime of their military and political careers.

Their political experience, hard won and tempered on the anvil of the Civil War, would now have been invaluable as once more England simmered, seeming to be continually on the brink of open strife. Discord amongst the nobility was never far below the surface and tensions continued to run high. Occasions to bind the nobility to the land were sought. In mid-1220 (prior to Ranulf's return to England) the bones of the sanctified Thomas Becket were moved to a new home in Canterbury Cathedral, while in September, at the end of a summer-progress through the north and Midlands, the young Henry was crowned once more at Westminster (or shown to his people in a 'crown-wearing' reminiscent of the Lionheart in 1194). All the court was there. It was an occasion to promote unity and the blessing of the mother church on the *status quo*.

Ranulf's return meant that he now had two years of personal backlog to clear up. Some matters simply needed crown ratification, such as re-confirmation of the honour of the earldom of Leicester, which came on 4 October, a moment chosen perhaps as much in a show of admiration for the English hero of the crusade as merely a rubber stamp for what was already his.[2] It is possible that before his departure for Damietta, and with no obvious heir, Ranulf had to place his various titles and offices in the hands of the Legate, in the event that he might not return. Ratification at this stage merely marked his resumption of his former place in society. He was also formally entrusted with all the lands of the earldom of Huntingdon, in safe-keeping for his late brother-in-law David's son, his nephew, John le Scot.[3] Although they were nominally in the purview of the King of Scotland (Alexander, son of the late William the Lion, a man still at odds with England but nevertheless bound by a new treaty and fealty to Henry), Ranulf was family and Henry consented, although his interests must also have been in Ranulf's mind. Joined by a stream of individual gifts, this gave Ranulf control of numerous manors in central and east Northamptonshire and Leicestershire (Dodford, the entire hundred of Willibrook; Nassington, Jerwell; Shepwick).[4] At the same time the King confirmed to Ranulf lands in Lincolnshire, including those which had been traditionally in the remit of his wife's family, the de Fougères, at Navenby, Limburgh and Long Benington. At the last, there seems to have been some serious decay or destruction (perhaps left over from the Civil War) as Ranulf was given leave to take quantities of timber from the King's forest (Brian de l'Isle as the new royal forester was ordered to offer him all assistance), apparently to rebuild his manor there, perhaps previously torched as belonging to hostile Bretons.[5] A further royal grant was made for such reconstruction work to take place at Ranulf's properties on Cannock Chase and St Mary's Church, Lichfield (Staffordshire).[6] Again, a similar facility was extended to Ranulf within the year at the King's forest at Mansfield (Nottinghamshire) where Brian de l'Isle again was ordered to provide fifty pairs of cruck-blades for Ranulf to rebuild his houses at Sutton Bonnington (Nottinghamshire).[7] The whole of the Midlands had suffered greatly in the previous six or seven years and Ranulf seems to have been making good some major rebuilding across his lands.

Ranulf was also newly placed at the centre of a number of law suits, some simply which had festered while he had been away, others which ought never to have been left unaddressed at his departure to Damietta.[8] He appears to still have been holding prisoners and hostages from the Civil War (such as Henry de Redenesses, whom he captured under John at York in the winter of 1216). The legality of his continued imprisonment was raised. In Staffordshire Ranulf became embroiled in a royal dispute over rights of appointments to the parish church of Stoke-on-Trent with the Prior of St Mary's Augustinian Priory, Kenilworth, which, despite the best attentions of his attorney, Hugh Goldsmith, dragged on for two years to be settled in compromise. Others concerned a plea made by the Abbot of Peterborough concerning the church of Normanby (Lincolnshire), while yet another was against the Abbot of Pershore over grazing rights at Chipping Campden (Gloucestershire). In all these, and other, lesser examples, the matter was ably handled by Hugh Goldsmith for Ranulf, although in the last case Ranulf won because the Abbot did not bother to turn up to set out his case. It seems that while there was an understanding that the interests of a crusader should not be undermined while he was in God's service, his return meant open-season for the advocates.

Hardly was Ranulf back in England than events around the court began to look gloomy once more. As the young King neared the end of his royal progress he reached Rockingham (Northamptonshire), where the castellan, William des Forz (his family originally from the Isle of Oleron off the Poitevin coast), Earl of Aumale, closed the gates and refused him entry.[9] William had still not received back all his lands (including Rockingham Castle) which had been forfeit after joining the rebels in the Civil War and he was supremely bitter. He was said to be a poor administrator and very harsh to his communities, a trait which had led to a widespread indictment against him across his lands in six northern counties, after only a short time in charge.[10] He was absolved by a promise to go on crusade. He had also just been excommunicated for holding a tournament in 1219 at Brackley (Northamptonshire), against Pandulf's express wishes.[11] But now he was unable to go anywhere since he had recently been chosen as one of the King's hostages for peace with Scotland. Many of his northern lands (such as his castles of Cockermouth, Skipton in Craven and Skipsea) were disputed by England and Scotland and he was afraid they were going to be bargained away in the new, albeit shaky, *entente* between the two.

The Royal Council's response to the Earl of Aumale's high-profile protest was to have Fawkes de Bréauté lay siege to the castle with the King's bodyguard. Given the chance to surrender or suffer the consequences, the Earl surrendered, since he had had neither opportunity nor finances to bring in provisions for a siege.[12] He was given the benefit of the doubt over his conduct (i.e. it was a mere protest) and Pandulf allowed him to pay a fine in lieu of going on crusade, which he was thus able to defer. To try to get him out of the way he was briefly considered as the new governor of Poitou – but Pandulf objected, presumably on account of his awful reputation for brutality. In the end he defaulted on his fine, but did not go on crusade either. He was a loose-cannon, plain and simple. However, he would not be the last protestor prepared to risk open strife. Pandulf was worried for the country which remained a Papal possession, so much so that in June all the southern ports were closed, from Dover to Plymouth. Pandulf wrote to his master, Pope Honorius III who, on 28 May 1220, replied in a letter that no one ought to hold more than two royal castles, a far-reaching conclusion indeed (for a man who had no hands-on experience of Anglo-Norman feudal tensions).[13] In fact it took some time to put into place since in 1221 the King's council met to consider the status of all castles, trying to decide which ones were lawfully built and which were illegal (or *adulterine*). Clearly the years of the Civil War had left some uncertainty. Aumale was about to ram home the nub of both the Papal directive and justify the need for the coming discussion perfectly; however – although he did not know it – he did so to everyone else's detriment.

A few days after the treaty with Scotland was concluded, orders were sent for the Earl of Huntingdon's castle at Fotheringay to be surrendered (by the young Earl Marshall, who held it by dint of his late father's custody for Henry a year or more before). He was twice more ordered to hand it to the Earl of Huntingdon (in the personage of Ranulf as ward of John le Scot, the earl-in-waiting, and all the Huntingdon lands). Ranulf only received the surrendered castle in late November 1220.[14] He was later formally made ward of Huntingdon in March 1221 by the King of Scotland.[15]

Now the Earl of Aumale, still not placated, and fearing Scottish gains in his own back-yard (Rockingham and the Scot's castle at Fotheringhay are close neighbours), refused to relinquish another of his castles at Bytham (Lincolnshire).[16] Matthew Paris simply relates that 'he wished to disturb the King's peace', in the formulaic language of the time used for rebellious lords. Nothing is ever so simple. Roger of Wendover, looking to apportion blame less pointedly, saw the hand of foreign meddlers at work.[17] Put under increasing diplomatic pressure to comply, he lashed out, wasting the villages of Edenham and Deeping (Lincolnshire) and at the end of December, with most nobles still enjoying the end of their Christmas courts, marched on Fotheringhay, now held by a small garrison of Ranulf's men. In bitterly cold weather, early in January, the garrison was surprised by the attackers who crossed the frozen moat and slipped in over the walls in the dead of night. Two of Ranulf's sergeants were killed and the rest of the garrison captured.[18] Ranulf meanwhile stood at the head of an increasingly worried baronial group who over the Christmas period wrote to Pope Honorius to try to make sure that those who had supported Prince Louis during the Civil War should not be allowed to return

The motte of Fotheringhay Castle (Northamptonshire), taken from Ranulf by the Earl of Aumale over a frozen moat in the dead of night, December 1220. (2005)

to England.[19] They were clearly worried about the present danger of undesirables re-opening old wounds and fomenting open revolt.

News from Fotheringhay reached a royal council on 25 January 1221, where Ranulf was said to be incandescent with rage. This not only threatened the understanding between England and Scotland but had now dragged his family into the argument. He joined Pandulf, the Archbishop of York, at least seven bishops and the Earl of Salisbury (who was implacably opposed to Aumale anyway) in excommunicating the Earl of Aumale (again!). His condemnation was thus unanimous. Ranulf joined in the ceremony, hurling a lighted candle to the floor as sentence was pronounced.[20]

The royal army marched to Fotheringhay which it reached on 3 February. However, finding it utterly deserted, they left it in the charge of Falkes de Bréauté and moved on to lay siege to Bytham. Ranulf was no longer present, instead choosing to pay scutage, probably because his family was so closely linked to both the English and Scottish crowns. On 8 February 1221 Bytham surrendered. Aumale was long gone. He was later tracked down to Fountains Abbey (North Yorkshire), where he had sought refuge. From there he was taken in chains and served a short exile.[22] It was another twenty years before he fulfilled his vow of crusade (and died at sea in the process), but he never gave the remarkably forgiving Henry another cause for concern.

With the moment of panic seemingly over, Ranulf's attention turned to the more leisured pursuits of chivalry, most particularly his passion for hunting. In 1222 the King gave him forty bucks at his hunting lodges of King's Cliffe and Brigstock from the royal forest of Rockingham (then a huge area of eastern and central Northamptonshire). Shortly after he increased the numbers in his gift to sixty breeding stock (bucks and does), for Ranulf to stock his own hunting park at Barrow-on-Soar (Leicestershire). Ranulf was to catch the animals himself.[23]

Ranulf's growing interests and the urgency of rebuilding across the Midlands were accompanied by a desire to increase revenues in the area and the King granted him a number of new opportunities. At his manor of Wainfleet (Lincolnshire) he was granted the right to hold a fair (which would attract custom from a radius of a day's ride and more); elsewhere he consolidated his mercantile gains at Olney (Buckinghamshire) and Waihill (Northamptonshire). Similar opportunities were given him at Chawton, near Southampton, a great potential source of tax-revenue on imported goods coming inland.[24]

It was never a good thing to take one's eye off the troubled western frontiers, however, and Ranulf took care to ensure that his core territories were provided for. Indeed Llewellyn had risen once more and attacked the lands of the new Earl Marshall (the younger); an able enough son and heir, but lacking his late father's charisma and the gravitas lent by his experience and many offices. Llewellyn took and burnt a number of castles, forcing a hasty truce which humiliated the young Marshall in September 1220.[25] It was perhaps only time before Llewellyn looked to the north and the Chester frontier once again. To this end in 1222 Ranulf was given custody of an additional castle, that of Whittington (Shropshire) while in the following year he gained the manor of Chartley (Staffordshire) to add to the castle there.[26] Ranulf already held Chartley amongst his family's possessions and was already refortifying it for his brother-in-law (Ferrers) to continue to hold. At Whittington, the hereditary castle of Fulk Fitz Warin, Ranulf began a new building programme which saw a completely new curtain wall with inner and outer wards, mural towers and double-towered gatehouses. It shared many characteristics with Chartley and other castles over which Ranulf now had control.

Within Ranulf's heartland the Earl's domestic politics once more began to assume a greater importance as he further consolidated the territorial gains made since the precarious end of the Civil War. It must be remembered that there was still simmering discontent, not just from the Earl of Aumale. New alliances were being forged and old ones cemented. In 1221 or 1222 the King (through the Regent) gave permission for Rose, the daughter of Ranulf's old Norman ally Nicholas de Verdun, to marry Perceval de Somery; the de Somery family held Dudley Castle, one of a network of strongholds behind Ranulf's border-lands.[27] Ranulf himself held the honour of Dudley. In fact the de Somery's would later marry into Ranulf's sister Mabel's family. All around was physical reconstruction, personal consolidation and a spirit of optimism seems to have pervaded the tone of Ranulf's efforts. In August 1222 he presided over the marriage of John le Scot to Helen, daughter of Llewellyn the Great, binding Huntingdon (and Chester) with the intention of cementing relations with the royal houses of Wales and Scotland.[28] A year before, John de Lacy, Constable of Chester, had married Ranulf's niece, the daughter of Robert de Quincy, a union probably eagerly sought by Ranulf since the death of the head of the house of Winchester, Saher de Quincy.[29] He was rebuilding for the future, giving more time to his lands, wasted by civil war and his absence overseas. For the most part, his enemies, principally Hubert de Burgh, were leaving him alone. However, elsewhere in England, his friends and allies were not faring so well and the country was about to teeter on the brink of a bloody rebellion which would test Ranulf's resolve and call his loyalty into question.

It was all a question of castles, 'the bones of the kingdom' as once described by William of Newburgh, and had been simmering since 1220 when Pandulph had received his 'maximum two castles' letter from the Pope. The King, with Pandulf to guide him, was becoming increasingly worried about young William Marshall, not least because his younger brother Richard had now entered the family's hereditary lands in Normandy and sworn allegiance to Philip Augustus, splitting their father's previous fealty to Henry. The partial return to Philip was dangerous since it opened up a family channel for correspondence and private dealings which Henry could not control. Rumours began to circulate of a plot against the King, centred on Peter de Maulay, Sheriff of Dorset and Somerset, Engelard de Cigogné and William Marshall the younger. Thus William Marshall was now required to surrender the castles he held of the King (Marlborough and Ludgershall). At Ludgershall, it was done relatively gently but with some royal cunning as the constable was ordered to hand over the forest surrounding the castle (known as 'the Earl's woods') to Ranulf. Thus the King threw a cordon around the castle, physically cocooning it in a loyal shroud. It was effectively under threat of blockade if Marshall might resist the order to surrender.[30] He did not. Engelard de Cigogné and Peter de Maulay were another matter, however. Cigogné was arrested and imprisoned, his royal castle of Windsor taken back into the King's hands. He had little chance to resist. His imprisonment implies his guilt and he may have confessed. De Maulay had for some time held the supremely strong royal castle at Corfe (Dorset), one of the very few strongholds to have successfully resisted Louis in the French invasion of 1216–17. There at Corfe he held a group of royal hostages, mostly left over from the Civil War. These included that hapless woman and perennial hostage Eleanor of Brittany, who now was seemingly guarantor of absolutely nothing yet probably still knew too much about just about everything to do with England's dirty dealings with France, from her mother's ill-fated marriage to Ranulf onwards – most definitely including her brother Arthur's murder.

Eleanor had now been a hostage for almost all her adult life, shunted from castle to castle. Ever the pawn, she was now said to be the centre piece of the plot, to be spirited away from Corfe to Philip Augustus (to whom she would tell all she knew). It is difficult to know whether she could have been of further use to Philip. Her ship was to be chartered by Peter des Roches, Bishop of Winchester (and still tutor to the young King Henry). Peter was supposed to be on pilgrimage to Santiago de Compostela but was rumoured to be consulting with Philip Augustus. His understudy as the King's tutor was Philip d'Albini, who became tainted by his close association. Once more Ranulf stood at the edge of the affair as erstwhile step-father to Eleanor and uncle to Philip d'Albini. Philip had many allies and Roger of Wendover described him in glowing terms (probably because of the suspicion) as 'A fearsome knight and noteworthy in his honest nature, he was the King's tutor, very learned and trustworthy'.[31] He had also masterminded the great naval victory over Louis of France off Sandwich in 1217; hardly the stuff of a natural rebel.

Corfe was duly surrendered to Henry and a week later De Maulay was released, the King seemingly satisfied of his innocence (or re-profession of allegiance). Peter des Roches, Philip d'Albini and Faulkes de Bréauté took the cross in April 1221, avoiding further suspicion and took themselves off, the former to Santiago, the last two to Damietta. There Philip wrote despairingly to his uncle Ranulf, addressing him as 'Respected lord and friend'. He related the dreadful conditions the crusaders were enduring as the tide of the war turned and the Muslim forces began to drive the crusaders out of Egypt.[32] Perhaps he hoped that Ranulf, who had achieved mythical status at Damietta, might return. While Albini stayed on, propping up the faltering crusade, its cause long since lost, de Bréauté returned home soon after, his rebellious star very much in the ascendant. Both remained very close to the Earl of Chester. Poor Eleanor of Brittany simply remained in custody; she continued to live as her station dictated but a prisoner nonetheless, still in her prime throughout the 1220s, incarcerated in a variety of castles, but principally Corfe.

As 1221 ended the King held his Christmas court at Winchester. The occasion should have been a time of peace and good will but a furious argument broke out between, on the one hand Ranulf and William, Earl of Salisbury and on the other, Hubert de Burgh, the Justiciar.[33] Ranulf was already implacably opposed to de Burgh, who now accused him in public of giving ear to the plots of 'foreigners' against the King, reminiscent of the very recent allegations against de Maulay, de Bréauté and de Cigogné. It is not altogether clear what the catalyst was on this occasion but Ranulf's blood was up and he had to be physically restrained when, probably with drawn sword, he threatened violence on Hubert. Both put their retainers on alert, to be ready for open conflict. The matter was quelled (if not settled) by the Archbishop of Canterbury, who had deliberately hung back for some time.[34] He called the warring parties together and threatened to excommunicate them both as disturbers of the King's peace. This did the trick, but the enmity continued to simmer.

By the middle of 1222 there was unrest in London and a French-inspired riot in the capital was put down by Faulkes de Bréauté and Philip d'Albini, aided by some extra-judicial executions which raised a number of hackles. A new feeling of unrest was speading from the nobility to the commons and England seemed to be heading once more towards civil war. In the summer of 1223 a conjunction of events sped the process.

First of all Llewellyn attacked from Wales, driving a wedge between the Chester lands to the north and the Marshall lands of the south, choosing the less-heavily-defended Shropshire part of the frontier. He quickly took Kinnerley castle and Ranulf's castle at Whittington, still unfinished. Shropshire was in turmoil and the whole of the Welsh Marches seethed. In order to try to calm things down, the King and the Justiciar reached Shrewbury on 7 March at the head of an army, moving to Ranulf's castle at Bridgenorth three days later. Steadying the ship as they went, they then moved south along the border with Wales to Bristol, whereupon the King headed back to London via Wiltshire and Hubert diverted to Ireland. Meanwhile, Ranulf came forward to mediate between England and Wales, offering himself as surety for Llewellyn's compliance with the King.[35] Meanwhile the Justiciar, having diverted to meet an army already under arms in Ireland, crossed the sea and marched into Wales. Llewellyn had little time to react and a small force under his son Gruffydd met them at Kidwelly. For want of supplies, they quickly withdrew before the larger English force.

At a peace council at Ludlow, Ranulf sought to divide the Welsh resistance. Since 1216 the sons of the late Gwenwynwyn, Prince of Powys had been the Earl of Chester's hostages in Bridgenorth Castle. They were now taken to the King at Gloucester Castle and the proposal was published that all who came to the allegiance of the two sons would escape the King's wrath, splitting Powys from Llewellyn's designs. By the end of October 1223 Llewellyn had made peace, but only aided by the marriage of his daughter Helen to John le Scot. So long as he lived, Ranulf now held a real balance of power in England's dealings with her closest neighbours. In addition, by means of the marriage he placed his nephew and his earldom of Huntingdon, now allied with Wales, at the centre of opposition to Hubert de Burgh (who held most of his lands on the troublesome Welsh border and whose recent fourth marriage to Margaret, sister of the King of Scotland, meant he too had acquired an ear at the Scottish court). His dealings were more than keeping pace with those of Hubert.

On 13 April 1223 Pope Honorius wrote to four groups of nobles and churchmen: Peter des Roches, the Justiciar and William Brewer, a noted judge; to Ranulf himself (who this year was a baron of the exchequer);[36] to Ralph Neville, Vice Chancellor; to the earls, barons and faithful of England. His letter pronounced that in the eyes of the Church Henry was now of age and able to rule with Papal blessing without a regent. Pandulf was recalled. What followed can only be described as a free-for-all, Hubert de Burgh making the first unsubtle move when he summoned Walter de Lacy and Ralph Musard to the King and refused them leave to depart (house arrest) until they had handed over their royal castles, Hereford and Gloucester.

There was an immediate reaction and anger spread throughout the baronial ranks, led by Ranulf himself, discerning the hand of Hubert de Burgh, now unchecked by Pandulf and taking advantage of the young King. Indignantly the disaffected barons marched on London, forcing the terrified de Burgh to spirit the King away. Ignominiously they barricaded themselves in Gloucester Castle, unsure of Ranulf's next move.

With some style and panache Ranulf marched on the Tower of London itself, stirring up the mob, which sure enough had the effect of grabbing the King and de Burgh's attention. They realised that if they lost London, the whole kingdom might rally to Ranulf. Disaffection could so easily turn to open revolt. They had to be careful not to force the birth of a new rebel faction which might threaten civil war. Quickly they returned to London to mediate with the disaffected lords, whose numbers had been swelled by the addition of Falkes de Bréauté, John de Lacy, William des Forz, Earl of Aumale, Brian de L'Isle, Robert de Vipont, Peter de Maulay, Philip Marc and Engelard de Cigogné and William de Canteloupe. This comprised the principal members of Ranulf's circle and included the core of the former Poitevin barony, whose very existence in England had so angered the rebels of 1215, leading to the embittered proscriptions of Magna Carta's last sentences.

Early in the year a letter (of unknown origin) was sent to the Pope, asking him to order 'on the King's behalf and in his interest', that Peter des Roches, Bishop of Winchester, Ranulf, Earl of Chester, Falkes de Bréauté, should all be forced to give up the royal castles they held. The author of the letter is unknown, although the apparent even-handedness, including men on both sides, might suggest it was Stephen Langton, Archbishop of Canterbury. It is understood only by the surviving reply the Pope sent, in full agreement, issuing a Papal bull against them, making reference to Henry having reached his majority.[37] In spite of the opposition, and emboldened by the Pope's support both for his stance and for his majority, the King summoned the named members of the disaffected party:

> To the Earls of Chester, Gloucester and Aumale, John, constable of Chester, Robert de Vipont, Falkes de Bréauté, Brian de L'Isle, Engelard de Cigogné ... you should come to us at London on the Sunday after the feast of St Andrew ... to speak with us ... at the Hospital of St John of Clerkenwell or at the New Temple Church of London, or somewhere other that we may provide better counsel to all.[38]

Fearing for their safety, Ranulf and his group did not turn up. In John's day that would have been grounds enough for open war, but Henry was more conciliatory, fearing that his whole baronage was rallying behind Ranulf. Eventually he reported with the others to the King at Waltham Abbey. Questioned by the King he asserted that his actions had been directed at Hubert de Burgh, who should be removed from the seat of power as a waster of the King's finances and an oppressor of the people. Hubert, who was present throughout, was incensed, blaming it on the weakest member of the group Peter des Roches, a move which might avoid Ranulf's power being brought into play. Equally incandescent, the Bishop of Winchester stormed out threatening violence against Hubert, followed by Ranulf and the others who remained united for the present.

Chastened by his experience and paying heed to the disaffected baronage, that month young Henry began to issue letters patent in his own hand and seal, instead of that of the Justiciar. The first was to proclaim a Christmas truce until 20 January 1224, enough time for the rage to cool. Ranulf and his party went to Northampton to make plans, but the King suspected they were still simmering and followed with the most sumptuous Christmas court seen for years. Feeling hemmed in by the approach of the court, Ranulf and his friends removed themselves ahead of the royal train to Leicester.[39]

The powerful and disaffected were suddenly conspicuous by their absence and Stephen Langton, Archbishop of Canterbury, wrote to the barons at Leicester to attend the King on pain of excommunication. Although reticent, they nevertheless obeyed (having first weighed up that the King possessed a larger force with him, according to Matthew Paris) and presented themselves at Northampton Castle, swayed by the threat of the ultimate spiritual sanction, backed up by greater force.[40] Once at court, with the festivities of Christmas behind them, the Papal letter was read out, the seal displayed and all, without exception, were required to surrender the royal castles. Most were required to give up a hat or a glove as token of their immediate compliance – in this only Ranulf and Hubert de Burgh were the exception.

Ranulf was to surrender Shrewsbury, Bridgenorth and Wallingford castles, together with the castle, county and honour of Lancaster. The first two were to go to Hugh Despencer, while the Lancaster elements went to Ranulf's brother in law, William Ferrers, Earl of Derby. Neither was a particularly difficult parting as both recipients were in Ranulf's close circle. The King retained Wallingford for the time being. With Lancaster, however, went considerable financial loss, but for Ranulf this was less an emasculation than for others. In all 25 castles changed hands. Of twelve displaced castellans, five had been in Ranulf's opposition to Hubert de Burgh, the other seven had been either neutral or in Hubert's camp. Further transfers took place until by March 1224 the total stood at 33 castles confiscated and redistributed.

Faulkes de Bréauté came off worst, losing control of six of his seven counties, keeping only the diminutive Rutland. The opposition to de Burgh was effectively finished. However, this merely created more rancour. De Bréauté himself later noted that 'while the Earl of Chester and his friends (actually) gave up their castles, the Justiciar and his party held onto theirs', confirmed by contemporary chroniclers.[41] With little more to be said for the moment, the Christmas court retired after hearing the re-issued (and diluted) Magna Carta read once more.

Ranulf and his party continued to try to undermine Hubert and sent messengers to the Pope. However, Langton intercepted the messengers and privately met Ranulf to seek his compliance. In any case the Pope was luke-warm and vacillated, leaving Ranulf's protest unanswered.[42]

On 15 May Henry issued letters of safe conduct for Ranulf and the disaffected nobles and at a council shortly after, agreement was reached.[43] Ranulf and his party backed down and gave their kiss as a sign of their promise of compliance. Hubert too backed down. All were allowed back into the King's Peace. Henry was willing to let bygones be bygones.

It was just in time. Since 1217 France had been at peace with England, chastened by its defeats in that year. In July 1223 Philip Augustus had died, succeeded by his son, Louis VIII. In April 1224 the truce had come to an end. Despite having promised to help England regain her Norman lands, Louis had not lifted a finger and never intended to. He now began to threaten Poitou and the remaining English lands on the continent, aided by Normandy and Brittany. In response to this the English sheriffs were ordered to seize all English lands of Normans and Bretons. Although the matter threatened to escalate, Louis was the first to back down, since his own interests were separately threatened by heretical Albigensian rebels in the south. A ten-year truce was agreed with England, although, ironically, England only sought one lasting four. However, this was not before a small (numerically insufficient) force was dispatched to reinforce La Rochelle, key to Poitou, under direct pressure, if not threat of siege.

The English nobility at this time seemed to have a talent for self-destruction. Soon after Easter a charge was levelled at Faulkes de Bréauté over an eight-year-old capital offence. Seemingly already politically emasculated, the hapless Faulkes was convicted and sentenced to a heavy fine. Faulkes' family rose up as one (he had six brothers or half-brothers and a sister), led by his eldest brother William, who was castellan of Bedford castle. William captured and imprisoned one of the judges, Robert de Braybrook on his way to court. It seems unlikely that Faulkes knew of the plan since, when Henry quickly laid siege to Bedford, Faulkes was nowhere near. He was, of course, under a vow of crusade, so could not be touched with impunity.

The Church quickly moved to excommunicate the Bedford garrison and what turned out to be an eight-week siege began. In those eight weeks, the English eye was distracted and the Poitevin towns began to crumble like a house of cards. Poitiers, Niort, St Jean d'Angely, La Rochelle (despite its reinforcement) all fell. Surrounded, Limoges and Perigord went over to Loius too. In the eyes of his enemies, Faulkes became associated with these awful events, somehow to blame for all England's misfortune. The King summoned the royal field army to reinforce him at Bedford. They met at Northampton but Henry found opposition to the siege was strong, led by Ranulf, who was openly unsympathetic.[44] With him were Aumale, Peter des Roches, Canteloupe, De L'Isle and De Maulay. Ranulf, excluded from the King's Council, left the muster and went home, complaining of his treatment.[45] He could still keep in touch with events as his wife Clemence's kinsman William de Semilly was serving with the King (his first reappearance in documents since the loss of Normandy).[46] Ranulf had not been unreasonable and the Pope later wrote to Henry, criticizing his treatment of the Earl of Chester.[47] More than once that spring Ranulf must have been very concerned for his future; it coincided with his wife Clemence attending to her own will, so dangerous had matters become.[48]

Faulkes meanwhile escaped the field army and fled westwards into Ranulf's lands. He was quickly becoming the prize every bit as much as Bedford itself. Although in the Civil War he had become known as 'The rod of the Lord's Fury' he now was being battered from pillar to post, his previous reputation counting for nothing.[49] He hid in safe-houses in Ranulf's lands, hoping to gather a force around himself before slipping back into the home counties.

Henry wrote to both Ranulf, appealing to his knowledge of the situation (and Faulkes' whereabouts) and to Llewellyn too (hoping to deny Faulkes any Welsh support). Ranulf's reply has survived, in which he expressed his sympathy for Faulkes' plight, gently admonishing his King for his actions, feeling him to have misjudged Faulkes. He reiterated his own loyalty and spoke of having secured a temporary truce on the Welsh frontier. His dignified words, in excellent and well-framed Latin, made him diplomacy personified 'now I shall help you with constancy and faithfulness ... just as faithfully and with such consistency have I always been at pains to offer help and assistance to your predecessors'. He closed with a degree of familiarity 'May you fare well and may your majesty increase always'.[50] Ranulf knew when to acquiesce quietly. The King's letter had been delivered to Ranulf at Chester by Alexander de Stavensby, Bishop of Coventry and Lichfield (one of Ranulf's most familiar clerics), who was now told where to find Faulkes nearby. At a meeting he and Ranulf persuaded him to return with them as far as Coventry (where Stavensby presumably guaranteed him safety in the nearly-completed Cathedral of St Mary or in Ranulf's manor at Cheylesmore ten minutes' ride from the cathedral). Only the fourteenth-century timber-framed gatehouse of Cheylesmore manor is visible above ground today. This, the manor's former north range, was restored in the 1960s and today is Coventry's Register Office. Once the manor was moated around and included a sturdy fortified south hall-range where Ranulf may have briefly entertained Faulkes. It was partly excavated in 1992, by the author, before being covered again by a new building. The manor once had a huge hunting park attached, now covered by the city's eponymous suburb of Cheylesmore.

There at Coventry on 12 August, Faulkes was given the King's letter of safe-conduct to Northampton, where finally news came of the fall of Bedford Castle – and a grisly execution for Faulkes' brother William and his fellow rebels in the garrison who had refused to surrender when they had the opportunity. Faulkes himself (who of course had been nowhere near throughout) was subsequently spared a similar fate, but the episode abruptly ended his career. He had had to be summoned under safe-conduct passes twice in three months, somewhat stretching the meaning of allegiance. He was a broken man whose finances were wrecked by the huge fines he had to pay. Even his goods were sold, raising about £950.[51] He died in exile only two years later.

With the Bedford diversion (it never really constituted an all-out rebellion) at an end Poitou and Gascony were reinforced and English authority re-established within the year, headed by the King's brother, Richard Earl of Cornwall (appointed Count of Poitou) and Ranulf's kinsman Philip d'Albini. With England in the ascendant, operations were brought to a sudden end by Papal decree; Louis was threatened by the Albigensian heresy down south, making his cause in support of the Holy Mother Church the priority. Within another year Louis himself was dead, succeeded by his ten-year-old son Louis IX. Like England's Henry III, his country would be ruled for some time by a regent during his minority, in this case his mother and widow of Louis VIII, the redoubtable Blanche of Castille. Eventually the youngster would grow into a great and celebrated king, best known for his spirituality (and ever since known as Saint Louis), but for the moment Blanche was in charge. She would become much reviled at court and France would be all the weaker for it.

10

TIME TO BUILD (1224–9)

The period following Bedford is in many ways the quietest of Ranulf's life, at least in terms of the national and international stage. It was, however, far from idle. For a man such as the Earl of Chester, constant activity characterised every period of his career. The King certainly came to miss him and soon after the siege of Bedford formally remarked of Ranulf that 'we are accustomed to having him and his friends in our deliberations' (contrasting now with his absence).[1] In that same year Ranulf, certainly still disgruntled at the rise of Hubert de Burgh, noted that he himself had been excluded 'from (the King's) private counsel'.[2] Seemingly both the King and Ranulf missed each other's company and advice, but neither could circumvent the wheedling Chancellor Hubert, whose power at court continued to grow.

Returning probably to Chester as his ancestral base of operations, Ranulf began to think about how to consolidate his position and redress the balance after his reverses at the hands of the young Henry III, whether still advised by Hubert de Burgh or not. Ranulf's star had clearly waned and he had lost face at court since the violent argument with Hubert in 1223. His lands too had been eroded by events; Lancaster had gone, as had the royal castles. In due course his guardianship of Huntingdon would go too, but only because his nephew John le Scot would come of age in 1227 and inherit his rightful patrimony, held in trust by Ranulf from the King of Scotland since 1220. This he could plan and prepare for.

His western frontier now held fewer concerns. At a notable tournament in 1225, at Hubert de Burgh's brand new Montgomery Castle (Powys), Ranulf was sealing the King's charters.[3] Since tournaments were places of unofficial court business and intrigue, someone in Ranulf's position would have been striking bargains and hammering out the detail of new ventures. It was probably no different at Montgomery since by 1226 he had reached agreement with Llewellyn in a three-way peace which also involved William Marshall junior. Ranulf went to Henry on Llewellyn's behalf, to be described by the King as his 'counsellor and friend'.[4]

A western peace was particularly helpful at this time since Henry had been experiencing baronial unrest, especially in Ireland by the restive Hugh de Lacy Earl of Ulster. He was, of course, related to Ranulf's friend and confidante, John de Lacy, Constable of Chester and in 1226 Ranulf was able to offer surety for the handover of Hugh's castles at Carrickfergus, Antrim, Ratour and Le Nober to the more reliable Walter de Lacy in a knock-on version of what all the English nobles had gone through in 1224.[5]

Ranulf continued to hold the largest number of lands of any magnate in England; with them came the bulk of the armed forces. Besides his ancestral earldom of Chester, the Honour of Chester stretched right across the Midlands, south into Gloucestershire and across Staffordshire and Warwickshire into Northamptonshire. Outlying lands attached to the Honour lay as far south as Devon and as far north as Derbyshire. His earldom of Lincoln was intact, stretching from Yorkshire to Leicestershire, while the honour of Leicester linked his northern lands with those in Northamptonshire. To these, of course, could be added the family lands. His brother-in-law Ferrers held the earldom of Derby and now the honour of Lancaster, while his nephew was Earl of Huntingdon. He was clearly secure in a Midlands which was once more at peace.

Throughout his lands Ranulf now raised a tax on goods and on persons to pay for ambitious construction works.[6] The tax was extended to everyone passing through his dominions (this would also affect everyone trading via the Rivers Dee and Mersey and via the Chester-dominated North Wales coast across to Ireland). Some chroniclers believe he had begun taxation as early as 1220 but the greatest opportunity to use it came now and he began to build on a grand scale. Bereft of his royal castles Ranulf began to build or re-build his own, at Beeston (Cheshire), Chartley (Staffordshire) and Bolingbroke (Lincolnshire). Ranulf Higden, monk of Chester, stated that building work had begun as soon as Ranulf returned from Damietta. If so then Ranulf's own part must have been limited by his attendance elsewhere until 1224. To the traditional list of projects can be added a new fortified manor house at Coventry (Cheylesmore), partly excavated in 1992 and dating from this period. At his Manor at Bugbrooke (Northamptonshire), a near contemporary chronicler records that he also built a new Hall (*aula*), still notable more than a century later.[7]

At Chartley and Bolingbroke the building projects constituted rebuilding existing sites. At the former a motte and bailey was extended and translated into stone, while at the latter a polygonal courtyard castle totally replaced a former old motte and bailey. Both were characterised by a set of towers in the latest projecting D-shaped style, mirrored at other castles being built under Ranulf's

Beeston Castle (Cheshire): the distinctive D-shaped towers of the entrance. (2009)

Chartley Castle (Staffordshire), rebuilt by Ranulf for his brother-in-law William Earl Ferrers from 1225. The characteristic D-shaped towers of the inner bailey during archaeological recording. (1997)

guidance, such as the much smaller Whittington (Salop) by Fulk Fitz Warin, and later in Wales by Llewellyn. Within the drum of each tower were mural rooms for archers and crossbowmen to cover the approaches to the castle and all Ranulf's military building projects of the 1220s share similarities of this kind.

Without a doubt, however, Beeston was intended to be a centrepiece of Ranulf's works. It was on a new site a couple of miles from its predecessor, a serviceable-enough large motte and bailey in the village of Beeston. The new castle stood and, although ruined, still stands on an eyrie of rock thrust up from the surrounding plain some ten miles from the bustle of Chester, but also curiously removed from the traditional flashpoints of the frontier with Wales. Its aspect and defensibility is breathtaking from the surrounding landscape, matched only by the wide prospect from its walls, in which the Welsh mountains form the western horizon. It has always been said to embody the latest quirks of castle building and set the tone for at least the next generation. Something similar can be said for Chartley, Bolingbroke and Whittington too as they all share characteristics built in by Ranulf. The castle perch at Beeston was everything Château Gaillard had been, high above the Seine. It must not be forgotten that Ranulf had served in person at Gaillard for some time and had witnessed its construction, the wonder of the age. It is surely no coincidence that both Gaillard and Beeston were known to their local contemporaries as, simply, 'The Rock'. Like Gaillard, Beeston's inner and outer court were now to be separated by a huge, precipitous rock-cut ditch, guarding the only possible approach, a distinguishing feature they both shared with the Knights Templar castle at Athlit in Palestine (now in Israel), the new so-called 'Pilgrim' Castle Ranulf had notably helped fund in

1219. Here too Athlit was only approachable from one direction, the remaining three sides being cliffs down the Mediterranean Sea. Only the castle at St-James-de-Beuvron enjoyed such natural defensibility amongst Ranulf's own former possessions, perched high on an oxbow in the River Beuvron, and again separated from the town and the wider approaches by a massive rock-cut ditch. Chartley too, was now divided into two by a massive ditch; less defensible perhaps than its more famous cousins but conforming to Ranulf's ideas he had learnt in so many construction projects and sieges. They all bear Ranulf's stamp as the culmination of his experience.

Chartley (Staffordshire), which strategically overlooks the main road north to Stafford, is a defensible position but far from commanding. Here, keeping the existing circular motte with circular keep, Ranulf rebuilt the bailey and ringed it with a substantial wall punctuated by the huge D-shaped towers with mural rooms, including two flanking the entrance from outer to inner bailey, wholly reminiscent of Beeston's design. Just as at Beeston, they sported the latest style fish-tail arrow-loops. A wide rock-cut ditch formed the outer ring. In 1266, a generation after Ranulf's death, Chartley Castle sustained a concentrated siege by the royal siege train. Consolidation of the surviving masonry in 1997–8 allowed archaeologists, led by the author, to note the original construction work of Ranulf's day, the extent of the siege damage, and look at the repairs and remedial work undertaken to get it back into shape.

At Bolingroke (Lincolnshire), like Beeston, Ranulf's castle was built from scratch, smothering a motte and bailey. It is an irregular polygon, each change in angle marked by the expected characteristic D-shaped tower. While the buildings of the interior were altered and rebuilt in the ensuing years, the enceinte of the castle is as Ranulf had it built. Topographically, it lies in a discrete hollow which is almost ringed a mile or so away by a high ridge, which describes a horseshoe-shape around three quarters of its prospect (high that is, relative to the flat Lincolnshire countryside beyond). Anyone toiling over the ridge with evil intent (and a siege-train in-tow) is thus clearly outlined on the skyline. Thus there is only one sensible approach to the castle, up the main road which crosses low-lying ground in front of it. Here are the earthworks of ditches and dykes providing every opportunity for deliberate defensive flooding. Part of the moat still survives and today forms a distinctive marshy band around the foot of the walls. The whole castle was (and is) an isolated place, perhaps deliberately so, but is a more inspiring centrepiece for the earldom of Lincoln for all that.

At Cheylesmore, (Coventry, Warwickshire) the manor house replaced much of the function of the former castle nearby, confiscated and slighted by Henry II after Ranulf's father Hugh had rebelled back in 1173. The new manor was a sub-square courtyard with a moat surrounding it. At least two ranges, the east and the north, were of timbered construction (although what survived of later, fourteenth-century re-building on dwarf-walls smothered most of this). However, Ranulf's south range was a rectangular hall-keep, with walls a believably defensible 3m thick. It was of at least two storeys and had arrow-slits in the long axes. The ground floor, partly excavated by the author in 1992, was probably for storage, while the Hall, its floor supported on a row of stone-set oak posts, would have been on the first floor.

Not forgetting his spiritual obligations, Ranulf also diverted moneys to the reconstruction of Dieulacres Abbey (near Leek,

Staffordshire), which had almost certainly spent the first ten years of its life in 'temporary' timber buildings, such as was the case with most Cistercian houses at the start of their lives. There was much engineering work to be done in Cistercian houses, which prided themselves specifically upon the water-management prowess of their order, turning unlikely and unpromising waste locations into the most fertile and profitable estate centres. Unfortunately today, though the site is undeveloped and is a Scheduled Ancient Monument, nothing survives to be seen above ground at Dieulacres. Professor Alexander has described Ranulf in matters spiritual as a 'pinchpenny patron'. Quite the opposite; with Dieulacres at the head, Ranulf's widespread benefactions combine with an extensive set of fairs, tax- and toll-exemptions to a large number of monasteries to form a view of a man who created the right economic conditions for monastic houses to thrive across his entire estates. He was a shrewd economist and knew how to make his money work for him and his friends and beneficiaries.

It is not always easy to follow Ranulf's commercial interests and discern who, beyond his immediate circle – his so-called *familiares*, who made up his first priority – just who were his beneficiaries on a day-to-day basis. Usually this is because of the paucity of surviving documentation (and the fact that the more mundane, everyday transactions draw little or no comment from contemporary secretaries and chroniclers anyway). However, from 1224–6 there survives a rash of documentation relating to Ranulf in the Close Rolls, connected mainly with his commercial dealings. Two incidents in particular stand out.

It has already been noted that Ranulf had previously received gifts from King John of various quantities of wine, usually Gascon. In the days before the loss of Normandy, even when in England,

Ranulf had even been attended in his court by a wine-maker or *vigneron*, Gerard Vinetarius. The Earl clearly took viticulture seriously. In 1224, no longer with his continental vineyards available, it becomes clear that Ranulf was buying large quantities of Gascon wine himself, perhaps for his many construction gangs who would be working on sites where sufficient wells were yet to be dug (and in any case clean drinking water could be hard to come by and wine was a common substitute). In this case it was from Richard Renger, Mayor of London, who had the wine shipped north along the east coast tax-free.[8] Unfortunately a ship was wrecked or beached off Orford (Suffolk), some of the sailors being drowned, losing the entire cargo. This was probably not a one-off shipment since shortly after, safe-conduct passes were issued through Ranulf to Matilda and Reginald de Berneval and Brother Thomas the Templar to land the cargo of Thomas German's ship, carrying Gascon wine.[9] His trading license had been issued by Ranulf, an interesting aside in its own right since Thomas German was a merchant of the castle of Vire in Normandy. He was almost certainly a spy for Ranulf in the heart of his former Norman lands, bringing information back and forth.

Secondly in 1224–5 the King conceded a favour to Ranulf. For many decades the Jews of England had been persecuted in a series of pogroms. King John had been particularly hard on English Jewry and his taxation of them had been severe. Not that the situation in much of western Europe was much better. The treatment of Jews had been a matter of expediency for the crown (since they were the principal source of bank loans), shot through with the Church's embittered thread, which entwined outright condemnation over their alleged collective part in the trial and crucifixion of Christ with an evangelising zeal. Henry seems to have espoused something of the last of these and, in contrast to his more vindictive father, set up a monastic-style house in London, specifically for Jewish converts to Christianity and possibly Messianic Jews (those Jews who both follow the Law and acknowledge Jesus as the Messiah).[10]

There seems to have been a move in the Midlands at that time to expel the Jews from their urban homes (most were city-dwellers where their congregation in ghettos offered some safety in numbers from frequent casual violence). Their detractors seem to have been most vehement in Coventry and Leicester, where Ranulf petitioned for and was granted permission to allow them to stay.[11] It is not clear why they were being expelled from Leicester at this time, but at Coventry it could have been connected with a missionary zeal which accompanied the completion of the Benedictine Cathedral Church in 1224. Their continued presence in an atmosphere of conspicuous self-congratulation may have been seen as a potential stain on the Church's new work.[12] The documents make it clear that while the Earl of Warwick (Henry de Newburgh) wanted rid of his local Jewry in Coventry (perhaps supporting the Benedictine Priory which held half of the city and counted the Earl of Warwick as a major patron), Ranulf had him overruled in court (Ranulf held the other half of the city of Coventry from his manor at nearby Cheylesmore). Why the Earl of Leicester is mentioned is unclear since the title had been held back by the King (Council) since Earl Simon de Montfort the elder's death in 1218 and, but for the Damietta interlude, Ranulf himself then held the honour (and would continue to until he freely chose to give it up in 1231). This anomalous mention might suggest that the House of Leicester was not altogether supportive of their temporary Chester overlord and the normal workings of the secretaries and officials who administered the earldom were actively anti-semitic, causing Ranulf to intervene personally.

Ranulf's reasons for this intervention in what was otherwise a pretty inexorable and shameful set of pogroms and expulsions is not at all clear. Ranulf's dealings with England's Jews are mentioned only infrequently. It is always in relation to finances, since like many of his contemporaries, he used the lending power of the Jews to finance loans. His documented repayments of his debts to them are notable and creditable occurrences (when so many debtors simply reneged and turned violent in refusing repayment). It is possible, however, that with his massive building programmes under way at his various castles and other major projects planned, he needed their continued banking expertise. He was in every way a shrewd economist.

Ranulf's support for the Jews would have brought benefits both for his enterprise and for the continued health and safety of the Jewish communities in Coventry and Leicester. Elsewhere his near-altruism was also manifest. In 1225–6 he began draining 500 acres of the Lincolnshire Fens, a huge undertaking not contemplated by anyone since the Romans and not again for many hundreds of years.[13] While the eventual benefits would be for the earldom of Lincoln as 500 more acres of cultivable farmland would produce crops to carry market tolls and bring tithes to the church, its immediate impact would be to enrich the lives of his dependent fenland dwellers whose existence was at the most basic subsistence level.

In 1227 Ranulf made his reappearance at court in a brief episode which flared up suddenly – and died down just as quickly. An argument arose between Henry and his younger brother, the relatively naïve Richard, Earl of Cornwall, who had just returned from the expedition to Poitou (leaving Philip d'Albini as governor there – a thankless job). The argument was over charters of forest liberties, which were in abeyance and Richard wanted restored;[14] others seem to have done so too since he was supported by Ranulf and (inevitably) his brother-in-law Ferrers. With little ado Richard was bought off with the gift of his mother's dowry and lands in England, taking the sting out of his supporters' bluster. Once more Ranulf had supported the rights of the individual against the King, this time seemingly with impunity. This may have been due to Hubert de Burgh being forced by the natural course of events to recede into the background somewhat. It is probably no coincidence that Hubert's gradual retirement from royal counsel, coincided with Ranulf's gradual return. In January 1227 Henry had been formally recognised as of age. He could now overrule his closest advisors, including Hubert de Burgh. His immediate plans were made abundantly clear: wishing to avenge his father, he had designs on France.

The King had been appealing for funds since December 1226, the fires of his fervour stoked by the death of Louis VIII on 8 November 1226 and the accession of the ten-year-old Louis IX, under his mother's unpopular regency. Matters were aided by the death of Pope Honorius III in March 1227. The policies of his successor Gregory IX were not yet clear and some nervousness ensued, even to the point that Ranulf's former adversary at Damietta, Coradin, still Sultan of Damascus, perhaps fearful of another crusade, had sent gifts of greeting by the end of 1227 to Henry. On 8 June 1227 the King wrote to Ranulf, bidding him assemble his troops, including those of Wales (with Llewellyn at peace) and Scotland, to prepare to move overseas to France, encouragement aided by the advancement of funds from the treasury towards the muster, just as John had done in 1206 and 1214.[15] In fact the muster came to nothing; plans were put on hold and Ranulf was still in Chester in August 1228.[16] In the same year Henry confirmed to Ranulf the honour of Leicester for life (he had held it anyway since 1218).[17] This continued to be a great source of revenue and it guaranteed the knightly service of Leicester for the King's enterprises overseas, placating Ranulf after his support of Richard of Cornwall.[18]

Much of Ranulf's money and that of his court, may well have been tied up at this time as his acumen was put to the test in 1229. In that year the Pope sent commissioners to raise a tax of his own across England, Scotland, Wales and Ireland, a tithe to pay his own debts. Matthew Paris records: 'The Earl of Chester alone stood against them, unwilling to submit his lands to servitude. And in his lands he did not permit the Papal assessors and the clerics to levy the tithe, in the same way that England and Wales, Scotland and Ireland were compelled to pay the tax'.[19] Ranulf's unwillingness to pay (his stubbornness took out Cheshire with the majority of Staffordshire, Warwickshire, Leicestershire and Lincolnshire, not to mention other numerous manors) may have hinted at a widespread inability on the part of his already over-taxed vassals to pay, but it did put much of England's (and thus Henry's) reserve out of reach of the Pope. Not even the King would be able to compel Chester to pay out since the Earl's authority outstripped that of the King in his own lands. That probably suited him since Henry was planning to use his reserve, both military and financial, against France and Ranulf was to lead the way. At the age of fifty-nine, Ranulf was back at the centre of operations.

11

BACK HOME (1229–32)

During 1229 intrigue on the continent came to a head. Although the boy King Louis IX would, in time, become an able enough ruler, celebrated for his spirituality and becoming known as Saint Louis, his early years were mired in the unpopular regency of his mother, Blanche of Castille, the late King John's niece. During this time the leanings towards England of Pierre Mauclerc, Duke of Brittany, had become well known. Louis' eventual biographer Jean de Joinville relates that at a council at Corbeil disaffected Norman barons met and unanimously agreed to raise up the Duke of Brittany against the regency and Louis.[1] They stated that if they were asked to make war on the Duke as a rebel, they would drag their heels and levy insufficient forces, leaving him free to defeat Louis and his much-disliked mother.

As part of this general desire to rid themselves of Blanche and Louis, old continental allies looked to England. Many French barons were perhaps unaware of just how chummy Mauclerc had become with the English, back in their fold since doing homage to Henry for Richmond in 1218 and now, just as they hoped, he now led the move away from France. Many would follow him willingly.

Matters would now move apace as it seemed clear that opposition to Louis was coalescing. This particularly fast-paced period in Ranulf's life is very well documented by state papers, royal letters and a small group of contemporary chroniclers whose accounts are in broad agreement (particularly Matthew Paris and Roger of Wendover, but whose grasp of the course of events is not always very clear).

On 26 July 1229, Henry III wrote to Ranulf ordering him to assemble his army and to come with his knights to Portsmouth by 14 October, which he did. He and the King's brother Richard, Earl of Cornwall, appear at the head of a list of 103 knights.[2] Henry, meanwhile, began to amass his army at Reading. The fleet, however, was taking some time to be readied and the winter closed in before embarkation could be arranged. The troops were sent home with a notice to re-assemble in the following April, which they did. Ranulf was able to secure the support of his nephew, John le Scot, Earl of Huntingdon, in the expedition and a contemporary observer with the force noted that there were a large number of Scots on the expedition (*Pictavenses*). Alongside them were Philip d'Albini and four earls: Gilbert de Clare of Gloucester, Aumale, the younger Marshall and the ever-loyal Ferrers. Having spent mid-October 1229 at Portsmouth, in late April 1230 Ranulf was there again, mustering his forces a second time. On 24 of that month the King ordered the Irish judiciary to lend aid to Ranulf's merchants to trade and buy merchandise freely in Ireland (usually corn) and freed Irish merchants to do likewise in England.[3] Clearly Ranulf's logistical efforts were a major part of the preparations and ongoing supply for the expedition.

News of Henry's imminent embarkation at the head of a major invasion fleet had a remarkable effect as Mauclerc led a widespread move to declare for England. On 1 May 1230 Henry departed Portsmouth, with Ranulf in charge of the royal army aboard a huge fleet. Mid-way they called and anchored overnight on the island of Jersey. On 3 May they docked in St Malo where they were met by Mauclerc in his Ducal flagship who there and then did formal homage to Henry for Brittany.[4] This must have been very satisfying indeed, both for Henry and Ranulf. Henry and the Duke disembarked and on 8 May after four days headed for Dinan, to pick up Breton forces; they then headed overland via Rennes to Nantes by 17 May where Henry was to meet his mother. At the same time Ranulf and the fleet carried on around the rocky coast of Brittany which juts far out into the Atlantic. Making final landfall at St Gildas-de-Rhuys, close to the fortified city of Vannes, they rode at anchor overnight and disembarked the following morning when the port was secure, news of Brittany's formal allegiance having reached the south.

Two sheltered coves rimmed by treacherous rocks constitute the port of St Gildas-de-Rhuys. Each is wide enough for perhaps a maximum of twenty ships to be beached side by side. Here the horses could be disembarked safely on one cove, the troops on the other. A short hillside walk took the army to the famed Benedictine Abbey in the village, last home and burial place of the hapless lover Abelard. Buried there too, in a plain granite coffin, is St Gildas, father of English historians. At the Abbey the leaders would have taken Mass and given thanks for a safe crossing. From there the road took the army to Pierre Mauclerc's new manor at Suscinio (begun in 1218). It was not yet the magnificent ducal castle into which his descendants made it, but the road led past its walls and through the attached hunting park (no doubt to Ranulf's delight) where supplies and forage could be found in abundance. All the movements of both the fleet and the army were only possible with Breton agreement. The way into St Gildas-de-Rhuys would be a death-trap for the ships, given long fingers of rock which lie hidden in the shallows, while the Breton interior east of the Gulf of Morbihan would see an unwary army mired in marshes and lost in nearly-impassable forest, prey to any ambush on the one road which led behind the shore. Pierre Mauclerc's support and the guidance of his pilots and scouts were paramount.

Within weeks, emboldened by the army's presence, Fulk Paynell the younger, Baron of Hambie and his brother William Tesson, Baron of Henneville (holding Ranulf's former Viscounty, St Sauveur-le-Vicomte) headed a group of Norman barons who petitioned Henry III to re-enter Normandy. The King, gaining a reputation for being impetuous, readily agreed. He had, after all grown up with the rancour of his father's loss of Normandy. He could not forget that.

Henry himself spent late May and all of June holding court at Nantes in a period of prolonged inactivity, during which he hoped to receive messages of allegiance. Ranulf and the army, however, were in Poitou, where they captured the castle of Mirebeau, scene of Eleanor of Aquitaine's dramatic capture so many years before and then laid siege to Verdun. The French were seriously worried and young Louis with his court sent an army south.

Henry was unhurried and moved south into the Saintonge and Gascony, reaching Bordeaux in early August before returning through the Saintonge to Nantes again in early September in a mini-tour of his western Angevin dominions. However by now he had found that funds were running low. On 27 June, with Henry about to head south from Nantes, Ranulf was at Rennes with Pierre Mauclerc. In the rear the Breton baron André de Vitré (who through his wife advanced claims to the Dukedom of Brittany) had declared for Louis and threatened allied supply lines across the duchy. His seat at the eponymous castle of Vitré was strongly held. Ranulf tabled proposals to lay siege to Vitré. However, for some reason this did not happen, possibly because events in Poitou continued to distract or because Mauclerc knew just how strong Vitré was. As a result they probably used the time to subdue the Isle d'Oleron at about this time.

Although most of Poitou and the Touraine had been won over during his summer court and progress, Henry's expedition funds were running dangerously low – despite taking with him in cash an unprecedented £13,200.[5] By early September 1230 he was beset by financial constraints and a growing number of calls for aid from new 'allies'. However, it did not stop him promising Pierre Mauclerc 6000 marks in recognition of his service, when he next came to England. It was money he could ill-afford which might otherwise have kept the expedition fed and watered through the winter. On 23 September he left Nantes and headed north into Brittany. Through October he and the court travelled seemingly aimlessly around the northern part of Brittany, via Guincamp, St Brieuc, Lannion and Morlaix before finally taking ship at St-Pol de Leon (nr Roscoff) on 26 October before the summer sailing season drew to a close, amidst rumours of an impending war in Wales.[6] His intention was to return in the spring of 1231 with fresh forces and a newly-filled war-chest. Unlike his father, John, it was not Henry's intention to abandon his allies on the continent and, in order to continue the campaign, he left a very strong force comprising Ranulf at the head of 500 knights and 1000 men-at-arms to aid Pierre Mauclerc in a well-motivated campaign fighting from home turf.[7] Ranulf was under the King's orders but Mauclerc could follow him to England whenever he liked.

Eventually on 9 October 1232 the government would issue letters of safe conduct for his passage.[8]

Louis wasn't done yet and continued a war of attrition where Henry had left a vacuum in Poitou. Having raised the siege of Verdun, he moved on to Henry's allies. In October, clearly taking advantage of Henry's long journey home (and probably Mauclerc's), he attacked and destroyed Thouars Castle, prompting a call to Ranulf for aid by Aimery, Count of Thouars (brother-in-law to Pierre Mauclerc). Louis hoped to draw the smaller English force out of its allied Breton territory and trap them in central Poitou.

However, believing the best form of defence was attack, Ranulf made his own move to cut off the French rear. The Anglo-Breton army made a determined thrust east out of southern Brittany into the northern Touraine, well north of Louis' army. They rode along the River Loire, through the region of Angers and up the tributary valley of the River Sarthe, where in quick succession they besieged the castles of Château Gontier and Châteauneuf-sur-Sarthe. Both were taken.[9] Their towns were sacked mercilessly, to deny supplies to the French army further south, although the English forces began to take casualties including Gilbert de Clare, Earl of Gloucester on 25 October 1230.[10] Winter was now coming on and neither army could feel secure far from home territory. The French were aware of the chaos Ranulf was creating in their rear while Ranulf was aware that an agitating de Vitré also left him insecure. An eclipse of the moon took place on 22 November, related by the superstitious (and usually anti-Norman) Matthew Paris. However, it was unclear as for whom this inauspicious event was meant to augur ill. Matters seemed finely poised with both armies carrying out offensive operations, but neither was able to gain the upper hand without the necessary pitched battle which neither was yet able to engineer.

Despite successes on both sides, winter had come before the two sides could maneouvre into favourable battle positions and the list of successful sieges remains as the best guide to a good year's campaign.

Ranulf, with lengthening supply-lines dangerously exposed to de Vitré, now took his force north for the winter, moving to the Breton-Norman border; safer, home territory. He made for St-James-de-Beuvron where Matthew Paris states that he strengthened his castle and, with the benefit of his resources, brought in troops, provisions and ammunition.[11] Clearly this was to be his base for the winter and, with such a strong garrison as he had, would be a safe bet if he was attacked. He was also surrounded by old allies, whose familial and political allegiances he had regained. Brittany was for England and with it Fougères; the west of Normandy had pointedly declared for the English cause, led by the Paynells (Pagnels). Both flanks were secure and the French would have to make the first move.

Ranulf's Christmas court at St-James must have enjoyed all the hope and frivolity of three decades earlier. However, he was now surrounded by a very different inner circle of knights, an energetic group which included a new generation of *familiares*, his courtly family. They were no longer Normans whose allegiance would be tested, but English knights and nobles, a generation removed from those who had abandoned Ranulf. Among these were names whose influence in England would last down the decades, Hugh Despencer, Ranulf's seneschal, Stephen de Seagrave, within a year made Chancellor of England (probably under Ranulf's influence), William de Canteloupe, the King's Steward and Ranulf's young cousin – Simon de Montfort the younger. As a close relative, Simon had come under Ranulf's increasing influence after the death of his own father, (Simon de Montfort the elder – and also Ranulf's uncle) in the Albigensian Crusade in 1218. He had an elder brother, Amaury, but he was in charge of the family's former French dominions in a typical family-split, either side of the Channel. Commentators have seen the younger Simon's relationship as one in which Ranulf assumed the role of adoptive father.[12] There is certainly evidence that he was fast becoming Ranulf's favourite protégé and during the winter of 1230 or spring of 1231 he petitioned Ranulf for his birthright of the honour of Leicester, which Ranulf had held since 1215 after his discredited father (who was financially broke) had had it confiscated by John after going over to Philip Augustus in 1204. Ranulf already held half the honour of Leicester from July 1200.[13] Ranulf had had them re-granted to him by Henry III for life in 1227.

Ranulf seems to have been amenable to Simon's request and the grant was effected (at least between the two of them) on the proviso that Simon did homage to Henry III on their return to England.[14] Money may have changed hands as we know that within a couple of years Simon declared a debt of £200 to Ranulf. On reflection this is perhaps also an indication that over a period Ranulf was becoming acutely aware of his own mortality; the last couple of years had seen a number of personal grants of large portions of his domain to members of his family and friends, which effectively saw him deliberately loosening his own grip on power. It had perhaps begun in 1227 (when Ranulf was 57) with massive grants to his knight Henry de Audley, particularly in Coventry.[15] Henry had administered Ranulf's western lands while he was on crusade and is said to have married Bertrada, the daughter of Ralph Mainwaring and Ranulf's half-sister, the late Amice – making him almost family. Audley was appointed Sheriff of Shropshire and Staffordshire at this time, so would handle much of Ranulf's finances in those counties for the King. His support was essential.[16] Although by comparison Ranulf himself had the gift of all the land between the Ribble and the Mersey confirmed to him in October 1229 (a source of tremendous knightly service), he also began to dispense with extraneous parcels here and there.[17] In February 1230 he passed the manor and town of Bingley (Yorkshire), which he had held since confiscated by default from Maurice of Ghent in 1218, to William de Canteloupe for the service of two knights. William, whose family came from Cantiloupe near Barfleur, was one of Ranulf's most loyal Norman knights, probably with him since before 1204. He was also a very valuable ally at court, being a steward of the royal household. Audley and Canteloupe had both come to know that they would be looked after by the Earl and their loyalty would be well rewarded.

The young Stephen de Seagrave, by comparison, held his manor and castle of Caludon, near Coventry, in return for his management of Ranulf's attached hunting park there. One of Ranulf's former knights, Philip Barbe d'Avril was ensconced at adjacent Stoke and held his retirement lands by service of provision of a pair of gilt spurs each year, thus keeping Ranulf himself in the finest hunting livery.[18] Philip and his father Milo, had been knights of St Sauveur-le-Vicomte and had been with Ranulf since before 1204. All Ranulf's former knights and current adherents there paid their tithes to the rector of St Michael's Church, Coventry. This was the post once held by Ranulf Mainwaring, Ranulf's brother-in-law (and now Henry de Audley's father-in-law). Clearly he still looked after his own, some very diligently for over 25 years.

Back at St-James, for the moment Louis' advisors and Andre de Vitré must have agreed that Ranulf was not to be trifled with while he lay up through the winter, since no attempt was made to attack him and the year drew to a close without further action. Matters were left to rest like this, as Ranulf waited through the spring of 1231 for Henry to return from England with funds and reinforcements. At this point it was the French who broke the deadlock and invaded Brittany, ending Ranulf's wait. Here, however, they were moving through hostile territory, exposing their lengthening supply lines, their flanks to either side bare to a largely hostile baronage. André de Vitré alone was not enough to form an effective rearguard at the eastern border. It was just the risky move Ranulf and Mauclerc (who had returned to the fight) had hoped for, exactly the move that they themselves had judiciously avoided the previous year.

The allies' patience had paid off; a united Brittany was a gigantic trap for the entire French army who obligingly rode in the front door, probably near Pontorson. Moving deep into allied-held Brittany their supply lines were cut behind them when Ranulf fell upon Pontorson and, following a brief siege, took it.[19] They shadowed the advancing army at a safe distance, south into Brittany before striking decisively at a pre-prepared place (probably as the French crossed the river Couësnon). Matthew Paris takes up the story:

> But when the Counts of Brittany and Chester learnt of (Louis') approach, they prepared an ambush; and outflanking him fell upon the army's baggage train containing the wagons, the provisions, arms and siege equipment, capturing the whole lot, together with a prize of 60 of the most valuable war-horses.[20]

As far as victories go, this was the best, almost bloodless but total. The entire French royal field army was caught with its pants down. Its flank guards had failed, its intelligence had let it down and it was now utterly powerless. To attempt to fight on would be suicidal. It would be quite some time before such a force could be raised again and there were some serious ransoms to be exacted for the release of many noble French prisoners. Since this was only sixteen years after the victory at Lincoln, this meant near financial ruin for many lesser baronial families who had to ransom their principal family members twice in one generation. Unsurprisingly, without making any further move (as if they had any they could make) the French signed a humiliating truce on 4 July at the castle of St Aubin-du-Cormiers, near Fougères, where they had taken refuge. It was gleefully signed on the allied side by Ranulf, with Richard Earl of Cornwall for England and Pierre Mauclerc for Brittany. It was to last for three years, the length of time estimated it would take France to recover such disastrous losses in material and finances.[21]

The castle of St Aubin-du-Cormier is not easy to find in a modern world, but its peaceful modern setting amidst parkland, fishing and water-sports (the water once part of its defences), gives no hint at its pivotal role in the final days of the Poitou campaign in 1231. The castle, although ruined, is based around the keep, with an agglomeration of different courts surrounding it. One half of a single round tower stands to almost its full height but everywhere advancing undergrowth is punctuated by barely-glimpsed woodland trails through old orchards staggering under the weight of unpicked fruit. Without warning they turn suddenly down fern-veiled stone stairs into the earth, which still hides far, far more of this castle's secrets.

Ranulf was rightly pleased with the closure at St Aubin and returned to St-James-de-Beuvron before crossing to England with his inner circle of knights in late July 1231. To judge from his benefactions, Ranulf was now increasingly aware of his own health, which may have begun to fail (he was now 61 years old). His thoughts of his family began to turn to making provisions for their well-being. Not only was the honour of Leicester passed to young Simon de Montfort, but he now laid the foundations for the transference of his earldom of Lincolnshire to his sister, Hawise.[22] Other movements were under way but this was by far the biggest pointer to a personal recognition that he was in the twilight of his life. As if to underline the end of a chapter, at St-James-de-Beuvron he deliberately left behind his armour.[23] This was surely a very symbolic act for a man who had spent much of his adult life at war. He was leaving St-James at peace, with Brittany secure and returning to an England also at peace.

On disembarkation in England Ranulf sought out the King, who was on the Welsh frontier, once more addressing the question of restive Welsh neighbours. He met the King and his court at Pain's Castle on the Welsh border where Henry was strengthening the defences.[24] For a while he seemed to be back in the groove, witnessing the gift of Wallingford Castle to Richard Earl of Cornwall but soon, during a short debate, it became clear that the young King and Ranulf were in grave disagreement over something and Ranulf, in a towering rage, stormed out of the King's court, setting off for Chester, which he reached on 21 August. Stephen de Seagrave, one of Ranulf's close family of knights (and Chancellor of England within the year) was sent after him and urged to placate him (he was apparently forgiven this slight to the royal person) and, if possible to recall him to the court.

Commentators are divided over the cause of this infamous argument. What most do agree upon was that Hubert de Burgh was embroiled in it. One side alleges that in a redistribution of manors by the nepotistic de Burgh to a relative, he forgot (or omitted) to consult Ranulf, within whose Leicester domain they all fell. This was both a snub to Ranulf and to Ranulf's new protégé, Simon de Montfort the younger.[25] Certainly, there remained no love lost between Ranulf and Hubert. As if to add barbs to family enmities, Hubert's kinsman Richard de Burgh arrested Ranulf's merchants in Ireland and impounded their merchandise at about this time (alleging their impending defection to Welsh rebels).[26] The King was forced just after Christmas 1231 to order Richard to release them and let them return to Chester, taking security for their allegiance.[27] The old enmity with de Burgh, which Matthew Paris relates began in 1214 over Hubert's preference to Ranulf as a hostage after the battle of Bouvines, was loathe to die down.[28] Nevertheless the King managed to placate Ranulf. Clearly some of his old stubbornness had returned. It was perhaps with the knowledge that his own days were numbered that in early 1232 he refused outright on behalf of himself and others when the King demanded financial help to raise another French expedition (despite the three-year truce).[29]

Within months Ranulf became ill. On 6 May 1232 his last will was proved; the timing was not coincidental as a royal tournament had to be postponed due to his infirmity.[30] Although no copy of his will now survives, some excerpts are to be found in other documents and charters.[31] There is also the evidence of what actually happened after his death which shows that he had put together a thoughtful formula for the legacy of his many dominions.[32]

By summer he was seriously ill and he knew it well. His last will and testament would have been partly formulaic: leaving, no doubt, his soul to Almighty God, Jesus Christ and all the Company of Heaven, he certainly expressed a wish to be buried wherever he ended his days but, wherever that was, his heart should be cut out and buried at Dieulacres Abbey. Despite failing health he kept going. He adjudicated in a dispute between one of his family's monasteries, Spalding (Lincolnshire) and its mother-house at Angers, witnessing the agreement at Brampton (Huntingdonshire) on 8 June.[33] Soon he was with the court at Woodstock (Oxfordshire) on 28 July. For the summer months of 1232 he was surrounded by his knightly family. His own last charters were consistently witnessed by some very influential men, mostly his juniors. The warrior-bishop of Winchester – and Henry III's former tutor – Peter des Roches, Alexander Stavensby, Bishop of Coventry and Lichfield (probably Ranulf's confessor) Richard Marshall Earl of Pembroke, William Ferrers, Earl of Derby (Ranulf's sole remaining brother-in-law), Stephen de Seagrave (Chancellor and Sheriff), Simon de Montfort, William Ferrers (Jun), Philip d'Albini, Henry de Audley and William de Cantiloupe.[34]

The end came at the royal castle at Wallingford in Oxfordshire on 26 October 1232. On 25 October word came to the King at Reading (where he had been for some time) that Ranulf was close to death. Straightway the Royal Charter Rolls for that day's business record a grant by the King at Reading of sixty shillings per annum out of the revenues of Newcastle-under-Lyme to St Werburgh's (Chester Abbey) for a chaplain to say masses for Ranulf. He seemingly hovered between life and death.[35] The next day in a poignant act of personal honour (otherwise without good explanation) the King suddenly moved his court from Reading to

Wallingford, undoubtedly to pay his respects at Ranulf's bedside. We do not know whether he arrived before Ranulf died but on the following day (27 October) he moved quickly on to Oxford, his brief business done. In any case, Ranulf died surrounded by his family circle. Peter des Roches, Alexander Stavensby, his trusty John de Lacy, Constable of Chester, Seagrave, Audley, Cantiloupe.[36] Also present were Fulk Fitz Warin (reconciled to the crown since John's death), Walter Deyville of Whitley (Coventry), Baldwin de Vere and Richard de Arden (Warwickshire). Two clerics, Simon and John, very likely a Chester Benedictine and a Dieulacres Cistercian, were also present to pray for his soul as he breathed his last. John de Lacy and Stephen de Seagrave were Ranulf's executors.[37]

There was real grief at his passing. Contemporary Englishmen knew they had lost a great statesman. The annalist, Thomas Wykes wrote:

> Ranulf Earl of Chester, a man who counselled great things and was foremost in military matters, died at Wallingford with his Earldom greater than ever and, with a level of honour previously unheard of, was borne to his homeland.[38]

Contemporary chroniclers, such as the Tewkesbury Annalist, relate the funerary arrangements which were not quite as Ranulf had previously set out in his wishes. In this we may see the hand of Clemence at work, perhaps with the monks of St Werburgh's (Chester Abbey) lodging a petition. In the custom of the day (as King John before him), his body was eviscerated and embalmed straightway, probably at the adjacent Holy Trinity Priory, Wallingford where such practices were second nature. There his entrails were buried. His heart was indeed cut out and buried at his Cistercian foundation, Dieulacres Abbey.[39] His body was taken to Chester's Benedictine Abbey, where it was laid to rest on 3 November 1232 in the chapter house, alongside those of his grandfather Ranulf de Gernons, fourth earl of Chester and his father Hugh Kevelioc, the fifth earl.[40]

Ranulf's personal legacy to his family was huge.[41] To John le Scot, via his mother Matilda, Ranulf's sister (who barely outlived Ranulf) went the earldom of Chester and its fabulous wealth. With it went Chester and Beeston castles, the latter still unfinished. John was confirmed as Earl on 21 November 1232 but enjoyed it for less than five years before his own death in 1237. To Ranulf's sister Hawise de Quincy went the earldom of Lincoln and all lands in that county, with Bolingbroke Castle as chief seat. Within days she passed it to her son-in-law, Chester's Constable John de Lacy. To Ranulf's nephew, the young Hugh d'Albini, Earl of Arundel in-waiting, went Barrow-on-Soar (Leicestershire, as chief seat), Coventry, Chipping Campden and Olney (actually in the King's custody for two years as Hugh was still a minor). To William Ferrers and his wife Agnes, Ranulf's sister, went Chartley Castle (Staffordshire) as their chief seat with the castle of West Derby (Lancashire, now Merseyside), all the land between the Ribble and the Mersey (including Liverpool, Leyland and Salford), Bugbrooke in Northamptonshire and Navenby in Lincolnshire. To his niece Coletta d'Albini he allotted a marriage-gift of £30 from out of his lands. Henry III decided this should come from Leeds, which was delivered to Hugh d'Albini in 1234.[42]

Something of the wider family's grief at Ranulf's passing can be gauged from two very personal debts paid to his memory. Henry de Audley, who some years earlier had founded the Cistercian Hulton Abbey in Staffordshire, now made a grant to this house to provide for a daily mass for Ranulf's soul to be sung by the full complement of the Abbey 'all the days of the world'. In Coventry, where Audley himself held lands Ranulf had given, Lady Agnes de Boscherville (of east-Norman descent but a descendant of Robert de Boscherville, Ranulf's knight with Coventry-associations) still held her lands in 1279 by virtue of a promise to keep a candle burning in the Earl's stables there. The effect of his death on Clemence must have run deep. She would, however, be taken care of. Her dower rights and manors, some inherited from Ranulf's mother Bertrada's own dowry, were preserved by the King and the Countess of Chester lived on in her widowhood, probably moving from home to home, Repton and Ticknall (Derbyshire), Long Benington and Foston (Lincolnshire), Kington (Oxfordshire), Witleford (Buckinghamshire) and Ippleden (Devon), until her death in 1251.[43] She was buried next to her husband's heart at Dieulacres Abbey.

Ranulf had also made enemies, perhaps not surprising for a man of war, many of whose dealings from youth were concerned with the Machiavellian politics of the Norman-Breton border. In England the most notable had been Hubert de Burgh, the Chancellor. In 1232, a few months before Ranulf's death but already ill, Hubert was ignominiously disgraced, replaced by Stephen de Seagrave, and taken in chains to London, stripped of his office on charges of maladministration and massive financial fraud.[44] He was shut up in a chapel where he sought refuge from the King. Henry wanted to stir up the people against Hubert and storm the place but Ranulf, in one of his last acts of counsel advised strongly against it (perhaps after the experience at the Tower of having once tried to rouse the mob himself!). Church privilege demanded that King Henry had to leave him alone in there and could not get him out. The Bishop of Dublin spoke up for him and although Henry initially wanted him dead, he offered alternatives such as banishment for life. It is with some surprise given previous enmity, that Ranulf defended him, when his contemporaries had already dubbed him 'that evil, treacherous earl' and 'a degenerate and wicked man'. Nevertheless, perhaps because of his magnanimity, Hubert seems to have warmed to Ranulf at the last. When, in his chapel-prison, he learnt of Ranulf's death (Matthew Paris calls him 'one of his greatest enemies') Hubert gave a sigh and cried ' 'May the Lord be merciful to him'; taking up his prayer-book he stood as usual before the altar in the chapel and prayed to the very end for the soul of the celebrated Ranulf'.[45]

His enemies could clearly be magnanimous although de Burgh was also contemplating his own fall and possible death, events forcing him into an unusually reflective mood (although he survived to be imprisoned at Devizes castle). Preserved in French archives is an apocryphal episode, described there as 'a curious legend which illustrates the spirit of the age and reminds us again of the reputation of the Earl of Chester', seemingly both as a devout Christian with much monastic patronage and as the bane of the French. I translate from the French:

> When the death of the Earl Ranulf became known, a hermit, who lived outside Wallingford, heard the cacophonous din of a crowd passing outside his cell, a sound such as is made by the entourage of a mighty person. The hermit questioned one of them and received this reply, 'We are demons and are in pursuit of the Earl Ranulf who has died, in order to accuse him for his sins'. The hermit pressed the demon to return about a month later and tell him more, in order to learn what sort of man Ranulf had been. The

> demon returned at the appointed time and told him, 'Earl Ranulf has been condemned for his crimes to the cruellest punishments in hell: but the dogs (i.e. monks) of Dieulacres, with many others of their kind, have barked (i.e. prayed) so much that they have filled our domain with their racket and thus our prince (i.e. the devil) has reached the end of his tether and has ordered us to throw the Earl out. He is now one of our most dangerous enemies, because the prayers which have been said for him have delivered many other souls from the prisons of hell.'[46]

No doubt Dieulacres and Ranulf's other monastic foundations and family monasteries received handsome bequests at his death. Ranulf did have outstanding financial dealings to be cleared up. Strangely, his personal papers had been lodged with the Prior of St Andrew's Priory, Northampton, a personality who does not otherwise figure in Ranulf's story. The King issued orders for their retrieval. A few personal debts were paid as late as 1237 and orders were given for Ranulf's armour to be retrieved from St-James for valuation for the estate to pay his executors, de Lacy and de Seagrave.[47]

The most poignant of all Ranulf's bequests was to his king. Ranulf's loyalty could never be doubted. The Dunstable Annalist relates that he gave to Henry III his castle at St-James-de-Beuvron.[48] It was a gift laden with pathos, Ranulf's favourite castle for his erstwhile young charge who longed to take back Normandy and avenge his father. This was despite the pangs, both of losing so many castles in 1224 and the long years of the preferment of Hubert de Burgh. Despite Richard's coolness in 1189, despite the burden of John's suspicion in 1203 and again in 1205, despite the machinations of a first wife, who had been a loose cannon at the heart of politics, Ranulf had weathered every storm and remained loyal to the crown of England when all around him had changed sides. Within a year or so Pierre Mauclerc occupied St-James and did homage to King Louis IX for this small but explosive part of what eventually became France. Some measure of the success of Ranulf and Mauclerc's last campaign out of St-James comes with the news that when in 1234 Mauclerc did homage to Louis (at St Aubin-du-Cormier once more) as the 1231 treaty expired, he also handed back Poitou, the county of Perche (Normandy), and the Isle of Olèron.[49] He continued to do homage to Henry for the earldom of Richmond. It was his last change of sides and he was readmitted into the French King's peace. Henry appealed to the Pope to regain St-James and even sent a small force to take it, but it was ineffectual. Too little, too late.[50] Thanks to Ranulf alone Henry III had held for little more than one year what he craved most, land in Normandy. It was small recompense for John's loss in 1204, but it had been one loyal servant's dying gift to his monarch.

To Ranulf himself the monks of Dieulacres paid their last respects and over the casket which held his heart wrote of Ranulf's inspiration and bravery and implored God to accept his soul into heaven. [51] On the evidence of the French story, they just might have succeeded.

12

OVERVIEW

Contemporary historians paid universal homage to Ranulf but, unlike the anonymous eulogist of William Earl Marshall, stopped well short of panegyric, or of examining any aspect of his life, whether personal, comital or military. Ranulf's peers and contemporaries were polite and proper in their address too. The most personal address known comes from Philip d'Albini in 1222, who, in writing from the Holy Land, addresses his uncle as 'Esteemed lord and friend, Ranulf.'[1]

A majority of historians in the twelfth and thirteenth centuries were monks, some anonymous, and, in their cloistered surroundings, we may assume a degree of collusion, often awaiting the same news to circulate from monastery to monastery, carried by the same messengers. Thus it is perhaps no surprise to meet with formulaic affectations and epithets for Ranulf being employed from one chronicle to another. For instance, Matthew Paris calls him both 'illustrious' and 'noble'.[2] The Dunstable Annalist, in relation to Henry III, described Ranulf as 'counsellor and friend'.[3] The same historian, writing of Ranulf's successful return from Damietta, noted his upright manner.[4] Walter of Coventry, of the same crusade, noted Ranulf was 'foremost in the army', probably reflecting his real rank in terms of the leadership he gave.[5] Gervase of Canterbury adds spiritual clout as the victor in a crusade, calling him 'venerable'.[6]

For the rulers whom Ranulf served, the mode of address could speak volumes, whether in praise or denigration. Although no personal address to Ranulf is recorded from either Henry II or Richard the Lionheart, this is probably due to a comparative lack of records; compared, that is, to John whose legacy on the page is huge, being a compulsive and effusive record-keeper of the minutiae of royal power, whether in England or Normandy. John regularly addressed Ranulf in his official documents and as a signing witness, Ranulf's movements with the court can be monitored, his absences noted. However, John used accepted epithets common to many magnates, and usually employed the royal 'We', which maintained a discrete distance from all his nobles. Thus 'Our beloved and faithful Ranulf' is the most common address, usually just after the King had called Ranulf's loyalty into question, but had been forced to back down.[7] John blew hot and cold and, when at his most suspicious, he dropped all affectation, addressing him simply 'Earl Ranulf'.[8] Henry III was the most affectionate, probably since his early years were spent with Ranulf in a major role in the inner circle of the royal council (with the Papal Legate, the Earl Marshall and the Bishop of Winchester), offering close support. Thus Henry describes him as his 'counsellor' in the most personal sense.[9] He also bemoaned his absence when he was not at court. When he went to Henry to broker peace with Llewellyn, Ranulf was described as the King's 'counsellor and friend'.[10] Few could claim that. Pope Honorius, with no axe to grind (but everything about the *status quo* to preserve), called him 'that noble man' in July 1217, before his crusading peak.[11] The annalist Thomas Wykes perhaps summed up contemporary views of Ranulf at his death most aptly, saying of him that he was 'a man who counselled great things and was the most prominent of military men'.[12]

The late medieval period brought one additional reference of note, by the Elizabethan Richard Johnson who called him one of the seven champions of Christendom: 'the Barron of Chester, a bolde and hardier knight they thought lived not then upon the whole earth'.[13] The origin of this late medieval tall tale, mixed with fantastic feats and deeds of little veracity, may lie in the same tradition as 'rymes of Randal, Earl of Chester' circulating from the early fourteenth century. The latter is mentioned most notably by William Langland in *The Vision of Piers Ploughman* and is quoted incessantly by modern commentators.[14] Since the rhymes are mentioned side-by-side with the myth of Robin Hood, we may assume that they grew ever more fantastic with each telling. It is notable, however, that on the one possible day in history when Richard the Lionheart could physically have met one Robin Hood (if he ever existed), 29 March 1194, Ranulf would certainly have been present, hunting at the King's side. It would be wonderful to discover the nature of such 'rymes'.

With the onset of modern historiography, comment concerning Ranulf has been more forthcoming. The great Victorian editor, Rev William Stubbs set the ball rolling. In regard to Richard's reign, he stated that '[the Earl's] policy halted between the temptation of being stepfather to a King (Arthur) and the hatred of his unfaithful wife (Constance)'.[15] Since this statement juxtaposes Arthur's nomination as Richard's heir-apparent (1190–93 at most) and Constance's disaffection (1196–9, and her marital infidelity before 1199 is questionable), his words are a sweeping generalisation and ill-chosen. For a brief while Ranulf was perfectly happy to claim the benefits of Brittany's dukedom although did not regularly style himself '*Dux Brittanniae*'. To many of his subjects, there would have been little point. Stubbs also made the mistake of believing the legend that Ranulf accompanied Richard on the Third Crusade.[16]

Of John's reign Stubbs was inconsistent in how he viewed the relationship between King and Ranulf. He states that Ranulf always hated John, yet the facts show us he served him loyally throughout.[17] He also states, seemingly oddly, (if Ranulf hated him, but forever kept it totally hidden), that John trusted Ranulf more than any other Englishman (or should that be *Norman*, given Ranulf's view of himself?).[18]

More recently, some commentators have been more forthright about Ranulf. Many rightly saw his power and influence as of supreme importance at key moments in the reigns of John and Henry III.[19] His landed power was second only to the King.[20] His detractors, however, have been notable. Holt wondered if his loyalty was quite as solid as it seemed, reliant (he says) on what was in it for him.[21] Painter too saw a selfish side, calling him 'haughty and turbulent', 'greedy and rapacious', but his standpoint was arguably to paint his subject, the Earl Marshall, in the best possible light, the colours of those around him dulled so that he shone all the brighter by comparison.[22] To some extent Alexander followed Painter, although his considered judgement was to perhaps damn Ranulf with faint praise, calling him 'restrained – a man who never let his pride and prejudices destroy his mental balance'.[23]

Powicke, noting events surrounding the angst-ridden coronation of the young Henry III in the dark days of autumn 1216, rightly points out that Ranulf's support was the one single cause why the nation, strained almost to breaking-point, did not disintegrate.[24] That many wished to wait until Ranulf arrived makes it clear that without him they were unsure of the wisdom and effectiveness of their actions.[25]

Ranulf's contribution to castle building has previously drawn little comment. His building schemes, assessed now by the portions which survive, were, however, clearly at the forefront of military design. He made numerous additions to existing castles, refortifying others during critical campaigns. However, many have subsequently been much altered, some razed, others still completely rebuilt. We are left with those few surviving examples which we know he substantially rebuilt or actually built from scratch, with the implication here that he chose the site also, or at least ratified its choice: Chartley (Staffordshire), Bolingbroke (Lincolnshire) and Beeston (Cheshire).

At Chartley the site of an existing timber motte and bailey was the biggest constraint and the rebuild of *c.* 1225 utilises this to the utmost, perhaps newly dividing the bailey into two wards by the cutting of a deep ditch across the site. The *enceinte* of the inner ward was rebuilt in stone, punctuated by massive mural towers and two D-shaped towers flanked the gate. Such a double D-shaped design can be seen at very slightly earlier sites in the Holy Land, such as at Arsuf, being rebuilt in the early thirteenth century and arguably at Château-Gaillard (although here such remains are fragmentary). Significantly the entrance to the citadel at St-James-de-Beuvron was similarly defended.

Constrained by an existing site at Chartley, a new round stone keep was built upon the old motte. The castle was the site of a brief but bitter siege only thirty years after Ranulf's death and the towers still bear the scars of the battering it took and the subsequent repairs. Other than the restrictions applied by the existing motte, the re-fortified wards at Chartley (divided by the ditch) have a vague air of the St-James-de-Beuvron or even Château Gaillard (in plan), to which they perhaps pay a canting allusion.

At Bolingbroke, similar towers to Chartley dominate a new idea (which rapidly gained ground), the keep-less enclosure, here hexagonal, presaging the polygonal and concentric defences of Edward I at the likes of Beaumaris more than a generation later. Here the views along the walls afforded by the principal towers give nearly complete coverage for the defenders of anyone beneath the walls, where the site was not a commanding one. The lack of a keep was an utterly new idea, seen mainly in the Holy Land, where a more strongly-fortified entrance gate served a similar function. Athlit (then Palestine, now in Israel), to which Ranulf contributed while commanding at Damietta, was conceived without a keep, being built from 1217. He may have taken a lead from such a radical design.

Aspects of Athlit's design, together with the nature of its site, can be discerned also in Ranulf's (surprisingly small) castle at Beeston. Like Athlit and Château Gaillard the castle was built on a rocky promontory, certainly not an uncommon location, although (unlike the coastal Athlit) the sea did not envelope three sides, nor was there an equivalent of the river Seine to guard far below. Nevertheless the promontory at Beeston was just as inaccessible on almost threee sides, due to its precipitous nature. The remaining side, facing the steep (but passable) approaches, was separated from the rest of the promontory (like Athlit and – just as significantly – St-James-de-Beuvron) by a deep rock-cut ditch, lined on the inside by a new curtain wall with strong D-shaped towers. The entrance was defended by D-shaped flanking towers. In common with Bolingbroke (and Athlit), there was no keep. The chosen location owes so much to Ranulf's good experience at Château Gaillard and less good at Mountsorrel.

In all this the greatest loss is the contemporary defences of Damietta, whose aspect in 1218–19 must have provided much food for thought for a generation of English crusader-knights.

There may have been many a defensive nuance which held up the Christian forces and which numerous individuals must have remembered in years to come on their return home. Ranulf in the later 1220s was not alone in the promulgation of new designs and the D-shaped towers and similar flanking gate-towers can be newly seen within a decade or so at Whittington (Shropshire) and Llewellyn's castles at Criccieth, Castel y Bere and his rebuild at Degannwy (all Wales). Notably all three can be said to lie within Ranulf's closest sphere of influence. Within a generation such gate defences were standard. Ranulf may have been the originator, or one of a number of similarly-influenced innovators.

Ranulf's spirituality has hardly been considered by previous commentators, other than for Alexander to dismiss him as a 'pinchpenny patron' in regard to his church benefaction.[26] This author is of the opinion that Alexander was unaware of much of Ranulf's patronage and took little account of either the disprate claims on his patronage or what damage the break with Normandy in 1204 did to existing patronage on that side of the Channel. Ranulf in fact was very free with the benefits he conferred on the churches and monastic houses of his wider family and the legacy of his forefathers, either side of 1204; plus of course, those which he espoused himself, being the founder of at least four. These included Coventry's Franciscan Friary just before his death, decided perhaps, by his experience of Francis of Assisi at Damietta in 1219. He met both the obligations begun by his forebears and added considerable commitments of his own.

In England, although his principal title had Chester as its origin, Coventry was in fact the spiritual centre of his earldom, since it was there that his Bishop had his seat, and with whom he must deal, whether it was the hateful Nonant or the trusted Muschamp and Stavensby. In France until 1204, he had had numerous spiritual centres beneath his sway from Mont St Michel to Hambye and from Bayeux to St Sever. Thus there may have been a tendency to dilute his efforts at benefaction with a multiplicity of competing claims to his patronage.

Furthermore, the events of 1204 laid understandable constraints on anyone who had dealt freely on both sides of the Channel. However, even in such circumstances, such as Ranulf's dealings with Savigny, the very disgrace of the de Fougères family was surely pivotal in persuading Ranulf to assume patronly responsibility for their Savignac interests in Lincolnshire. While he would undoubtedly benefit spiritually from their religious ministrations (and a cynic would note undoubted temporal benefits), his inaction would have meant embarrassment for his wife, who remained a scion of the de Fougères. It is notable that these Lincolnshire Savignac properties, no passing whim, remained bound with the Honour of Chester until long after Ranulf and Clemence, to be given by Richard II (as Earl of Chester) to the Carthusians of Coventry in the late fourteenth century.

Moreover, it is likely that the Church's acclamation following Damietta or, previously, the Pope's recognition of Ranulf in his letter of 1217, would ever have been anything like as fulsome, had he suffered a dubious reputation as miserly with his gifts to the church. Such bad reputations spread very widely (such as happened to the Tosny family of Conches-en-Ouches in Normandy) and were difficult to divest. At the level of an individual monastic house, Ranulf could not have felt sure, buffeted by a fierce mediterranean storm while returning from Damietta, that the monks of Dieulacres would have been praying earnestly for his soul at a given hour, had he not made sufficient provision for their well-being, especially since a crusade, more than any other form of warfare, was as likely as not to mean his untimely demise. Again, in 1232, when he died, the anecdote concerning the incessant prayers of Dieulacres' monks, being as annoying as barking dogs to the demons of hell, is not one borne of half-hearted devotions in return for miserly patronage. Coming, as it does, from a French source, one might even discern a little embittered jealousy at such a peak of devotion from Ranulf's favourite Cistercians.

Today, St Sever is a surprise, combining the earls of Chesters' spirituality and their possessions. The town looms very suddenly astride an otherwise seemingly never-ending straight Norman road, fringed by vast plantations and *forêts communales*. The town's streets seem to branch out of that one main arterial road, along which flows the lifeblood of today's Norman agriculture. Clustered around the market square are the *Mairie*, the *Syndicat d'Initiative* and the former Benedictine Abbey of which Ranulf and generations of his family were patrons. Most of this is late medieval or later. However leading off the north aisle is a small chapel, surrounded by a peaceful garden. Here, before an altar lie the bones of Hugh Lupus, 1st Earl of Chester, Baron d'Avranches and Ranulf's great-great-grandfather who died in 1101 after a short monastic retirement in the Abbey. The locals take their link with their former baronial family very seriously and even today every street sign in the town centre sports the arms of the Earl of Chester.

Ranulf's relationship with Normandy seems never to have changed all that much. Given (with hindsight) the finality of events of 1204, that might seem a strange assertion to make. Naturally the loss of his ancestral homelands in that year would have hurt but he seems never to have given up hope of their return, witness not least his readiness to serve in so many of John and Henry III's expeditions, in 1206, 1214 and 1230, being instrumental in both their logistics and their execution. Likewise, his relations with Brittany, which might have been ended by his irreparable break with his first wife, Constance, the proverbial loose cannon of her generation, merely continued through his second wife Clemence and her family. Admittedly Constance continued to cast a long shadow over Brittany as her subsequent brief third marriage to Guy de Thouars produced twins (before she herself succumbed to leprosy). The elder of these, Alice, married Pierre Mauclerc and thus re-founded (successfully) the dynasty of the Breton Dukes, jeopardised so spectacularly by John's murder of the boy Arthur and a lifetime's imprisonment of the hapless Eleanor. If Arthur's murder defined the final course of the war for Normandy, Eleanor's deperate lifelong existence in a velvet prison defined the ongoing strategic importance of Brittany as Normandy's unpredictable neighbour. She could not be allowed to bear potential rival claimants to Brittany while that claim challenged that of the King of England. Her incarceration through the years of her stifled fertility (and beyond, up to her death in 1241) meant her family's immediate claim was literally and metaphorically barren. Ironically, after 1213 even Mauclerc could have no benefit from an Eleanor freed, since her ongoing Anglo-Breton claim to Brittany was a threat to his own Franco-Breton claim.

Ranulf's family relationship with the Breton nobility was one of being hereditary neighbours, not enemies and whatever England made of Brittany (and vice versa) the Viscounts of Avranches traditionally got on well with their neighbours across their western border, especially at Fougères whose former friendship had gone back to the rebellion of Earl Hugh (1173) and before. If the lands of western Normandy were ever to be recovered, antagonizing the neighbours would not help, so Ranulf's continued diplomacy in Brittany was a prerequisite.

Professors Painter and Holt saw Ranulf's return to John's side in 1204–5 and his agreement to lay down Richmond in 1218 without protest as being intimately connected with avarice in the first instance and stoical acceptance in the second.[27] He was far more likely to have been placated in 1205 by a promise of help to recover what was lost by the conferral of Richmond (since his loss of his homeland was compounded by the impasse he experienced over Clemence's dowry lands). It must never be overlooked that Clemence was a Breton lady, also dispossessed of her cultural roots both by the events of 1204 and by her mean-spirited great uncle, William de Fougères. She surely rued at least one of these.

Painter also omitted to point out that four months before Pierre Mauclerc received Richmond (May 1218), Ranulf was himself dealing personally with Mauclerc's steward to ensure the smooth handover of Richmond to Brittany, the honour being granted in January jointly to him and Mauclerc's steward.[28] It is clear that Ranulf was moving in a sensible, measured manner, not at all the actions of the disenchanted.

From October 1216 to Ranulf's departure for Damietta, no royal grant or favour came from the boy-king Henry, but from the inner council who advised him, under the watchful eye of the Papal legates, firstly Gualo and later Pandulf. Thus to suggest that Ranulf was disadvantaged by the council's acts is to miss the point that Ranulf was an intimate part of the decision-making process. When Mauclerc got Richmond, it was with Ranulf's full knowledge and implicit agreement – and just in time since Ranulf left on his long-planned crusade within four weeks of Richmond's handover, a timing surely not without significance as he surely laid aside other titles and responsibilities to the royal council at this time, insurance in the event of his death. Most were resumed on his return.

Ranulf's royalist part in the Civil War of 1215–17 was clearly instrumental. John had sought his favour and backing and, when he got it wholeheartedly, had rewarded him. His prowess at Lincoln had been noteworthy, as had his assertion of his right as a Norman to fight in the front rank, pointing out just how he saw himself, despite having been without his Norman patrimony for more than a decade by then. Whatever his rights, he knew that at that time he held only English lands and that others (whether still friends or turncoats) sat in his ancestral halls and castles in Normandy. That he still saw himself as Norman says much about his sense of traditional hierarchy in the court but also about longings for his lost birthright. For seventeen years he had been used to John's royal court where Normans, English, Anglo-Normans, Poitevins, Gascons, Brabançons and generally 'foreigners' (as the last three groups were viewed by the first three) and paid mercenaries or '*balistarii*' (literally crossbowmen or artillerymen) had had to vie with eachother for the King's favour. In what remained of the *status quo*, Ranulf had no such posturing to perform; however, victory for the rebels would mean drastically rearranging the pecking-order. He had a huge amount to lose by mid-1216.

After John's death, Ranulf's backing of the boy King Henry was, without doubt, the deciding factor which defeated the rebellion that had begun with Magna Carta. Although clearly Ranulf came around to Magna Carta's benefits, he was fully aware that those behind it had ulterior motives; indeed Ranulf refused to endorse it in its earliest, most rabid and xenophobic form – perhaps objecting as much to the petitioners as to the petition. It is only with the benefit of many hundreds of year's hindsight that Magna Carta has been viewed as a first faltering step to some kind of modern democracy. At the time it was an unmitigated disaster for England since it made measure of just how wide was the gulf between the unpredictable John and the majority of his baronage. That Ranulf stood by him is a credit to his loyalty and his belief in the right of kings, however much his king had abused him. Such constancy clearly impressed his contemporaries. In the vacuum following John's death, to a council contemplating the hasty (and unprecedented) coronation of the child Henry, the words 'Wait until the Earl of Chester comes' ring down the centuries. His backing, his military might and his counsel were indispensable. In spite of this, that Henry's coronation at Gloucester did go ahead without him, irked many, but not Ranulf himself. He had already attended two coronations, standing in positions of great honour, and he knew the form. He also trusted his old ally, the Earl Marshall, implicitly. His late arrival might even have been planned, dallying a day or so outside Gloucester: certainly if other, less powerful magnates coalesced without his military backing, the move to crown Henry would be seen as strong enough already. With his backing, the coronation received a separate, very deliberate ratification and sent a message that the loyal barons of every ilk were both united and supported by Ranulf with the army. Certainly the effect of Henry's coronation on the rebel camp was electric. The Dauphin Louis was said to be incandescent with rage, since he had figured the loyalists would cave in without John to lead and cajole them. He perhaps overplayed John's role and underestimated the influence of Ranulf and the Earl Marshall in standing firm with Gualo and the Church. Although there would be more English reverses and many a castle would yet fall to the rebels, the move to rally behind Henry meant the beginning of the end for the French invasion.

On the two occasions when Ranulf did lose real power and influence, in 1204 and 1218–20, it was simply because he was not where he ought to be when events took a dangerous political turn. In the last days of 1203 he followed John to England when he needed to be in Normandy. His judgement may have been questionable in this case, or he might have been asked by a seriously-panicked John to accompany him. Commentators have previously all stated that Ranulf was charged at Montfarville with holding the western frontier – so why did he follow John to England within the week? It seems likely that he knew the situation was hopeless. By departing and saving his Norman vassals the issue of swopping allegiance 'to his face', he may have spared his ancestral lands from considerable destruction; certainly the handover to new French-backed overlords seems to have been amongst the smoothest in the Duchy. Commentators all note that the castles of the western frontier mostly capitulated without any of the bitter sieges which had characterised the fall of eastern and central Normandy. It seems plausible that Ranulf's departure had effectively declared them all to be 'open' towns, the individual decisions on new allegiances left to his vassals, the Barbe d'Averils, Tesssons, de Hambyes, Harcourts and the rest. It may be this single aspect which made the same towns (and for the most part the same former vassals of Ranulf) so amenable to Henry III and Ranulf on their expedition to Brittany in 1230.

In 1218–20 Ranulf was in Damietta. His absence was unavoidable but it was during this time that his place at court came under the most serious and lasting threat. It was undoubtedly made worse by his being accompanied on crusade by so many of his former friends and allies, such as William d'Albini and Saher de Quincy, who had been so supportive as family, despite their being for a while on opposite sides in the Civil War. Both died in the crusade, which also claimed other less-reliable rebels, such as the brutal Robert FitzWalter, joint architect of Magna Carta. Meanwhile back in England a new legate was in post, Pandulf, who had barely any time to get to know Ranulf before he departed. In 1219 the Earl Marshall died. Aged and dignified, his counsel had carried the weight which the regency needed to steer the ship of state when a strong rudder was required. With his death,

Pandulf turned increasingly to the ambitious Hubert de Burgh, whose antipathy towards Ranulf was well-known from 1214 onwards, although as one of the erstwhile gaolers of the teenaged Arthur of Brittany, the aggravation towards Hugh may have begun as early as 1202. His antagonism would crop up again and again in the years to come and his designs would eventually be his own downfall under an older and wiser Henry. But for the moment he had the ear of Pandulf unopposed and it must be supposed that reports he gave of an absent Ranulf were less than flattering. No doubt the triumphal nature of Ranulf's return from Damietta would have rankled and cast the Earl of Chester in a new light for Pandulf. However, damage had been done and the years after Damietta became a struggle for Ranulf as England once more teetered on the brink of civil war.

The castles affair of 1223–4 was begun by a letter from the Pope but Pandulf was withdrawn to Rome before he could carefully ensure that the royal castles were handed back to the King. Unfortunately none of the factions which still existed at court were happy to oblige and even de Burgh, who forced the issue with the handover of the first two castles, would lose ground. Thus Ranulf's rancour would not have stood out but for his breathtaking march on the Tower of London. For a brief while the stupefied kingdom held its breath – this one event sending de Burgh scurrying to the King's side and their ignominious flight to Gloucester. Stephen Langton, Archbishop of Canterbury, acting as a worthy unofficial legate, seems soon to have been instrumental in ensuring that no one party held the upper hand and the power of young Henry's majority was assured. That Henry quickly began to issue charters under his own seal (eschewing that of de Burgh who was gradually prised from his singular position of counsel) may have saved the day since it became clear that Henry would be nobody's puppet in his majority.

Ranulf's response to Faulkes de Bréauté's treatment over Bedford in 1224 is notable for its dignity. He clearly respected Faulkes but was careful not to alienate the King, and deliberately renewed his oath of allegiance, while at the same time offering his help and assurance of safety to the would-be rebel, whose own world began to fall around his ears with every passing week. That Ranulf's persuasion and personal assurances ended up ensuring Faulkes' custody may have rankled since Faulkes was quickly dispossessed, exiled and died a broken man. This was surely not Ranulf's intention. His diplomacy did ensure, however, that he himself was left untainted by his reluctance to get involved at Bedford.

Ranulf's relative retirement from court after Bedford is as much to do with his attentions being elsewhere as it was a loss of face, whether real or perceived. This period saw his replacement of his former royal castles with his own new ones at Beeston and Bolingbroke, his refortification of Chartley and a new fortified manor at Coventry. Further influential construction work at Whittington and the consolidation of his decade-old foundation at Dieulacres took time, money and effort which could not be expended at court. It is also the period of his greatest commercial ventures, not least draining 500 acres of the Lincolnshire Fens and defending the Jewish communities of Coventry and Leicester against a tide of anti-Semitic feeling. He seems to have been touchy about finances at this time, possibly because he had little left and was noted by contemporaries as being alone in refusing outright to pay a major Papal taxation of 1229. His stance succeeded.

His return to the battlefield in 1230, aged sixty, represented a last campaign for the most celebrated soldier of his generation. With Brittany as the bait, Normandy beckoned once more and, however questionable were the lasting effects of the campaign, his own conduct showed he was still a formidable leader in the field. His cooperation with an immensely able commander, Pierre Mauclerc, made for an irresistible combination which within a year won back Brittany, parts of western Normandy, the Touraine and the Isle d'Oleron for Henry III. Successful sieges across Brittany and the Touraine and an almost bloodless ambush and capture of the entire French baggage train emasculated the French army in one fell swoop, forcing Louis to the negotiating table, his position as weak as it could possibly be. The treaty Ranulf signed in July 1231 with a chastened King Louis, penned in St Aubin-du-Cormier, put a seal upon a great military career.

Although his final months saw disagreement with Henry (inevitably due to the agitating of Hubert de Burgh), Ranulf's affairs were at the last dominated by his own impending death. We do not know the details of his final illness, just where and when he died, but his affairs make it clear he knew he was dying and that for some time he had been making steady provision for the handover of his legacy to his heirs. After his death the immediate effect was for the crown to be presented with a *fait accompli* in terms of the legacy and ratification of each portion was swift. Although, perhaps inevitably, the beneficiaries would quarrel in the years to come, all who benefited from his generosity, whether family, friends or feudal vassals, came to enjoy great stability. The towns where he had invested his time and money – Chester, Lincoln, Coventry, Leicester, all enjoyed huge success, laying economic foundations which underpin them still. The success of the earldom of Chester would never quite be the same again, however. Henry III saw it as too important to continue as an independent fiefdom. Therefore, following the death of Ranulf's nephew and heir, John le Scot, only five years later, the King appropriated the earldom to the Crown for good. There it remains to this day, a title conferred upon each Prince of Wales in succession.

Ranulf might so easily have seen the second half of his life as being one in which his cultural heritage had been torn up by its roots. Scrutiny of his charters shows that more often than not, before 1204 he was careful to have official documents greet his men, 'both French and English'; after 1204 this distinction is noticeable by its absence. He was realistic about Normandy. He certainly never gave up hope of its restitution but he moved across his English possessions with ease and with a concern which saw him rebuild after war and construct always with the future in mind. He appeared to care for those who lived under his sway and stood up for those who could not defend themselves. He stood up for individuals who were wronged, regardless of their standing, and seemingly without heed of the damage he might sustain in the process. It is one aspect of the chivalric code his class was expected to live by but so few did. In a world of complex allegiances, we see God, his family and his king increasingly at the fore in so many of his decisions. That he never had children of his own was perhaps to the detriment of his dominions.

Rev Stubbs once stated that with the death of Ranulf passed the last feudal link with the Norman Conquest. If Ranulf himself could have realised his own legacy, having noisily asserted his Norman birthright at Lincoln in 1217, he might have been amused that, ironically, more than any other he had helped bring about the birth of an independent England.

NOTES

The following textual endnotes are pertinent to the documents dealing in particular with the acts, involvement and whereabouts of Ranulf, Earl of Chester. They are not intended to be comprehensive notes to all the affairs of state going on around Ranulf. The reader is referred to the Bibliography for researching wider issues.

Preface

1 Perhaps, in particular Warren, Norgate and others
2 Such as Gillingham (1989), McLynn (2006)
3 Except perhaps Powicke (1961)
4 Yann Brekilian

Chapter 1: Earl in waiting (1170–89)

1 Barraclough (1951, 1988), Husain (1973)
2 Powicke's survey of the principal Anglo-Norman nobility 1189–1204 is unparalleled (1961, 331–7)
3 Ranulf's birth is recorded in the Chester Annals (Christie 1887)
4 See Harris (1975, 101) for a fuller discussion of Oswestry and its unlikely association
5 See Christie (1887)
6 For Roger de Cestria see, for instance, Barraclough (1988, 187, 222 (doc 221) and 258 (doc 259)
7 For a lengthy biographical note see Cronne (1937); for his military career White (1976)
8 National Archives E164/21 f76.2, Charter confirmation (1162–73) by Earl Hugh
9 Chester Annals in Christie (1887 intro *et seq*)

10 Roger of Hoveden in Stubbs (1870, II 51); Ranulf Higden in Lumby (1876, VII 50)
11 Roger of Hoveden in Stubbs (1870, II 55, 61, 65)
12 *Ibid* (68, 118)
13 For Hugh's treatment by Henry II see Benedict of Peterborough in Stubbs (1867, I 135, 161). For Geoffrey's campaign, *Ibid* (I, 83). For Bromfield, Chester Annals in Christie (1887)
14 Chester Annals in Christie (1887, 28)
15 Roger of Hoveden in Stubbs (1870, II 265); Chester Annals in Christie (1887); Benedict of Peterborough in Stubbs (1867, I, 277)
16 Constance may have had at least two brothers (Everard 2000, 43). It is also possible that she had a twin brother, Richard, who was a witness of one of her charters. It is complicated by the existence of two contemporary knights known as Alan and Richard, the twins. See Round (1899, charter 10)
17 For the marriage, Benedict of Peterborough in Stubbs (1867, I, 7, 59)
18 Barraclough (1988, 246)
19 The Savage family are known later in 1195 (Stapleton 1840, 150)
20 For the debate on Amicia's legitimacy see Christie (1887, xvii-xviii)
21 For Mainwaring's career see Christie (1887) and Franklin (1988). There remains a possibility that there were two separate Ralph Mainwarings, although that both resided in Ranulf's close circle makes this unlikely
22 Simon's death is recorded in Chester Annals (Christie (1887), amongst others
23 Gerald of Wales II, 11 in Dimock (1877, VI:141)
24 Barraclough (1988, 242 doc 243)
25 For Bertrada and Hugh as joint monastic benefactors, see Coyd and Stenton (1950, doc 348); Bertrada's death is recorded in Chester Annals (Christie 1887)
26 Harvey and McGuiness (1996, 53 and fig 48) *c.* 1200. see also Heslop (1991, 193–5)
27 Arthur's naming was widely supported; Benedict of Peterborough in Stubbs (1867, I: 358)
28 For Constance's ironic ancestry, see Round (1899, 291)
29 Hoveden in Stubbs (1870, II: 265); Benedict of Peterborough [Hoveden's nom-de-plume] in Stubbs (1867, I: 358); Ranulf Higden in Lumby (1876); Christie (1887)

Chapter 2: Into the Limelight (1189–94)

1 Barraclough (1988)
2 *Ibid* (1988, 229 doc 229)
3 Alexander (1983, 4); Cheshire Sheaf 10233
4 Coggeshall in Stephenson (1875, 23)
5 For arguably the best modern account of Richard's reign see Gillingham (1989); more recently McLynn (2006)

6 Matthew Paris in Madden (1866, II: 7)
7 For his sister see Great Roll of the Pipe for 1 Ric I in Hunter (1844, 223); For Constance and Eleanor *ibid* (61, 197). As a babe in arms, Arthur warrants no separate account
8 The best account of the arrangements is still that by Stubbs (1902)
9 For Richard's full itinerary 1189–99, see Landon (1935)
10 Glover (1865, 252). Arthur was at that time briefly styled by Richard as 'Duke of Britanny' (Hardy 1885, 8)
11 Menard (1897, 31). However it is not clear why Ranulf was quite so fêted at Richard's coronation if he resented his marriage
12 For Constance's 'twin' Richard see Round (1899, 10)
13 Menard (1897, 33 n1)
14 For Nonant, see Franklin (1988); Stubbs (1902). For his trouble at Coventry Priory see also Rylatt and Mason (2003)
15 Barraclough (1988, doc 219); Franklin (1988, xxxix)
16 Richard of Devizes in Stubbs (1864, 73)
17 *Ibid* (37)
18 Matthew Paris in Luard (1876, II: 371)
19 For Richard's movements in captivity, see Landon (1935)
20 Franklin (1988, 134–5); Landon (1935, 80–82)
21 Pipe Rolls 5 Ric I
22 Hoveden in Stubbs (1870, III: 217–20)
23 Powicke (1961, 95)
24 Landon (1935, 83)
25 For Hugh and Robert Nonant, see for instance Franklin (1988); Contemporaries include Hoveden in Stubbs (1870, III: 233)
26 Farrer (1924, II: 299)
27 Hoveden in Stubbs (1870, III: 237–9) recounts the siege. The deaths at Acre of William Ferrers the elder and Ralph de Fougères, are noted (long after) by Matthew Paris in Luard (1876, II: 370)
28 This volume, Chapter 8
29 Hoveden in Stubbs (1870, III: 238–9)
30 This was the day on which romanticists portray Richard's fanciful meeting with Robin Hood. The latter's very existence remains unproven, the meeting almost certainly pure fabrication
31 Hoveden in Stubbs (1870, III: 248)
32 Pipe Roll 5 Ric I
33 Landon (1935, 88–90)

Chapter 3: War under Richard (1194–9)

1 For Nonant, Franklin (1988)
2 Landon (1935, 93–4); Ralph of Diss in Stubbs (1876, II: 115)
3 For Tosny and Stafford see Soden (2007)

4 The first mention of her wardship at court is 1189–90 (Hunter 1844, 197); eventually it became imprisonment until her death in 1241. She is surely the saddest of political prisoners, a lifelong victim
5 Great Roll of the Pipe in Hunter (1844, 61, 197, 223)
6 Great Roll of Normandy in Stapleton (1840, cxlvii and 154 m2)
7 Landon (1935, 100)
8 Glover (1865, 252)
9 Menard (1897, 31–2) from the Cartulary of Montmorel Abbey. Cf Landon (1935, 101) who confirms the date but omits the list of witnesses, also inexplicably mistaking the venue for St Jacques-de-la-Lande. Unusually in French, the town has never been St Jacques but the anglicised St James
10 Gillingham (1989, 260)
11 Widely reported, but see for example Hoveden in Stubbs (1870, IV: 7). Harris (1975, 103) says by these actions Ranulf appears to have started a war; if so it was just one scrap amongst wider hostilities
12 For instance Barraclough (1988, doc 224)
13 Thus halting Constance's assertions of Breton independence (Powicke 1961, 111)
14 Landon (1935, 112)
15 Barraclough (1988); Landon (1935); Menard (1897)
16 For Ranulf's stays at Château-Gaillard, see Landon (1935, 113, 118, 119, 133, 134) for Ranulf as witness to royal charters June 1196, June-July 1197, August-September 1198; also 1199 (Round 1899, 495)
17 Hoveden (Gillingham 1989, 263)
18 Stapleton (1840); Landon (1935, 117)
19 Stapleton (1840, cxlvii)
20 *Ibid* (cxxxvi-vii)
21 Alexander (1983, 7); after Pipe Roll 6 Ric I 119, 210, 258
22 Powicke (1961, 125ff). Brittany too was ravaged by war and the same storms (Everard 2000, 163)
23 Powicke (1961, 206ff)
24 *Ibid* (125ff)
25 Hoveden in Stubbs (1870, IV: 7)
26 Barraclough (1988, 244)
27 *Ibid* (305–7, docs 308–9)
28 Glover (1865, 274); Hoveden in Stubbs (1870, IV: 54, 86)
29 Hoveden in Stubbs (1870, IV: 86–7)
30 Glover (1865, 274)
31 Dimock (1864, 296–7)
32 For the date of her final departure see Hoveden in Stubbs (1870, IV: 97)
33 Ranulf's oath of allegiance: Charter Rolls (I pt 1) in Hardy (1837, 30b); At Rouen, *ibid* (31a); His presence confirmed by Round (1899, 495). Hoveden says he held back, uncertain of John's intentions (Stubbs 1870, IV: 88)
34 Ranulf's second oath at Northampton in Burton Annals (Luard 1865, I, 199)

Chapter 4: Normandy in tatters (1199–1204)

1 Stapleton (1840, clxxiii)
2 Barraclough (1988, 318 doc 317)
3 Hardy (1835^{3}, 43); For the ill-fated dowry agreement, see Coyd and Stenton (1950, 171–3; doc 236) where the full surviving Latin text of the charter is printed
4 Hardy (1835^{2}, 1) – 23 Sept 1199. See also Stapleton (1844)
5 *Ibid* (7)
6 Ranulf witnessing the King's charters: Charter Rolls (I pt 1) in Hardy (1837, 57b–74b)
7 Barraclough (1988, 319 doc 319). He read the venue not as Semilly but as a mis-spelling of Martilly, near Bayeux. While Martilly was in Countess Bertrada's purview, so not impossible, Semilly makes far more sense at this time
8 *Ibid* (1988, 269 doc 271)
9 Stapleton (1844, lii and 537); Hardy (1835^{1}, 39)
10 *Ibid* (clxv)
11 The long list of witnesses is given by Barraclough (1988, 278 doc 279). He was unaware of their significance in the coming years
12 Barraclough (1988, 277 doc 275) for Abbé. Roaud and de Louvigny in Stapleton (1844, ccxiv)
13 Calendar of Charter Rolls for Henry III, I: 1226–57, 334, 353. Caley and Lemon (1803, 20, 70)
14 Stenton (1926); Curia Regis Rolls 1201, m13
15 Hoveden in Stubbs (1870, IV:160–1)
16 Savage (1926, 103–4 doc 223): At Bonport 13 July 1202
17 Such a spate can be seen in Stenton (1926). One suit against Ranulf pre-empted his return in 1202, being still 'overseas in the service of the Lord King' (*ibid*, doc 200)
18 Powicke (1961, 139)
19 Burton Annals in Luard (1864, I: 208–9)
20 Hardy (1885, 12)
21 Perhaps the most eloquent and considered is Powicke (1909)
22 Powicke (1909); Philimore (1913, II: 109)
23 Ralph of Coggeshall in Stephenson (1875, 143–4)
24 Hardy (1835^{1}, 96–7)
25 Stapleton (1840, clxxiii)
26 Hardy (1835^{1}, 96–7); Hardy (1835^{2}, 28)
27 Hardy (1835^{2}, 29)
28 He had waited at least two years for this (Hardy 1875, 44)
29 The figures are preserved in Stapleton (1844, 536–7), discussed *ibid* (ccxlii)
30 Coggeshall in Stephenson (1875, 211)
31 Hardy (1835^{1}, 77)
32 Hardy (1835^{2}, 30), 31 May

33 He witnessed his last Charter in Normandy at John's Château de Gonville, 29 November 1203 (Hardy 1837, 114)
34 Charter Rolls, in Hardy (1837, 118–35; 26 January – 3 August 1204)
35 For instance Coggeshall in Stephenson (1875, 143–4; also Warren (1997, 86–96) for a good modern appreciation
36 Alexander (1983, 17)
37 Powicke (1961, 259) pays this scant attention
38 For these relationships, Thompson (1895)
39 Some listed by Powicke (1961, 330–57); others gleaned from subsequent documents, especially State-confiscations of 1205 in Hardy (1835[1], 87)
40 Hardy (1835[1]; 1837)
41 These figures are widespread, but see especially Stapleton (1840, lviii, xci-iv; 1844, ccxli) and Powicke (1961)
42 Stapleton (1835[1]) and Menard (1897)
43 Powicke's calculation (1961, 335)

Chapter 5: Consolidation (1204–9)

1 Powicke (1961, 259)
2 Holt (1961, 205)
3 Cal Charter Rolls Henry III; I: 1226–57, 257
4 Holt (1961, 205)
5 Hardy (1835[2], 48)
6 Ayscough and Caley (1802, 2)
7 For Ippleden and Witleford, Hardy (1833, 135)
8 Constance's grandfather, Count Alan, was a benefactor (Round 1899, 291). Clemence's first husband (Alan de Dinan) had helped settle some of the Abbey's disputes (*ibid*, 300). Ranulf's charter assuming responsibilities is in Round (*op cit*, 308), and Barraclough (1988, 334). Clemence persuaded him to donate some of the new Long Bennington land.
9 Powicke (1961, 331)
10 For some of this list see Hardy (1835[1]). Wm de Humet: Waddington (Beds/Bucks), Easton-by-Stamford and Grafton (both Northants), Esseby (Lincs). The de Humets later returned to the King's peace. Wm de Semilly: Princes Risborough (Beds/Bucks). Robert de Harcourt: Elmdon (Warks), Burstall and Sileby (Leics), Wellingborough (Northants), Benson (Oxon), Cherbury (Kent), Ludham (Suffolk), Sherston (Wilts). Jean de Harcourt: Rothley (Leics). Wm de Préaux: Henington, (Som). Jean de Préaux: Stoke by Shutlanger (Northants); Great Tew (Oxon). Pierre de St Hilaire: Carston (Som). Fulk Paynell: Duddington (Northamptonshire), Bingham (Nottinghamshire) (He gained these back in 1214 when he rejoined the English). Ralph Tesson: Watele (Nottinghamshire). Hugh de Colonces: Stepbinges (Essex). To this could be added William de Fougères, whose lands at Twyford, Witleford, Westkinton, Long Bennington, Repton, Ticknall and

Ippleden, were all beyond reach, many now held by Ranulf – as had been his right in the disputed dowry.
11 Hardy (1833, 18b, 59, 60)
12 *Ibid* (66b)
13 For Bishop Muschamp, see Franklin (1998)
14 For Lancaster, Ayscough and Caley (1802, 6); For Leicester, *ibid* (6b)
15 Powicke (1961, 342)
16 Hardy (1835[2], 68)
17 Curia Regis Rolls IV (1205–6), 199, 201, 214, 219, 267
18 Royal seal on proceedings in Hardy (1833, 106b)
19 Hardy (1837, 141–75)
20 Rylatt, Soden and Dickinson (1992)
21 Ranulf was witnessing royal documents throughout; for the Channel Islands see Hardy (1835[2], 68)
22 Hardy (1833, 84)
23 Hardy (1833, 74b, 84)
24 Farrer (1902) after Hardy (1835[3], 81)
25 Barraclough (1988, 284). Alexander (1983, 57) states that he later became Ranulf's chancellor
26 Hardy (1885, 15)
27 *Ibid*
28 Barraclough (1988, 355)

Chapter 6: Wales, France and the right of kings (1209–1215)

1 Hardy (1875, 147)
2 Gervase of Canterbury in Stubbs (1879, 106)
3 *Ibid*
4 Barraclough (1988, 280 for instance)
5 Bridges (1812 VIII, 41–2); Coyd and Stenton (1950) for the grant of power over the circus folk of Cheshire (*magistratum omnium leccatorum et meretricum totius Cesterskirae*), later passed by the de Lacy's to the Dutton family
6 Sweetman (1875, 439); Hardy (1833, 122b)
7 Farrer (1902) lists the military preparations
8 Stephenson (1875, 408)
9 Roger of Wendover in Howlett (1889)
10 Hardy (1835[2], 98)
11 *Ibid*, (100)
12 Hardy (1833, 147)
13 *Ibid* (163)
14 Rothwell (1975, 307); Cheney and Semple (1953, no 67)
15 Ranulf witnessing John's charters 1213–14 in Hardy (1837, 191–5)
16 For Dieulacres see VCH Staffs III and Fischer (1967)

17 Matthew Paris in Madden (1866, 231)
18 Thompson (1895, 211). Probably in relation to his attempts with unseemly haste to marry his son to the ravishing Ela, Countess of Salisbury *c.* 1225 when rumours spread of her husband's death at sea returning from Gascony. Although shipwrecked on the Ile de Ré, he was in hiding and returned in an epic journey of many months. Ironically he had previously shown great kindness to the Earl of Salisbury when he was very ill in 1220, who thanked him (Shirley 1862, 135). Salisbury died in 1226
19 John Capgrave in Hingeston (1858, 147), who said John 'put her under the kepyng of foure men, that there shuld be no frute of her wombe,' a policy presumably formed after Arthur's death
20 Warren (1997)
21 For all these places February-September 1214, see Hardy (1837, 196–201)
22 Stapleton (1844, lvi)
23 Hardy (1837, 201–4)
24 Doyle (1886); Stubbs (1879, 109)
25 Thompson (1895)
26 Hardy (1837, 202–13)
27 Rothwell (1975, 324)

Chapter 7: The defence of England (1215–18)

1 The period is covered by Norgate, Warren and Painter. However their perspective is largely royal, not baronial
2 Hardy (1835², 137, 153, 164)
3 Hardy (1833, 251b; 1835², 175, 193)
4 Hardy (1835², 186)
5 Stenton (1940, doc 1181) – '*occasione barbicane site in eadem terra ante porta castri de Bruges*'. It was defended for Ranulf by a Norman knight from the Ouches, Robert de Damville
6 Hardy (1885, 22); for Middleham see Alexander (1983, 33), following Painter
7 Hardy (1833, 251)
8 Hardy (1833, 233b, 241b). Later confirmed in Henry III's minority by the Council (*ibid* 296, 310)
9 Stapleton (1844, lvi); Hardy (1833, 286)
10 The subject of much debate. See, for instance Barraclough (1951), Husain (1973). Party the result of Cheshire's peculiar, often-debated status as almost 'independent' of the crown later on. This is not a debate for this book!
11 Hardy (1833, various)
12 Sweetman (1875, 624)
13 Hardy (1833, 289)
14 1212: Farrer (1902, 435)

15 Stenton (1934, doc 494n)
16 Painter (1933, 259)
17 On her death in 1221, Mauclerc continued to hold Brittany in trust for their young son. When he came of age (1237) Mauclerc retained the lesser title 'Count of Brittany'. The son was Duke Jean I
18 Hardy (1833, 350, 361b)
19 For Durham: Hardy (1837, 219); for Berwick: Farrer (1902, 258)
20 For the Isle of Axholme and Lincolnshire, generally, Stubbs (1872, 231)
21 Luard (1864, I: 62; 1865, IV: 406); Stenton (1934, docs 1151, 1257)
22 Hardy (1833, 280, 282)
23 Meyer (1891–1901, 209–69) for the proceedings of the Council, in Rothwell (1975). It was commissioned and unashamedly written as a panegyric of the Earl Marshall, his part in matters is naturally to the fore. The importance of this document cannot however be overstated
24 The Waverley Annalist alone states that Ranulf was actually present throughout (Luard 1865, II: 287). This is now thought to be a fabrication, its source, here or lost elsewhere, now unknown
25 Meyer (1891–1901), followed by Turner (1904, 1907) and others ever since
26 Alexander (1983, 74)
27 Dryden (1927)
28 Matthew Paris in Madden (1866, 206ff)
29 Nichols (1800, 85–6); Dryden (1927, opposite 124)
30 Meyer (1891–1901, III)
31 Most chroniclers recount the battle of Lincoln, such as Wendover (Howlett 1889, II: 208). The finest account is that of the Earl Marshall's eulogist, translated by Meyer (1891–1901, lines 16203 ff). This includes Ranulf's posturing to lead the attack, which is made to sound petulant, possibly because he had had to quit Mountsorrel rather ignominiously and been criticised by an annoyed Earl Marshall
32 Hardy (1833, 355)
33 Burton Annals in Luard (1864, I: 224)
34 Hardy (1833, 361b)
35 The letter preserved in Shirley (1862, 532)
36 Stenton (1937, xxxiii; docs 315, 1133)
37 *Ibid* (34)
38 Granted 6 May 1218; joint administration from 25 January 1218 (Hardy 1833, 350)
39 Wendover, in Howlett (1889, II: 227)

Chapter 8: Damietta (1218–20)

1 The Dieulacres Chronicle wrongly states that Ranulf accompanied Richard I on the Third Crusade in 1190 and enjoyed similar adventures. Most now accept this as fabrication, although Stubbs (1902, xxxii) seemed to believe it

2 Hardy (1885, 23)
3 Luard (1864–5, II: 289)
4 Tyerman (1988, 202); this was partly in recompense for his outlay in holding so many of the King's castles through the civil war (Dryburgh and Hartland 2008, 18, doc 69)
5 For Ranulf's departure, Chester Annals in Christie (1887); for Jocius, Coss (1986, 21)
6 The list of principal English participants is given by Matthew Paris in Luard (1876, 40–41). Other details are given by Oliver of Paderborn and Roger of Wendover (Oliverus [transl Gavigan, 1980]; Howlett 1889). Oliver of Paderborn is the principal source for the siege of Damietta, which he relates in detail, his work being largely written during the campaign. Arguably the best secondary source remains Runciman (1966) but the reader is also pointed to Van Cleve (1969) and Tyerman (1988)
7 Thompson (1895, 211)
8 Joinville in Johnes 1848 (1807 translation); see also Evans 1938
9 '*L'estoire de Eracles empereur*' in Eales (2004, 58)
10 Hoveden in Stubbs (1870)
11 See note 6 for this Chapter, above. Hereafter simply called Oliver
12 Oliver (Ch 12)
13 *Ibid* (Ch 13–14)
14 Their arrivals were separate (Van Cleve 1969, 402)
15 'Outremer' – over the sea, ie the Holy Land; Oliver lists many (Ch 16)
16 Jacques de Vitry, letters
17 The flooding is narrated by Matthew Paris in Luard (1876, 41–2) and by Oliver (Ch 19)
18 Oliver (Ch 20)
19 Oliver's translator, Gavigan (32, and Ch 20, n1)
20 Oliver (Ch 22)
21 *Ibid* (Ch 23)
22 *Ibid* (Ch 25)
23 *Ibid* (Ch 26)
24 *Ibid* (Ch 27)
25 *Ibid* (Ch 28). His brevity is all the more astounding since he is normally given to a verbose style. This was a real setback, best glossed over at the time
26 *Op cit* (Ch 29)
27 *Ibid*
28 Joinville in Johnes 1848 (1807 translation); see also, for instance Evans (1938, 66), but whose translation now (or even then) reads as very anachronistic
29 *Ibid*
30 For Hulton, Browne in Klemperer (2004, 133–4); for Coventry, Soden (2005, 137–8 and fig 45) and Anderson in Rylatt and Mason (2003, 130–5)
31 Oliver (Ch 29); Matthew Paris in Luard (1876, 49)

32 Van Cleve (1969, 414)
33 His audience is the subject of many medieval and later depictions, not least across France. My thanks to Brother Ninian Arbuckle, OFM, from the Franciscan International Study Centre, Canterbury for his help in this. For the whole incident see Armstrong *et al* (2000), which draws on the two main sources, Thomas of Celano (*Life of St Francis*) and St Bonaventure (*The major legend of St Francis*)
34 Ranulf began the foundation of a Franciscan Friary at Coventry in 1232, next to his manor house of Cheylesmore. The foundation was completed by the de Montalts. By then, although never a priest in life, Francis was already a Saint
35 Oliver (Ch 30)
36 *Ibid* (Ch 31)
37 *Op cit* (Ch 37–8)
38 Walter of Coventry in Stubbs (1873, 240)
39 Oliver (Ch 39)
40 *Ibid* (Ch 39–40)
41 *Op cit* (Ch 42)
42 *Op cit* (Ch 45)
43 Luard (1876, 56)
44 Farrer (1924, 396–7. One has to presume that David's death on the same day as the Earl Marshall's was a coincidence, although the shock of losing bulwarks against Wales and Scotland on the same day must be viewed with suspicion. In both cases Hubert de Burgh stood to gain as he was angling to marry Margaret, David's sister (and that of the Scottish King) and his English lands bordered both Wales and the Earl Marshall's. The marriage went ahead
45 William's own words are preserved in a letter to de Burgh in Shirley (1862, 135)
46 Dunstable Annalist in Luard (1864, III: 55)
47 Various mentions of his returning companions, such as in Luard (1864, 60)
48 For instance Matthew Paris in Luard (1876, 56)
49 Fischer (1967)
50 Farrer (1924, III: 13)
51 For the date, Dunstable Annalist in Luard (1864, III: 60)
52 Chester Annals in Christie (1887)

Chapter 9: A question of castles (1220–24)

1 Painter (1933) records the Earl Marshall's last days in tear-jerking detail. For the original, see Meyer (1891–1901, III)
2 Hardy (1833[1], 431b)
3 *Ibid* (1833[1], 596b)
4 *Op cit* (1833[1], 430ff)
5 *Op cit* (464)

6 *Op cit* (465)
7 *Op cit* (561)
8 For lawsuits, Curia Regis Rolls (10:1221–2; 11: 1223–4). Earlier suits had been brought but adjourned since, as his attorneys stated, Ranulf was still in Damietta '*quia dominus comes est in servicio dei in terra Jerusalemitana*' (8: 1219–20, 238; doc 315)
9 See for instance Coggeshall in Stephenson (1875, 188)
10 He had received his lands no earlier than November 1214, so with the Civil War, had had precious little time to do anything with them, good or bad. See Turner (1907)
11 *Ibid.* Tournaments were considered prime places for fomenting unrest
12 Wendover in Howlett (1889, 65)
13 Shirley (1862, 121)
14 Farrer (1924, 396–7)
15 Hardy (1885, 26)
16 Coggeshall in Stephenson (1875, 188)
17 Wendover (Howlett 1889, IV) in Norgate (1912); Matthew Paris in Madden (1866, 243–4)
18 Wendover in Howlett (1889, II: 255)
19 See Denholm-Young (1945) for a full discussion of the letter
20 Norgate (1912, 165); also Turner (1907)
21 Hardy (1833, 475)
22 Coggeshall in Stephenson (1875, 188)
23 Hardy (1833, 492, 531)
24 *Ibid* (626)
25 Hardy (1885)
26 Hardy (1833, 470, 520b)
27 *Ibid* (531)
28 Christie (1887)
29 *Ibid*
30 Hardy (1833, II: 52)
31 Wendover in Howlett (1889, IV, 75)
32 Shirley (1862, 249)
33 Norgate (1912); Coggeshall in Stephenson (1875, 203)
34 Partly beacuase his own brother Archdeacon Simon was embroiled up to his neck (Denholm-Young 1945)
35 Dunstable Annalist in Luard (1864, 82)
36 For Ranulf as Baron of the Exchequer, see Curia Regis Rolls (11: 1223–4, doc 1107)
37 Shirley (1862)
38 Calendar of Patent Rolls I, 481–2; Norgate (1912)
39 Matthew Paris in Luard (1876, 82–3) for this whole episode
40 Matthew Paris in Madden (1866, 260)
41 Shirley (1862); Norgate (1912); Coggeshall in Stephenson (1875)
42 Norgate (1912, 216)
43 Ayscough and Caley (1802, 13)

44 Shirley (1862, 233)
45 Baldwin (1913, 21)
46 Hardy (1833, II: 10b)
47 Shirley (1862)
48 Ayscough and Caley (1802, 22b)
49 The epithet coined by Matthew Paris. For de Bréauté's hopelessness see Matthew Paris in Madden (1866, 265)
50 Shirley (1862, 233)
51 Tout (1920, 234)

Chapter 10: Time to build (1224–9)

1 Baldwin (1913, 20)
2 *Ibid* (21)
3 At a muster called by the King (Hardy 1833, II: 31)
4 Dunstable Annalist in Luard (1864, 82)
5 Sweetman (1875, docs 1015, 1110, 1372–3); Hardy (1833, 527b)
6 For the tax see Chistie (1887); Also Higden in Lumby (1876)
7 For the castles, Keen in Ellis (1993, 94); Thompson (1991, 104–5); Soden (1998); for Bugbrooke, Henry de Bray writing in the 1330s, for which see Willis (1916, 20)
8 Hardy (1833, II: 21b)
9 *Ibid* (110b)
10 Hardy (1885, 32)
11 Hardy (1833, II: 123)
12 Savage (1924, 179; doc 360)
13 Barraclough (1988, 415–7; doc 421)
14 Matthew Paris in Madden (1866, 296)
15 For funds: Liberate Rolls Henry III; for muster: Hardy (1833, II: 211); for Llewellyn's peace: Dunstable Annalist in Luard (1864, III: 100)
16 For Chester: Barraclough (1951, 50); Royal progress halts: Hardy (1885, 30)
17 Maddicott (1994, 8); Fox (1939)
18 Ranulf was also receiving gifts from the Treasury; see for instance Devon (1837, 6)
19 Matthew Paris in Luard (1876, 189)

Chapter 11: Back home (1229–32)

1 Johnes (1848; 1807 transl) from Joinville; see also Evans (1938, 22–3).
2 Shirley (1862, 356; no 295); the nationwide summons lists all the knights by name in Critchley (1971, 88–95) from National Archives: Scutage C72/2 m12, but who turned up is not recorded. Others may have joined in the 8–10 months before the expedition finally set sail. Many had their debts cancelled as an inducement to serve overseas, such as John de Lacy.

However, even at the last moment, others chose to pay a fine and join up later on (National Archives: Fine Rolls C60/29 m6 etc)

3 Sweetman (1875, docs 1801, 1812)

4 The army's itinerary is laid out in the royal letters volume by Shirley (1862, I: nos 301ff). It is in accord with Matthew Paris who relates the campaign but in less detail. The letter in question is from Richard, Earl of Cornwall (the King's brother) to the Bishop of Carlisle

5 Tout (1920, 198)

6 Walker (1972, 483)

7 Matthew Paris in Madden 91866, 327); French sources follow Matthew Paris

8 Hardy (1885, III: 34)

9 Wendover in Howlett (1889, III:8); Matthew Paris in Madden (1866, 327)

10 Walker (1972, 482); On the day of Gloucester's death in the Touraine the King was in St-Pol de Leon, Brittany, about to embark for England. News of his death reached the court at Westminster on or before 6 November – 13 days (National Archives ref MSS book: The Itinerary of Henry III; 942.034 PRO). Other baronial casualties can be gleaned from contemporary national archives of early November as the lands of the deceased devolved quickly to the crown pending hearings on the age and fitness of the heirs (National Archives: Fine Rolls C60/29)

11 Opera cit (1889, III: 6; 1866, 327)

12 Madicott (1994, 352)

13 Caley and Lemon (1803; for 1236)

14 For Simon's dealings with Ranulf see Madicott (1994). Many of Ranulf's *familiares* seem to have attached themselves to Simon after 1232

15 Caley and Lemon (1803, 36; for 1227)

16 Carpenter (1976, 12)

17 Caley and Lemon (1803; for 1227)

18 Lancaster (forthcoming; prepared for publication by Peter and Angela Coss). Original in National Archives (E164/21, 59b.4, 76b.1, 76b.2). The Barbe d'Averil family remained prominent members of society at St Sauveur-le-Vicomte well into the modern period. Different branches had clearly held on to both camps from 1204

19 Wendover in Howlett (1889, III, 8); Matthew Paris in Madden (1866, 327)

20 Matthew Paris in Madden (1866, 333)

21 *Ibid*; also Ménard (1899, 36), citing French sources ('to the feast of St John the Baptist, 1234'). The French sources accord with Matthew Paris

22 Barraclough saw Ranulf transferring the earldom of Lincoln at this point. A charter of the first half of 1232 makes provisions for his body in the event of his death (Barraclough 1988, 392; doc 386)

23 Later part of the settlement of his will (Cal Close Rolls 12 January 1233)

24 Matthew Paris in Madden (1866, 333); for Ranulf witnessing the gift of Wallingford, Hedges (1881, 303)

25 See Eales (1986); otherwise, the King and Hubert were taking a lot of land into royal hands (Fine Rolls Henry III C60/30)
26 For economic sanctions against Wales, see Walker (1972, 489)
27 Sweetman (1875, docs 1801, 1930)
28 Matthew Paris in Luard (1876, 231)
29 For Ranulf's refusal see Paris in Madden (1866, 339)
30 Barraclough (1988, 310; doc 310); Cal Patent Rolls (1225–32, 473)
31 *Ibid* (1988, 392; doc 386)
32 See Farrer (1924) for the simplest formula for dividing the inheritance
33 National Archives (DL25/49)
34 Barraclough (1988, 310; doc 310)
35 Caley and Lemon (1803, 169); There has been disagreement over 25 or 26 as the date of his death. The Fine Rolls suggest he died on 26 October, surely corroborated by Henry III's sudden departure on that day from Reading to Wallingford. (Itinerary of Henry III: National Archives MSS book 942.034 PRO)
36 Audley was now Sheriff of Shropshire and Staffordshire for life; Seagrave was Chancellor and Sheriff of Bedfordshire, Buckinghamshire, Northamptonshire, Warwickshire, and Leicestershire. Their financial dealings were key to the smooth handover of Ranulf's dominions to his beneficiaries
37 Barraclough (1988, 393; doc 387)
38 Thomas Wykes in Luard (1865, IV:73)
39 Burton Annalist in Luard (1864, I:87)
40 Chester annals in Christie (1887)
41 For very lengthy discussions of the legacy and its dispersal from 1237, see for instance Stewart-Brown (1920) or Farrer (1924); more recently Eales (1986)
42 These are a small selection. As previously see commentators in note 41
43 For de Audley, Greenslade (1970, 235); for Agnes de Boscherville, Coss (1986, 390 doc 768 fol 111b); for Clemence, Caley and Lemon (1803, 20, 70)
44 Matthew Paris in Luard (1876, 227–8); Coggeshall in Stephenson (1875, 203)
45 Hubert's demise and personal magnanimity to Ranulf's memory is related by Matthew Paris in Luard (1876, 229–30). Also in Madden (1866, 347). However, as a monk of Hubert's own monastery at St Albans, he would see every benefit for Hubert's soul in ascribing him a generosity of spirit which may not have been quite so effusive
46 For the French, Ménard (1899, 36 n3 – 37n)
47 The armour is noted in the Patent Rolls 12 January 1233
48 Dunstable Annalist in Luard (1864, III: 132)
49 Johnes (1807 Translation) from Joinville; see also Evans (1938, 70–71)
50 A letter of the 1227 betrothal of his daughter to Louis' brother, Jean; text of the Peace Treaty of Paris, December 1234; Henry III's letter to Pope Gregory IX, 25 February 1235, all in Ménard (1899, 420–23)
51 Cheshire Sheaf 52 (1957), 24; Alexander (1983, 100)

Chapter 12: Overview

1 Shirley (1862, 242) '*Reverendus dominus et amicus, Ranulphus*'
2 Luard (1876, 40, 56) '*illustris; nobilis*'
3 Luard (1864, III, 82) '*Familiaris et amicus*'
4 *Ibid*, (55) '*tota ecclesia praedicat extollit comitis Cestriae probitatem*'
5 Stubbs (1873, II) '*primus in exercitu*'
6 Stubbs (1879, II 109) '*venerabilis et illustris vir: comes Cestriae*'
7 Hardy (1835[2], 29, 30, 71) '*Dilectus et fidelis noster Ranulfus Comes Cestriae*' (8/5/1203, 31/5/1203 and 1207/8 etc)
8 *Ibid* (1835[2], 7, 28) '*R/Ranulfus Comes/Com Cestriae*' (23/9/1199 and 14/4/1203)
9 Baldwin (1913, 20) '*familiaris*'
10 As n3, above
11 Shirley (1862, 532) '*nobilis vir*'
12 Luard (1865, IV, 73) '*vir magni consilii, et in bellicis rebus strenuus*'
13 Johnson [ed Fellows] (1596, 112)
14 Such as Eales (2004, 59) as the latest in a line
15 Stubbs (1902, 450)
16 *Ibid* (210); also see Alexander (1983, 4). For the silence of his business as Duke, see Everard (2000, 150)
17 Related by Alexander (1983, 7–8)
18 Stubbs (1883, 47)
19 Such as Powicke
20 Labarge (1962)
21 Holt (1961, 242)
22 Painter (1933, 227, 259)
23 Alexander (1983, 9, 12)
24 *Ibid* (70)
25 Powicke (1908)
26 See Appendices for Ranulf's monastic benefaction
27 See n 22 and 23, above
28 Hardy (1833, 350)

APPENDIX A

RANULF'S CASTLES

Ranulf came of age in 1189, inheriting his family's existing castles by virtue of hereditary titles and responsibilities as Earl of Chester, Viscount of Bayeux, Viscount of Avranches, Viscount of the Vau-de-Vire, Baron of St Sauveur-le-Vicomte, Baron of St Sever. He also held 138 manors at his death, listed by Farrer (1924).

All English and Welsh castle sites are related to their modern counties or unitary authorities. French sites are related to their modern *Départments*.

England

Chester, Cheshire (1189–1232; de Lacy hereditary garrison)
Beeston, Cheshire (commenced building 1225–1232, incomplete at Ranulf's death), replacing a nearby motte and bailey
Chartley, Staffordshire (1189-[commenced rebuilding 1225]–1232)
Bolingbroke, Lincolnshire (1198-[commenced rebuilding 1225]–1232)
Coventry, Warwickshire (1189–1232 but partly ruinous since 1174; replaced as residence by a new Manor House at nearby Cheylesmore)
Oversleyford, Cheshire (Masci hereditary garrison)
Pulford, Cheshire (Pulford hereditary garrison)
The Peak, Derbyshire (by gift of John, August 1215–1224)
Lancaster, Lancashire (by gift of John, January 1216–1224)
Richmond, NorthYorkshire (by gift of John, June 1216–1218)
Newcastle-under-Lyme, Staffordshire (by gift of John, 1214–1224)
Bridgenorth, Shropshire (by gift of John, 1216–1224) Ranulf built a new barbican there
Mountsorrel, Leicestershire (1217)

Wallingford, Berkshire (now Oxfordshire) (1217–1224) Ranulf may have been behind the new castle hall, built *c.* 1220
Fotheringhay, Northamptonshire (at behest of Henry III, 1221–2)
Shrewsbury, Shropshire (by gift of John 1216–1224)
West Derby, Lancashire (by gift of John 1216–1232)

Wales (but considered at the time to be part of the honour of Chester)

Degannwy, Conwy
Trefynnon, Holywell, Flintshire
Wrexham, Wrexham
Twt Hill, Rhuddlan, Denbighshire
Hoseley, Wrexham
Prestatyn, Denbighshire
Hawarden, Flintshire (de Montalt hereditary garrison)
Mold, Flintshire (de Montalt hereditary garrison)

Normandy

St-James-de-Beuvron, Manche (1189–1204, 1214 (1230)–32)
St Sauveur-le-Vicomte, Manche (1189–1204 Barbe d'Averil hereditary garrison)
Briquessart, Calvados (1189–1204)
Vire, Calvados (1189–1204)
Barfleur, Manche
Avranches, Manche (by gift of John, 1203–4)
St Pierre de Semilly, Manche (by wedding gift of John, Sept 1199–1204)

Castles and towns besieged and taken by Ranulf in sole or senior command

Nottingham, Nottinghamshire 1194
Dol-de-Bretagne, Ille-et-Vilaine 1203
Tours, Indre-et-Loire 1203
Le Mans, Sarthe 1203
La Suze, Sarthe 1204
Miléçu, Charente-Maritime 1214
Mervant, Vendée 1214
Vouvant, Vendée 1214
Nantes, Loire-Atlantique 1214
Richmond, Yorkshire 1216
Middleham, Yorkshire 1216

Worcester, Worcestershire 1216
Lincoln, Lincolnshire 1217
Damietta, Egypt 1218–9
Vitré, Ille-et-Vilaine 1230 (siege proposed but probably not invested)
Mirebeau,Vienne 1230
Châteauneuf-sur-Sarthe, Maine-et-Loire 1230–31
Château Gontier, Mayenne 1230–31
Pontorson, Manche 1231

Sieges by Ranulf relieved before they were successful

Roche-aux-Moines 1214
Mountsorrel 1217
Verdun 1230

Sieges involving Ranulf ended by negotiation

Windsor 1193
St Aubin-du-Cormier 1231

Castle-defence in which Ranulf was involved (whether Ranulf was present or not)

Château Gaillard (L'Ile d'Andelys or Ile de Château – the Island fortress; probably garrison rotation) 1196–7
Verneuil 1199 (probably garrison rotation)
Twt Hill, Rhuddlan, Gwent 1210 (relieved)
Fotheringhay 1222 (lost) – Ranulf not present
Athlit Castle (AKA The Pilgrim's Castle), Palestine 1220 (Ranulf helped fund the construction by the Knights Templar – he is not known to have visited but discussed the castle while at Damietta)

Ranulf's known hunting parks

Darnhall, Cheshire
Cheylesmore, Coventry, Warwickshire
Caludon, Coventry, Warwickshire
Barrow-on-Soar, Leicestershire
Trevières, near Bayeux, Calvados, Normandy

APPENDIX B

RANULF'S MONASTIC BENEFACTION

All English and Welsh sites are related to their modern counties or unitary authorities. French sites are related to their modern *Départments*.

New foundations by Ranulf

St Giles Leper Hospital, Boughton, Chester (Augustinian) *c.* 1181 or later
St John the Baptist's Hospital, Chester (Augustinian) 1190s
Dieulacres Abbey, Staffordshire (Cistercian) 1214
Coventry Franciscan Friary (Order of Friars Minor) 1232

Hereditary or new personal benefaction

England:

Benedictine
Chester Abbey, Cheshire
St Mary's Nunnery, Chester, Cheshire
Clerkenwell Nunnery, Middlesex
Coventry Cathedral Priory, Warwickshire
Spalding Priory, Lincolnshire
Minting Priory, Lincolnshire
Westwood Nunnery, Worcestershire
Polesworth Nunnery, Warwickshire
Shrewsbury Abbey, Shropshire
Bardney Abbey, Lincolnshire
Birkenhead Priory, Lancashire
Long Bennington Priory, Lincolnshire

Augustinian (Hospitals nominally followed the Augustinian Rule)
Spon Leper Hospital, Coventry, Warwickshire
Trentham Priory, Staffordshire
Rocester Abbey, Staffordshire
Wellow Priory, Lincolnshire
Kenilworth Abbey, Warwickshire
Lincoln Leper Hospital, Lincolnshire
Norton Priory, Wirral
Repton Priory, Derbyshire
Cistercian
Combermere Abbey, Staffordshire
Stanlow Priory, Cheshire – later moved to Whalley, Lancashire
Greenfield Nunnery, Lincolnshire
Basingwerk Abbey, Flintshire
Bordesley Abbey, Warwickshire
Revesby Priory, Lincolnshire

Knights Hospitaller
Maltby Priory, Lincolnshire

Normandy:

Benedictine
Abbaye de Mont St Michel, Manche
Abbaye Cathédrale de Bayeux, Calvados
Abbaye de St Sever, Calvados

Augustinian
Abbaye de Ste Marie, Montmorel, Manche

Premonstratensian
Abbaye de Ste Marie, Ardenne, Caen, Calvados

Cistercian
Abbaye de Ste Marie, Savigny, Manche
Abbaye Ste Marie, Aunay, Calvados

Egypt:

Church of St Edmund the Martyr, Damietta (re-consecrated mosque)
Church of St Thomas à Beckett, Damietta (re-consecrated mosque)

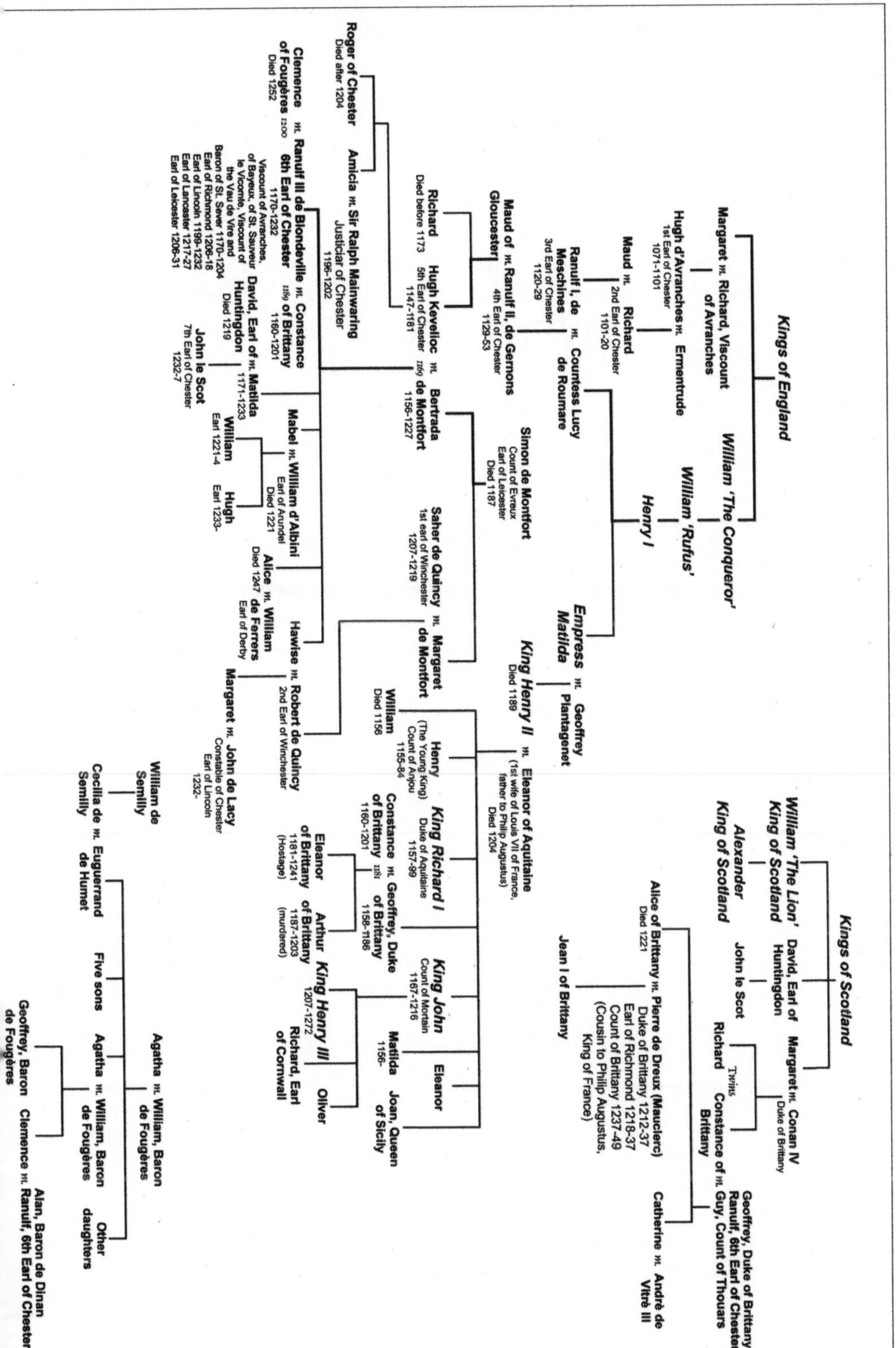

ppendix c. Ranulf's family tree

BIBLIOGRAPHY

Alcock, L. 1967 Excavations at Degannwy Castle, Caernarvonshire, 1961–6, *Archaeol. J.* 124, 190–201

Alexander, J.W. 1970 new evidence on the Palatinate of Chester, *English Historical Review* 85 (no 377, Oct 1970) 715–29

Alexander, J.W. 1983 *Ranulf of Chester, a relic of the Conquest*, Athens University, Georgia Press

Anderson, T. 2003 'The human bone' in M. Rylatt and P. Mason (2003, 130–5)

Armstrong, R., Hellman, J., Wayne A., and Short, W.J. 2000 *Francis of Assisi: early documents*, New York

Ayscough, Rev S. and Caley, J. (ed) 1802 *Calendarium Rotulorum Patientium in Turri Londinensi*, Records Commission

Baldwin, J.F. 1913 *The king's council in the middle ages*, Oxford University Press

Barraclough, G. 1951 'The Earldom and County Palatine of Chester', *Trans Hist Soc Lancs Cheshire* 103, 23–57

Barraclough, G. 1957 'The Annals of Dieulacres Abbey', *Cheshire Sheaf 3rd Series* 52

Barraclough, G. 1988 *The charters of the Anglo-Norman Earls of Chester, 1071–1237*, Rec Soc Lancs Cheshire 126, 205–438

Bateson, M. 1899 *Records of the Borough of Leicester; I: 1103–1327*

Berger, E. 1893 'Les Préparatifs d'une invasion anglaise et la déscente de Henry III en Bretagne', *Bibliotheque de l'école des Chartres* 54, 5–44

Boyd, D. 2004 *Eleanor, April Queen of Aquitaine*

Bradbury, J. 1992 *The medieval siege*, Woodbridge; Boydell Press

Bridges, E. 1812 *Collins's Peerage of England* (9 vols)

Brown, M. 2004 *The wars of Scotland*, Edinburgh University Press

Browne, S. 2004 'The burials' in W.D. Klemperer and N. Boothroyd, 2004 *Excavations at Hulton Abbey, Staffordshire, 1987–1994*, Soc. Medieval Archaeol. Monograph 21, 115–34

Caley, J. and Lemon, R. (ed) 1803 *Calendarum Rotulorum Chartarum et Inquisitions Ad Quod Damnum*, Records Commission

Carpenter, D.A. 1976 The decline of the curial sherifff in England 1194–1258, *English Historical Review* 91, (no 358, January 1976), 1–32

Cheney, C.R. and Semple, W.H. (ed) 1953 *Selected letters of Pope Innocent III concerning England (1198–1216)*

Christie, R.C. 1887 *Annales Cestriensis: Chronicle of the Abbey of St Werburgh at Chester*, Lancs Cheshire Rec Soc Trans (1886) 14

Coss, P., 1986 *The early records of medieval Coventry*

Coyd, L.C. and Stenton, D.M. 1950 *Sir Christopher Hatton's Book of Seals*, Northants Rec. Soc. XV (Trans for 1942)

Critchley, J.S. 1971 Summonses to military service in the reign of Henry III, *English Historical Review* 86 (no 338, January 1971), 79–95

Cronne, H.A. 1937 'Ranulf de Gernons, Earl of Chester 1129–53', *Trans Royal Hist Soc (4th Series)* 20, 103–34

Darlington, R.R. 1968 The Worcester Cathedral Priory Cartulary, *Pipe Roll Society* 38 (1962–3)

Delaborde, M. 1882 *Oeuvres de Rigord et de Guillaume le Breton*, Paris; Société de l'Histoire de France

DeLisle, M. 1867 *Histoire du château et des sires de Saint-Sauveur-le-Vicomte*, Valognes

Denholm-Young, N. 1945 'A letter from the Council to Pope Honorius III 1220–21', *English Historical Review* 60, 88–96

Denholm-Young, N. 1947 *Richard of Cornwall*, Oxford

Dimock, J.F. (ed) 1864 *Magna vita S Hugonis Episcopi Lincolniensis*, Rolls Series

Dimock, J.F. (ed) 1877 *Opera Giraldi Cambrensis; VI*, Rolls Series

Douglas, D. 1946 'The earliest Norman Counts', *English Historical Review* 61, 129–56

Doyle, J.E. 1886 *The official baronage of England; I*

Dryburgh, P. and Hartland, B (ed) 2007 *Calendar of the Fine Rolls of the reign of Henry III preserved in the National Archives; I: 1–8 Henry III, 1216–1224*, Boydell/National Archives

Dryden, A. 1927 *Memorials of old Leicestershire*

Duby, G. 1984 *Guillaume le Marechal, ou le meilleur chevalier du monde*, Fayard

Eales, R. 1986 'Henry III and the end of the Norman Earldom of Chester' in P.R. Coss and S.D. Lloyd (ed) 1986–92 *Thirteenth-century England: proceedings of the Newcastle-upon-Tyne Conference*, 4 vols; I, 100–113

Eales, R. 2004 'Ranulf III' *Dictionary of National Biography*, Vol 46, 56–9, Oxford
Evans, J.(Transl) 1938 *The History of St Louis by Jean, Sire de Joinville*, Oxford University Press
Everard, J.A. 2000 *Brittany and the Angevins: province and empire 1158–1203*, Cambridge studies in medieval life and thought 48, Cambridge University Press
Farrer, W. 1902 *The Lancashire Pipe Rolls and early Lancashire charters*
Farrer, W. 1924 *Honours and Knight's Fees; II: Chester and Huntingdon*
Fisher, M.J.C. 1967 *Dieulacres Abbey*, MA thesis, Keele University
Fox, L. 1939 'The Honour and Earldom of Leicester: origin and descent 1066–1399', *English Historical Review* 54 (July 1939) 384–402
Franklin, M.J. 1998 *English Episcopal Acta*; 17: Coventry and Lichfield 1183–1208, British Academy: Oxford
Fretton, W.G. 1879 'Memorials of the Franciscans', *Transactions of the Birmingham and Warwickshire Archaeological Society*
Gillingham, J. 1989 *Richard the Lionheart* (2nd ed), London
Glover, J. 1865 *Le livere de reis de Britannie e le livere de reis de Engleterre*, Rolls Series
Greenslade, M.W. 1970 *Victoria County History of Staffordshire; III: The religious houses*
Hardy, T.D. (ed) 1833 *Rotuli Litterarum Clausarum in Turri Londinensi*; Vol 1: 1204–27 & Vol 2 (1844): 1227–3., Records Commission
Hardy, T.D. (ed) 1835[1] *Rotuli Normanniae in turri Londinensi asservati Johanne et Henrico Quinto Angliae regibus; I:1200–1205 and 1417*, Records Commission
Hardy, T.D. (ed) 1835[2] *Rotuli Litterarum Patientium in Turri Londinensi asservati; I (i): 1201–16*, Records Commission
Hardy, T.D. (ed) 1835[3] *Rotuli de oblatis et finibus in turri Londinensi asservati tempore regis Johannis*, Records Commission
Hardy, T.D. (ed) 1837 *Rotuli Chartarum in turri Londinensi asservati; I (i) 1199–1216*, Records Commission
Hardy, T.D. (ed) 1875 *Liberate Rolls: John*, Rolls Series
Hardy, T.D. (ed) 1885 *Rymer's Foedera;* I: (1066–1377), III: Appendix & Index, Records Commission
Harris, B.E. 1975 Ranulf III, Earl of Chester, *J. Chester Archaeol. Soc.* 58, 99–114
Harris, B.E. (ed) 1980 The *Victoria County History of the County of Chester*; III
Harvey, P.D.A. and McGuinness, A. 1996 *A Guide to British Medieval Seals*, British Library and Public Record Office
Hedges, J.K. 1881 *A history of Wallingford*, 2 vols
Heslop, T.A. 1991 The seals of the 12th-century Earls of Chester, *J Chester Archaeol. Soc* 71

Hingeston, F.C. (ed) 1858 *Chronicle of England by John Capgrave*, Rolls Series

Holt, J.C. 1961 *The northerners: a study in the reign of King John*, Oxford

Howlett, H.G. (ed) 1889 *Flores Historiarum Rogeri Wendover*, Rolls Series

Husain, B.M.C. 1973 *Cheshire under the Norman Earls 1066–1237*, Chester

Johnes T., (1807 Transl of Joinville) in Anon, 1848 'Memoirs of Louis IX, King of France, commonly called St Louis', in *Chronicles of the Crusades*, Bohn's Historical Library; London

Johnson, R. 1596 *The seven champions of Christendom*, (ed J.Fellows)

Jolliffe, J.E.A. 1937 *The constitutional history of medieval England*

Jones, M. 1981 'The defence of medieval Brittany: a survey of the establishment of fortified towns, castles and frontiers from the Gallo-Roman period to the end of the middle ages', *Archaeol. J.* 138, 149–204

Keen, L. 1993 'The castle: history and structure' in Ellis, P. 1993 *Beeston Castle, Cheshire: Excavations by Laurence Keen and Peter Ellis 1968–85*, English Heritage Archaeological Report 23

Kettle, A.J. 'Religious Houses', in Harris (1980), 124–87

Labarge, M. Wade 1962 *Simon de Montfort*, London

Lancaster, J.C. (forthcoming) *Coventry Priory Register* (Edition of NA E164/21, prepared for publication by Peter and Angela Coss)

Landon, L. 1935 The itinerary of King Richard I, *Pipe Roll Society* 51 (New series 13)

Luard, H.R. 1864–5 (ed) *Annales Monastici; I: Margan, Tewkesbury, Burton; II: Winchester, Waverley; III: Dunstable, Bermondsey; IV: Oseney, Thom. Wykes, Worcester*, Rolls Series

Luard, H.R. (ed) 1876 *Matthaei Parisi Chronica Maiora*, Rolls Series

Luard, H.R. (ed) 1890 *Flores Historiarum*, Rolls Series

Lumby, Rev J.R. (ed) 1876 *Polychronicon Ranulfi Higden, monachi Cestrensis*, Rolls Series

Madden, F. (ed) 1866 *Matthaei Parisiensis, monachi Sancti Albani, Historia Anglorum (Historia Minor)*; II: 1189–1245

Maddicott, J.R. 1994 *Simon de Montfort*, Cambridge UP

McLynn, F. 2006 *Lionheart and Lackland: King Richard, King John and the wars of conquest*, Jonathan Cape; London

Menard, V. 1897 *Histoire, réligieuse civile et militaire de Saint-James de Beuvron*, Réimpression 2002; Luneray

Meyer, M.P. (ed) 1891–1901 *L'histoire de Guillaume le Maréchal*, 3 vols

Michel, F. (ed) 1840 *Histoire des ducs de Normandie et des rois d'Angleterre*, Paris; Société de l'Histoire de France

Nichols, J. 1800 *The history and antiquities of the county of Leicester; III, part I*, 85–6 (1971 ed)
Norgate, K. 1902 *John Lackland*, London
Norgate, K. 1912 *The minority of Henry III*, London
Norgate, K. 1924 *Richard the Lionheart*, London
Oliverus, Bishop of Paderborn (1980) *Historia Damiatina*, University of Pennsylvania (transl J.J. Gavigan 1948; repr 1980)
Page, W. (ed) 1906 *Victoria County History of Lincolnshire; II: The religious houses*
Painter, S. 1933 *William Marshal: knight-errant, baron and regent of England*, Baltimore (repr 1966)
Painter, S. 1937 *The scourge of the clergy: Peter of Dreux, Duke of Brittany*, Baltimore
Painter, S. 1949 *The reign of King John*, Baltimore
Le Patourel, J. 1976 *The Norman Empire*, Oxford UP
Phillimore, W.P.W. (ed) 1912 *Rotuli Hugonis de Welles; I*, Lincs Rec Soc 3
Phillimore, W.P.W. (ed) 1913 *Rotuli Hugonis de Welles; II*, Lincs Rec Soc 6
Powicke, F.M. 1906 'The Angevin administration of Normandy; I' *English Historical Review* 21, 625–49
Powicke, F.M. 1907 'The Angevin administration of Normandy; II' *English Historical Review* 22, 15–42
Powicke, F.M. 1908 'The Chancery during the minority of Henry III', *English Historical Review* 23, 220–35
Powicke, F.M. 1909 'King John and Arthur of Britanny', *English Historical Review* 24, 659–74
Powicke, F.M. 1910 'The pleas of the crown in the Avranchin', *English Historical Review* 25, 710–11
Powicke, F.M. 1961 (2nd ed) *The loss of Normandy 1189–1204: Studies in the history of the Angevin Empire*, Manchester University Press
Rothwell, H. (ed) 1975 *English Historical Documents 1189–1327*, London
Round, J.H. 1898 *Dictionary of National Biography*, 729–33
Round, J.H. 1899 *Calendar of Documents preserved in France, 918–1206*, Records Commission
Runciman, S. 1966 *A history of the Crusades; III: the kingdom of Acre and the later Crusades*, (esp pp150–204), Cambridge University Press
Rylatt, M. & Mason, P. 2003, *The archaeology of the medieval Cathedral and Priory of St Mary, Coventry*, Coventry City Council
Rylatt, M.E., Soden, I. & Dickinson, J.E. 1992 *Excavations at Cheylesmore Manor, Coventry, 1992*, Coventry Museums Archaeology Unit Report
Savage, H.E. 1926 *The Great Register of Lichfield Cathedral, known as Magnum Registrum Album*, William Salt Archaeol Soc transactions for 1924

Seidschleg, B. 1939 *The English participation in the crusades*, Privately printed, Wisconsin

Shirley, W.W. (ed) 1862 *Royal Letters of the reign of Henry III; I: 1216–35*, Rolls Series

Smith, D.M. (ed) 2000 *The Acta of Hugh of Wells, Bishop of Lincoln 1209–1235*, Lincs Rec Soc 88

Soden, I. 1991 *Excavations at the Castle Bakehouse, Coventry, 1991*, Coventry Museums Archaeol. Report

Soden, I. 1998 *Building Recording at Chartley Castle, Staffs 1997*, Northamptonshire Archaeol. Report

Soden, I. 2005 *Coventry: the hidden history*, Tempus: Stroud

Soden, I. (ed.) 2007 *Stafford Castle II: the excavations*, Stafford Borough Council

Stacey, R.C. 1987 *Politics, policy and finance under Henry III, 1216–1245*, Oxford University Press

Stapleton, T. 1840 *Magni Rotuli Scaccarii Normanniae sub Regibus Angliae*; I: 1180, 1195, London: Soc Antiqs

Stapleton, T. 1844 *Magni Rotuli Scaccarii Normanniae sub Regibus Angliae*; II: 1198, 1203, London: Soc Antiqs

Stenton, D.M. (ed) 1926 *The earliest Lincolnshire Assize Rolls 1202–9*, Lincs Rec Soc 22

Stenton, D.M. (ed) 1934 *Rolls of the Justices in Eyre for Lincolnshire 1218–19 and Worcestershire 1221*, Selden Society 53, London

Stenton, D.M. (ed) 1937 *Rolls of the Justices in Eyre for Yorkshire 1218–19*, Selden Society 56, London

Stenton, D.M. 1940 *Rolls of the Justices in Eyre for Warwickshire, Gloucestershire and Staffordshire 1221, 1222*, Selden Society, London

Stephenson, J. (ed) 1875[1] *Gesta Fulconis Filii Warini*, Rolls Series

Stephenson, J. (ed) 1875[2] *Ralph of Coggeshall*, Rolls Series

Stewart-Brown, R. 1920 'The end of the Norman earldom of Chester', *English Historical Review* 35, 26–53

Stubbs, W. (ed) 1864 *Chronicles and memorials of the reign of Richard I; I: Itinerarium peregrinorum et gesta Regis Ricardi auctore, ud videtur, Ricardo Canonico Sanctae Trinitatis Londoniensis*, Rolls Series

Stubbs, W. (ed) 1867 *Gesta Regis Henrici Secundi Benedicti Abbatis. Chronicle of the reigns of Henry II and Richard I 1169–92; II: Benedict of Peterborough*, Rolls Series

Stubbs, W. (ed) 1870 *Chronici Magistri Rogeri de Hovedene*, Rolls Series

Stubbs, W. (ed) 1872 *Walter of Coventry: II*, Rolls Series

Stubbs, W. (ed) 1876 *Radulfi de Diceto decani Lundoniensis Opera Historica: II*, Rolls Series

Stubbs, W. 1879 *Gervase of Canterbury; II*, Rolls Series

Stubbs, W. 1883 *Constitutional History of England; II*

Stubbs, W. 1902 *Historical introductions to the Rolls Series*

Sweetman, H.S. 1875 *Calendar of documents relating to Ireland; 1171–1251*, Rolls Series
Tait, J. 1920 *Cartulary of the Abbey of St Werburgh, Chester*, Chetham Society 79 and 82
Thierry, A. 1861 *History of the conquest of England by the Normans;* II (Transl W. Hazlitt)
Thompson, E.M. 1895 *A history of the Somerset Carthusians*, London
Thompson, M.W. 1991 *The rise of the castle*
Tout, W.F. 1903 'The Fair of Lincoln' *English Historical Review,* 18
Tout, W.F. 1920 *Chapters in Medieval administrative history 1*, Manchester University Press
Turner, G.J. 1904 'The minority of Henry III; Part I', *Trans Royal Hist Soc*, (NS), 18, 245–95
Turner, G.J. 1907 'The minority of Henry III; Part II', *Trans Royal Hist Soc* (3rd series), 1, 205–62
Tyerman, C. 1988 *England and the Crusades 1095–1588*, Chicago University Press
Van Cleeve, T.C. 1969 'The fifth crusade' in R.L Woolf and H.W Hazard (ed) *A history of the Crusades; II: The later crusades 1189–1311*, 377–428 (Gen Editor K.M Setton)
VCH, *The Victoria County History of the Counties of England;* Cheshire: III, Staffs: III, Warks: II,VIII, Lincs II.
Vitry, Jacques de (1219) *Epist.v. Zeitschift für Kirchengeschuchte* XV, 580
Walker, R.F. 1972 Hubert de Burgh and Wales 1218–1232, *English Historical Review* 87 (no 344, July 1972), 465–94
Warren, W.L. 1997 *King John*, (3rd edition) Yale University Press
White, G. 1976 King Stephen, Duke Henry and Ranulf de Gernons, Earl of Chester, *English Historical Review* 91 (no 360, July 1976), 555–65
Willis, D. (ed) 1916 *The estate book of Henry de Bray of Harlestone, Northants (c1289–1340)*, Camden Soc. 3rd Series 27

ACKNOWLEDGEMENTS

Sitting in a warm home at a desk and computer-screen lit by electric light, or relaxing over my notes in welcoming gîtes from Normandy to the Saintonge, I forget so easily the historian and the clerk of the twelfth and thirteenth centuries labouring with stylus and ink on vellum or parchment, straining to see by the light of a small writing-cell window or the flicker of a candle. Their efforts began all this.

I am indebted to the staff of Northampton Central Library (Local Studies) and Birmingham Reference Library for their help and use of their superb reserve stocks of medieval texts and State Papers, to the Northamptonshire Record Society for their library and the peace and quiet of their facilities. I record my thanks to the staff of Northamptonshire Library Service for the long-suffering trails they have blazed in search of almost-forgotten volumes via Inter-Library Loans and the fabulous national institutions of the British Library and the National Archives, whose collections enable such research as this to continue, when many other libraries sadly declare whole collections surplus to requirements. I am also happy to record the help offered at the libraries and Record Offices at Chester, Stafford, Coventry and Warwick together with the various *Syndicats d'Initiatives* throughout Normandy and Brittany who have pointed me to the more overgrown relics and documents of Ranulf's homeland.

I register my thanks to Paul Mason and Sallie Gee for reading my draft text and offering constructive comment. I hope I have done both them and all who have taught me justice. I apologise for any of my mistakes which remain. Also my gratitude goes to Jacqueline Harding for her expert rendering of my maps and drawings. The photos are my own, except for Bob Fielding's of the excavations I directed at Coventry Cathedral Priory in 1999–2000, and the 'old master' painting of Damietta. For the latter I thank the Frans Hals Museum in Haarlem, and in particular Susanna Koenig, for her generous help.

Finally, but most of all, I gratefully acknowledge the encouragement and forbearance of my wife and sons who for three years have accompanied me and my notes across England, Wales and France in search of Ranulf, sixth Earl of Chester.

This book is dedicated to the memory of Gunner Harry Harley RA, 1893–1981, my maternal grandfather (Somme, 3rd Ypres, 2nd Somme, Aisne), and to William Soden, my father, whose avionics work helped hone Britain's edge. They are my heroes.

INDEX